$3.74

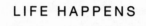

LIFE HAPPENS

RANDOM HOUSE

NEW YORK

Life Happens

AND OTHER
UNAVOIDABLE
TRUTHS

Connie Schultz

Published in the United States by
Random House, an imprint of
The Random House Publishing Group,
a division of Random House, Inc., New York.

RANDOM HOUSE and colophon are registered
trademarks of Random House, Inc.

LIBRARY OF CONGRESS
CATALOGING-IN-PUBLICATION DATA
Schultz, Connie.
Life happens: and other unavoidable truths /
Connie Schultz.
p. cm.
ISBN 1-4000-6497-X
1. United States—Social life and customs—
20th century—Anecdotes.   2. United States—
Social life and customs—20th century—Humor.
I. Title.
E169.Z83S38 2006
973.931—dc22   2005046693

Printed in the United States of America
on acid-free paper

www.atrandom.com

2   4   6   8   9   7   5   3   1

FIRST EDITION

Book design by Barbara M. Bachman

For Andy, who is gentle and wise.
For Caitlin, who is fiery and brave.
For Sherrod, who is my *hero, too.*

CONTENTS

he title for this book came about long before I knew I was going to write it.

In 2000, I was disappointed to be turned down yet again for a columnist position at *The Plain Dealer* in Cleveland, where I had worked for the last seven years. Where I saw failure, Ellen Stein Burbach, the paper's *Sunday Magazine* editor, saw opportunity. She took me to lunch and, right after we ordered, pulled a sheet of paper from her purse.

"I want you to write essays for our magazine," she said, sliding the paper across the table. "Here are some deadlines I have in mind." I looked at the list to discover that she had mapped out quite a plan for me for the next few months.

"We'll start with that," she said.

It was one of those moments when I felt that someone bigger than both of us was telling me that sometimes life happens only when you give it a nudge, so I agreed. She told me to come up with a name for the page where my essays would regularly appear.

I went for a long walk that weekend, which prompted the memory of another walk I had taken in 1998, only days after forty-one-year-old Lisa Hearey had died from a rare form of cancer that attacked her appendix. I met Lisa right after doctors told her she had only days, maybe weeks, to live. She agreed to let me chronicle her life and death, and then follow her family for a year. She was smart and beautiful. She loved her husband and three young boys, her career and her neighbors, and a glass of chardonnay at the end of the day. Like most of us in the throes of daily living, she thought she had all the time in the world. Until it was clear that she didn't.

She died before daybreak on a beautiful autumn day in October—in Cleveland, where fallen leaves gather around tree trunks like petticoats and the wind whips cheeks until they glow. I awoke from a dead sleep and sat straight up in bed the moment Lisa died. Even before the phone rang minutes later, I knew that she was gone.

On the first anniversary of her death, I was walking through piles of crisp leaves when I spotted a parked car's bumper sticker that said SHIT HAPPENS.

I stopped in my tracks and stared at that bumper sticker. I thought about Lisa, how hard she fought to live, how unfair it seemed that her life was so short. Then I thought about the afternoon when she told me she was ready to go. Her distraught husband, Clem, had finally been able to tell her it was all right for her to die. Her final burden had been lifted.

"It's time," she told me, smiling for the first time in days.

Now, there I was, a year later, staring at that bumper sticker's bleak take on the events that form our lives.

"No," I said out loud. "*Life* happens."

And so "Life Happens" was born.

When I began sorting through my *Plain Dealer* columns for this book, I started thinking about how every life has a beginning and an end but we have no memory of either of those moments in our own lives. For the story of our birth, we are completely dependent on someone else's account. When it's our turn to die, we are the only one in the room who won't have a story to tell when it's over.

And so it's the middle, that time between the beginning and the end, where our stories take shape, where life happens to the best of our recollection. Those are the stories I try to tell.

My mother always used to say I was a bright child, but you have to question her gift for assessment when you consider that I was sixteen before I realized an essential truth about my own beginning.

It was my mom's turn to host the monthly Canasta Club, where a half dozen or so women brought various versions of chip dip and settled in for a few hours of cards and kvetching. They were deep into loud chatter when one of them asked my mom, "Janey, when did you and Chuck get married?"

"February 1957," my mom answered.

She hadn't seen me standing on the stairs a few feet away, but a nod from one of her friends prompted her to look in my direction. I didn't notice her, either, because I was caught in a *wait-a-minute* freeze as I began counting splayed fingers toward the birth of her first child—that would be me—in July of that very same year.

"You keep those fingers to yourself!" she snapped.

The women erupted in laughter, my mother rolled her eyes, and I ran out the screen door into a world that would never look quite the same.

My parents' story is as old as love itself. Mom got pregnant, Dad got a union card and a marriage license, and the rest of their life was harder than they'd ever thought it could be. Twenty years later, Bruce Springsteen found a way to make their story rhyme, and their oldest child got to thinking maybe she could one day write, too, about how life happens.

I was the first in my family to go to college, the first to write for a living, too, if you don't count the little blurbs my paternal grandmother used to pen for the village newspaper so that other parents knew what was happening at the local school. My grandmother died before I was three, and I never knew she wrote until three years ago, when my father gave me an old red scrapbook of his mother's clippings. They look like box scores, these little yellowed squares of text, but they must have mattered a lot to her because she took the time out of mothering ten children to paste her tiny stories in neat rows across the black pages.

"By Mrs. Harry L. Schultz," the byline reads.

Not long after my father gave me that scrapbook, I finally started writing a column for *The Plain Dealer*'s Arts and Life section.

It was the fall of 2002. We were on the brink of a war most women opposed. Soon after it began, the ensuing battle for who would be our next president turned into a debate over who was and who wasn't a war hero. This had nothing to do with what most women cared about, such as health care, education, and every worker's right to a living wage, not to mention the human cost of the war.

It seemed to me that, since women cared about all these issues, and I was one of them, maybe I ought to write about them and all the other life that was happening around us. A Cleveland anchorwoman made headlines across the country after she stripped on the air to increase the show's ratings, a spokesman for the far right was quoted in more than a hundred newspapers denouncing women who were "deliberately childless," and Ohio's secretary of state was making registering to vote only slightly less difficult than childbirth.

I watched these and other events unfold, and decided there was no way I could be what others might define as the typical "arts and life" columnist. Instead, I would try to write about the art of living, and all that entails.

So, twice a week I started talking to readers about whatever was in the news or on my mind. I wrote about registering to vote, how to tip so the server actually gets the money, why women started grieving long before the war in Iraq had actually begun. I wrote about sex, too, and, let me tell you, that's an interesting endeavor when you're a middle-aged woman whose picture tops the page. But how could I not address our right to control our own reproductive health when we had a doctor on the FDA's Advisory Committee for Reproductive Health Drugs who opposed birth control for unmarried women and suggested we could just pray our cramps away?

Over time, I also wrote about my own life, in part because my editor, Stuart Warner, said readers would be more open to my opinions if they felt they knew a little about me. That theory has borne out, as an increasing number of readers who don't share my politics or religious beliefs nevertheless assure me that they love the stories about my friends and family.

Early in 2003, I started dating Ohio congressman Sherrod Brown because, as I joked with friends, my life as a single mom and full-time newspaper columnist wasn't complicated enough. Falling in love at my age, and with a politician, was quite a surprise to many—especially me. The curiosity we generated rivaled panda bears at a city zoo, and when it became clear that our relationship was becoming fodder for gossip columnists and radio talk shows, my editor suggested I own my own life for a little while longer and write about love in midlife. These columns generated some of the biggest reader response to come my way. Their calls and letters were often tender, sometimes confessional, and they offered glimpses into the lives lived all around us. There's no deadline on love, no age when it stops being worth the effort.

People often call or write to tell me, "You keep writing, we'll keep reading." That's mighty good news from where I sit. I guess over time, column by column, we've decided that we have a lot more in common than we might have thought possible. What a nice discovery to trip over on the rocky road of discourse we navigate these days.

Some people, mostly men, have grumbled about my choice of topics. In the newsroom and out in the community, they argued that I wasn't writing the kind of stuff that belonged in what has typically been viewed as "the women's section."

But I knew that women care about everything, and so that's what I was going to write about—everything.

Women, of course, have weighed in by the thousands. That's the thing about women. We're just full of opinions.

These are some of mine.

1.

Life Happens

I *grew up thinking* you had to hate what you did for a living.

That single belief of my childhood probably explains more about who I am and how I became a writer than anything else I could tell you.

My first eighteen years were spent in a small Ohio town that most people passed through on their way to somewhere else. It's called Ashtabula. You Bob Dylan fans may recall it was his creative reach for a rhyme to "Honolulu" in his song "You're Gonna Make Me Lonesome When You Go."

There are so many other towns just like Ashtabula all over the country. These towns are anonymous places where most of America does its living and dying. It's funny, really, how much all of us, from big-city folks to little-town people, resemble one another at the end of the day. In my town we didn't have Central Park or Hollywood Boulevard, but we did have the lady down the street leave her husband for her sister's husband, and don't even try telling me that isn't the stuff of made-for-TV movies. Hubert Humphrey even visited our town once. Dad shook his hand and got him on a home movie, which we always watched right before the scene of me putting my doll in the toilet.

Without meaning to, my father taught me early that work was something you just had to put up with so you could enjoy the few hours you had left in any day, any life. He was one of those workers who showered at the end of the day, after his shift at the plant was done. For thirty-six years he worked for the local utility plant, and for thirty-six years he despised his job and what he was sure it said about him as a human being.

Most nights, Mom and all four of us kids would join Dad at the dinner table and, likely as not, he would tell another story from his day on the job. He included funny tales about coworkers and pleas for a different Hostess pie in his lunch pail, but mostly he talked about abusive supervisors and backbreaking work in temperatures that easily topped 100 degrees in the summer. He offered up his stories as mounting evidence of just how much he didn't matter.

"Do you know what that bastard did to me today?" he'd say, not waiting for an answer before describing yet again how he was worse than invisible to the man ordering him around day in and day out.

"You kids are going to college," he'd say, over and over. "You kids are going to be somebody."

It was an order.

I am his oldest child, and over the years it grew harder and harder to watch that hurt masquerading as rage getting such a choke hold on my father's view of himself and his life. He was my dad, the man I most respected and feared. He filled up our house in that way that ferocious men do, but he was nobody out there, in that hulking factory where he spent the bulk of his days and too many overtime nights.

I used to envy the bankers' kids, the lawyers' and doctors' kids, even the kids whose dads were just insurance salesmen. I didn't envy their fathers' professions, just their access. Their fathers had offices their children could visit, secretaries and receptionists who would look up at them from tidy desks and say, "Your dad's on the phone, honey. Have a seat until he waves you in."

My dad worked in a place we could only see from the shores of Lake Erie. Sometimes, my mother would take us to a small patch of beach called Lake Shore Park. Gathering her chicks around her, she'd point to the smokestacks puffing huge gray clouds into the sky several miles away.

"Your daddy's over there," she'd yell. "Wave real hard and maybe he'll see us."

There we were, four skinny kids with the same bony knees, flapping and yelling, "Hi, Daddy!" as if he could actually hear us over the roar of the plant. One of those times, when I was about ten, I looked back at my mother as we hooted and hollered and saw that she wasn't waving anymore. She just stood there, staring at those ugly smokestacks with a face I'd never seen her wear before. Through her eyes, I had just seen the enemy.

I never waved at the plant again.

Whenever my father talked about work at the dinner table, my mother would quietly listen, but the look on her face told me all I needed to know about what she was really thinking. Here was her big, burly husband, the only man she would ever love, and, oh, how she loved him, being mistreated in ways she would never visit on a dog. That's a hard thing for a woman who loves her man, and I still wince at the memory of my tiny mother trying to lift up her fallen giant.

"They don't know you like I know you," she'd say, passing him a second helping of mashed potatoes, maybe asking if he'd like some canned peaches for dessert. I'm sure that, at such moments, there must have been an occasional look of tenderness between them, but I only remember my father staring straight ahead, his eyes narrowed in disbelief that this was his life.

At the beginning of my senior year, my high school guidance counselor, Joe Petro, asked me what I wanted to study in college. I'd never given it much thought, since all I really knew about college was what my parents told me: I had to go for four years, and I'd better have a job at the end.

"Well," I said, "I thought I'd be a social worker."

He frowned, shook his head. "I know you, Connie. You'll burn out."

He looked down at my test scores and tapped his finger on the page. "You're good in English, and your writing scores are great. Have you ever thought of going into journalism?"

He looked at my blank face and smiled.

"You're going to be working for a long time," he said. "You'd better pick something you really like to do."

Just like that, life happens: a sudden wide-awake flash changes, not just what you are, but who you are. Until that moment in Mr. Petro's dingy office, it had never occurred to me that I could love what I do for a living. In an instant, there it was: my brand-new life.

Before I became a columnist, I was a reporter for more than twenty years. It was a career dug in the rich soil of other people's lives, and that is fertile ground. Like many journalists, I am often asked how I get people to open up and talk so much, as if we keep some sort of magic dust in our pockets that we can scoop out and sprinkle around.

Truth be told, I spend a lot of time just paying attention. There are few people, indeed, who feel really heard on a regular basis. Who among us have enough people in our lives who hang on our every word, who know how life happened for us, and how it happens still? Good journalists ask great questions, but the best stories come about only when we shut up and listen. I haven't met a person who doesn't have at least one good tale, and if I leave an interview without hearing it, I always feel the blame is mine. Keeps the standard high.

All these years later, I still can't quite believe I get paid to do this for a living. I left behind my working-class life, but its roots run long and deep, and they keep me tethered to values that steer my every step. While we're clearly a country deeply divided, I find myself constantly stumbling onto common ground.

You might spot someone you know in the stories here. Maybe you'll even find a glimpse of yourself. Yes, yes, I know, each of us is unique, but life happens in ways that bind us like Gorilla Glue. There's something universally comforting in the folds of a worn denim shirt or a house that promises to hold on to our memories no matter how far we move. Maybe you, too, have been stopped dead in your tracks by a sign that assures us there's something bigger at work than our own stubborn will.

No matter where we live, we all have those moments when a sudden reminder of life's brevity changes us, at least for a little while. In that quiet moment of surrender, life happens.

THIS FOUR-LETTER WORD
IS A MALE LAND MINE

M*en, I'm going to share* with you a little tip that could change your life.

Women hate the f-word.

We especially hate when you use it, because your timing couldn't be worse if you were the mistress making a toast at her boyfriend's wedding.

At the precise moment when we are at our most vulnerable, our most needy, anxiously standing before you and hanging on your every word, you fling the f-word at us like a hunk of day-old hash and then wonder why we're reaching for the nearest steak knife.

"What?" you always say. "What did I do? What did I say?"

Learn from this story:

One of my friends walked over to my desk recently with his head hanging lower than the tail of a freshly neutered hound dog. Naturally, I was concerned.

"Now what did you do?"

He shook his head, mumbled his wife's name. "I don't know what's wrong with her."

"What did you do?"

He threw his hands up in disgust. "Nothing. Absolutely nothing."

"Again, I ask you, what did you do?"

He sighed, avoided eye contact. (A dead giveaway.)

"Okay," he said. "I'm standing in the kitchen minding my own business, cookin' a little oatmeal, drinkin' a little coffee, when she waltzes in wearing some new outfit and says, 'How do I look?' "

Oh, no.

He shrugged his shoulders. "So, I said, 'You—' "

No, no.

" 'Look—' "

No, no, no.

" 'Fine.' "

There it is: the dreaded f-word.

"I can't help you," I told him. "If you had insulted her mom, maybe. If you had forgotten her birthday, perhaps. But you said she looks fine. There's nothing to be done now."

How does this happen? Most men I know can launch into an hour-long lecture on everything from how much air belongs in my tires to the precise wattage of lightbulb that should be screwed into every socket in my house. These same men turn into monosyllabic goofballs when asked to comment on the appearance of the woman they supposedly love.

Fine? We look *fine*?

When we ask, "How do I look?" we want a response rivaling the great ardor of your brothers across the sea. We want the passion of Italy, the romance of France, the fervor of Greece.

You give us Switzerland.

When you say, "You look fine," and perform that little palms-up flip, our creative minds kick into overdrive. We hear:

"I've seen *Wide World of Bowling* highlights more exciting than you in that dress."

"(*Yawn.*) I'm sorry, were you talking to me?"

"Whoa, when did the back-fat thing happen?"

None of these will ever land you on the right side of the heart-shaped tub.

One of my male friends tells me, "Look, when we say 'fine,' all we mean is, 'We're running late, get the keys, let's go.' "

It is to laugh.

That wouldn't explain those grunts from the Bimini BarcaLounger during Sunday football games, would it? Nor does it shed any light on why you say it right before we meet your mother or head into the gym for your high school reunion populated with twenty of your old girlfriends.

(Neither of these happened to me, but I did bear witness to these unfortunate moments and both times "you look fine" made for one very long night for men named George. I'm not saying you Georges of the world are more likely to commit the crime, but you do seem to get less benefit of the doubt than men named Preston, say, or Kip.)

Now, I know the next question: Well, if you don't like the f-word, what should we say?

So glad you asked.

You are hereby encouraged to use the m-f word.

Here's how it works:

She says, "How do I look?"

You say, "You look mighty fine."

My work is done.

A GIFT THAT MOM WOULD HAVE LOVED

For some years now, I have meant to frame a square little black-and-white photo of my mother.

It rests against another framed photo by my bed, its sides slowly curling toward an eventual union. She is peering playfully around the corner at the top of a stairway, her right leg extended to show off a little calf under the poufy skirt. Her right arm stretches straight out, too, and she is holding her high-heeled party shoes in midair, a striking rebuff to the scruffy slippers on her feet.

It was 1958, and she was the twenty-one-year-old mother of one-year-old me. She is flirting with the man behind the camera—her husband, my father. He, too, was twenty-one.

This is my favorite photo of my mother, even though it sometimes makes me sad, especially in the middle of the night when I can't sleep. I flick on the light, and there she is. It is a perfect snapshot of where she came from and where she hoped to go, a tidy composition hiding a messy start.

On the night of this photo, I imagine my parents thinking that maybe everything was going to be all right. You don't know from looking at the smile on my mother's seamless face that their young marriage began with a doctor's surprising news and an elopement in the middle of the night across state lines. You don't know that the stairway doesn't belong to them, but to the great-aunt who kindly took them in. And you don't know that the girl in the picture hoped to be a nurse one day but never was.

All you know from that picture is what she wrote in her own loopy backhand on the back: "Chuck and I had just got home from Ma Schultz's—Sun. eve."

My mother always said her life was a good one. She raised four kids, loved four grandchildren, and told me a week before she died that she still got butterflies when my father walked into the room. But over the years, she gave up on her bigger self, the one who was going to go to night school to get a degree.

I still remember the night she surrendered. I was in high school when she enrolled in a typing class. She was so flustered after the first session that she drove up an exit ramp to the freeway.

"That's it," she told me later that night, her hands trembling as she wiped away tears. "I'm just not good enough." And that was that. She worked as a nurse's aide the rest of her life, in a hospital and then later for a hospice. She was only sixty-two when she died. More than eight hundred people attended her wake.

Nearly six years later, my father is slowly sifting through the cards and letters, the photos and Post-it notes that chronicle my mother's daily life. A recent batch he mailed to me included a folded, handwritten list that began, "I AM SOMEBODY!"

The list continues: "I AM A HUMAN BEING . . . I AM AN IMPORTANT PERSON . . . GOD LOVES ME . . . I AM SOMEBODY!"

I imagine her tucking this into her purse, or slipping it into her Bible, someplace where she could easily find it and pull it out as a reminder of something we obviously failed to make clear. I stared at the list in my hand, then looked over at that photo of her, the one where she seems so full of her young and capable self.

"How?" I wondered aloud, shaking the list at her. "How could you not have known this?"

Sunday is Mother's Day. I could rattle off a whole list of the gifts I bought her, the cards I mailed. But I can't describe a single time when I sat my mother down on that special day and asked her even one question about her life. She would have loved that, and by showing an interest in her life I would have learned so much about my own.

A month after my mom died, my daughter asked me a question about my childhood while I was driving.

"You know," I said, "I don't know. We'll have to ask Grandma."

My daughter stared at me as I slowed the car for a moment and sucked in air.

"Mom?" she said.

"I'm okay."

"Mom?"

Only after my mother was gone did I realize how much of me she held captive in her memories. Now, whole parts of me are lost to her for good.

My mom was somebody.

Yes, she was.

A PLANE IS MISSED,
BUT TIME IS NOT LOST

We *have a rule in* our marriage that if you screw up, you know you've screwed up, and you're even willing to admit you screwed up, the other person isn't allowed to rant about how you just screwed up.

This rule evolved from our previous marriages—one each, long ago—which had devolved into the blood sport of blame.

As rules go, it comes in handy, especially at our ages, when opportunities abound to discover anew its redemptive powers.

Take earlier this month, for example. We had just outrun the rising sun to stand at an airport ticket counter when the chirpy desk clerk said, "Oh, your flight left a half hour ago."

"No," said my husband.

"Yes," she said, nodding her head.

He looked down at the printed schedule in his hand, looked up at me, looked down again.

"Oops," he said.

Oops? *Oops?*

I had just packed a suitcase in the time it takes me to brush my teeth and showered so fast I still had soap bubbles popping in places I dare not name. I walked our tiny dog so fast that she tumbled headfirst into a fresh deposit from the neighbor's Rottweiler, and then I compounded her trauma by barely missing her head when one of my clogs flew off.

And now the best my husband could muster in response to the news that we were stuck at the airport for four long hours until the next flight to New York was "Oops"?

He smiled weakly. "I screwed up."

Then he did that eyebrow thing. "I'm really sorry."

Clever boy.

We were at Akron's airport, which is small and friendly and offers passengers no real escape from one another. My husband and I sat in chairs along the wall of the main walkway, and there we piled our newspapers and books and settled in for what we tried to tell ourselves was not a colossal waste of time.

It took the grace of a stranger to make me grateful for the wait.

I first noticed her because of her hair, which was merely fresh stubble in varying shades of gray.

Cancer, I thought. *She's just finished chemo.*

Then I noticed the little granddaughter tugging on her hand. The woman leaned down and chatted with her, nose-to-nose. The child's parents watched. The father smiled, but the young mother dabbed at her eyes. The grandfather hovered, took a few noticeably deep breaths, then laid a hand on the woman's bent back. When she stood up, she too wiped her eyes, and he looked away for a moment, sucking in air.

I wanted to look away, too, but there they were, right in front of me, a small family reunited for a while but now saying good-bye—to how much, they didn't yet know.

I told myself that this simply could be one of those prolonged good-byes after a happy reunion, the latest of many the older parents have endured since their own baby girl married. But I couldn't ignore her hair, the clenched tissue in her hand, the tears that insisted on betraying her smile.

The woman stood and watched her family until she couldn't see them anymore. She watched as they slipped off their shoes and piled them into one of the plastic tubs for the security check. Every time the little girl looked back, the woman waved and made a grandmother face, the one where the nose wiggles and the eyes crinkle to half their size.

When they disappeared, the woman surrendered. She lowered her head for a moment and didn't bother reaching up for the tears that fell. Her husband stood behind her with his hands on her shoulders for a bit, then leaned in and whispered something in her ear. She nodded, and together they turned toward the exit. Her soggy wad of tissue fell to the floor. Her husband stopped, scooped it up and tucked it into his pocket, as only a beloved would do.

I looked over at my husband, his eyes cartoon-large behind cheap reading glasses as he pored over yet another editorial page. I grabbed his hand, he squeezed back. Then I leaned my head against the wall, closed my eyes, and tried to pretend I had all the time in the world.

NEVER BLUE IN A DENIM SHIRT

*G**et this.** The New York Times* has declared that denim shirts are back in style.

Whoa, sorry. Should've warned you to sit down for that one. Anyone who's lived twenty minutes in the Midwest knows denim shirts never went out of style.

A denim shirt is the must-have, can't-do-without staple of our wardrobe. It is the sure thing, the old reliable, the one real piece of evidence that God wants us to be happy in this lifetime.

I'm not talking about the new denim shirt from Barneys New York that costs $190. Not the one with Ralph Lauren's little pony insignia, either. Those are denim wannabes worn by never gonnabes. Think Levi. Gap. Eddie Bauer. That's as pricey as it should get. Otherwise, you just look like a bank president trying to party on.

And guys? Don't starch it. Try not to iron it. Instead, steam it in the bathroom while you shower. And if you don't yet own a denim shirt, hear me when I say it's the only shirt that will ever inspire her to purr, "I just want to sleep in it while you're gone."

You're welcome.

My first denim shirt belonged to my high school boyfriend. He offered me his class ring. I said I'd rather have his shirt. It was a beauty, ever-so-slightly frayed at the collar and soft as a bubble bath. There was just something about all that denim wrapped around me like one long hug. I've had one ever since.

My oldest denim shirt carries more memories than a photo album. I wore it for most of my law school exams, and it was the first thing I pulled on the day I decided to drop out. When my daughter was a baby, I wrapped it around her after bath time whenever I forgot a towel. When she was a little older, it was her favorite shirt to snuggle in when she was sad or landed on the time-out step.

At the risk of sounding like a country singer, I swear that denim

shirts are loyal, too. The leather pants of my youth feel like sausage cas-
ings now, and spiked heels make me walk like an ostrich on roller
skates, but I'll never outgrow my denim shirt. And I feel twenty years
younger just by sliding into its sleeves.

Most of my friends own denim shirts. It's not a requirement of
friendship, but it helps when they need the benefit of the doubt.
Women sometimes dress them up with pins or pearls, guys pull on a tie
and head for work. My friend John says his denim shirt is the only one
he owns that works as well for raking leaves as going to church, and
there aren't many things in life you can say that about.

And here's a secret: Women—the right kind of women, anyway—
can forgive a lot of sins in a man who knows how to wear a denim shirt.

Occasionally, I am rendered speechless by such a man.

Just the other day, my boss noticed the steady stream of traffic at my
desk and decided I was distracted from the deadline looming over my
head like a giant mushroom cloud. "Why don't you take your laptop
and go to a coffee shop for a while?" he said. I couldn't bring myself to
argue with him, a lapse in willfulness I blame totally on the fact that I
was not wearing my denim shirt. (I'm just a fireball when I wear that
thing, I swear.)

I went to one of those places that offers coffee in sizes called
Grande, Mucho Grande, and Latvia, or some such nonsense. Being a
denim shirt kind of woman, I asked for a size mee-dee-um and then
settled down at a table by the window. I was typing, typing, typing,
clickety-clak, clickety-clak.

And then I saw him.

The Man in a Denim Shirt.

He set his laptop on the table, looked over at me, nodded and
smiled. I started to give him my very-very-very busy smile until it became very-very-very obvious that he was about to roll up the sleeves of
his denim shirt.

Right there in the middle of the coffee shop, there he was, rolling up
to that spot just below his elbow.

Well, I'm tellin' ya. Sitting here and thinking about it, even now, I
find that I.

That I. Well.

Just give me a minute . . .

Watching my grown son laugh with his mother took me aback. I was caught off guard by how right it felt, after all these years.

I watched Andy place a hand on her shoulder and lean in to share a whispered bit of mischief. She leaned in, too, and then suddenly stepped back and howled with laughter.

He glanced over and saw me watching.

I flashed him my best "I'm fine" grin. I meant it, too. It had taken Susie and me far too long to reach this patch of common ground that Andy longed for, but finally, in his thirtieth year of life, we had found our way.

Andy was barely seven the first time I met him, and I remember that day with the clarity of a mother recalling the first time she held her newborn child. He was a round, freckled chatterbox full of knock-knock jokes whose cowlick tickled my chin whenever he sat on my lap.

His father had taken us to a basketball game. I don't remember a second on the court, but I still recall nuzzling his soft little neck and breathing him in.

His father and I married, and Andy spent most of his time with us. The energy I had for a career I poured into my family instead, never thinking about how all my new-mom enthusiasm would hurt his already wounded mother.

Susie had the schedule of an accomplished lawyer. I was a stay-at-home mom who had the time to serve on the Mothers Committee and pick up Andy every day at three.

I stitched patches for his worn-out knees and made Halloween costumes from scratch. I taught him how to hit a ball, helped him memorize his dinosaurs, and signed him up for karate after he swore new glasses made him a nerd.

I thought I was tending to my stepson's needs, but Susie read my efforts as a harsh judgment of the choices she had made for her life. I could have done more to assure her otherwise, but I, too, was defensive. I had given up a career for her son. Where was the gratitude?

How foolish.

The lines were drawn, and the only one unsure of the boundaries was the little boy who just wanted to love everyone.

When Andy was eleven, I became pregnant, and Susie moved out of state but never out of mind. Once my daughter was born, I finally comprehended the magnitude of Susie's loss.

With my baby's every milestone, I was forced to think about how it had been Susie, not I, who had witnessed these same hallmarks in Andy's early life. So much had happened with Andy before I ever knew him. So much, and Susie had been there for it all.

The lines in the dirt we guarded so jealously began to blur. I mailed copies of Andy's report cards and pictures of milestones Susie had to miss. She sent me some of Andy's baby clothes, including a coat my daughter wore through two long winters.

When Andy was about to leave for college, Susie called me. "Thank you for raising our son," she said.

I hesitated, and she tried again. "I mean our son, as in yours and mine."

"Thank you for letting me," I said.

Somehow, we started to forgive each other for words we wished we had never said. Somehow, we found common ground.

We're divorced from the same man, and both of us are now married to men who love us. We're both former stay-at-home moms, too, who started careers later than most.

And we both love our son.

Last month, Susie and I drove 150 miles from opposite directions to converge in the city where Andy lives and works. He asked us to share a big event in the life of the woman he loves. We said we'd be there.

The first time Andy introduced Susie and me as "my two mothers," I looked at her and held my breath. But she made her peace with that dragon long ago. She just smiled and nodded, extending her hand.

By the end of the evening, we were standing side by side, watching our son hover over this woman who makes him smile.

I touched Susie's arm. She patted my hand. We were two proud moms of the same young man.

And for the first time, it felt just right.

A FOND LOOK BACK AT A HOME FOR TWO

If anyone had ever tried telling me I'd miss my days as a single mother, I would have laughed them out of the room to keep from crying.

For a long time, my most enduring memory of ten years as a single parent was of me pacing in the middle of the night, a ghost in my own house silently asking for a sign that we were going to be okay.

So many demons conspired to rob me of my sleep, night after night. There were all those financial debts, but there was that even bigger debt, the one I owed my little girl who deserved never to know how much her mother worried.

Could I pull this off, I wondered. Could I be as mighty and strong as she needed me to be?

It comes as quite a surprise to feel nostalgia tugging on my arm as I pack up the rented house, box by box, that my daughter and I called home for eight years. Memory is calling, gently turning my face back to take in the view one last time before I set my sights on the road ahead.

Last year I remarried, and now that Caitlin has graduated from high school, we are moving into a house that can accommodate the dreams of a hopeful middle age. Life is good, but dismantling the home this mom and her daughter built together reminds me that life's been pretty great all along.

The three-story duplex was a sorry sight when we moved in, its rooms full of peeling paint and dingy windows darkened by bushes masquerading as trees. The landlord was a kind man who just shrugged his shoulders and smiled at my many projects.

"Just take the supplies off the rent," he'd say.

Gray walls turned corn-silk yellow and robin's-egg blue. We painted the upstairs hallway the lightest shade of lavender to match the lilacs that bloomed out back, only feet away from where we played catch all summer long. We painted my bedroom sea-foam green after we returned from a beach vacation and my daughter realized my room was the only one we hadn't helped.

"You deserve a nice room, too, Mom," she said. I can still see the spots her young hands missed around the window ledge.

A friend once asked me why I bothered to fix up the place.

"You rent," she said. "It's not even your house."

But it was my daughter's home, and she inhabited every inch of it. Her first bedroom became my office after she decided it was too big. Her second bedroom turned into a guest room after she turned fifteen and moved to the third floor, insisting she needed her space. Through most of high school, her footfalls on the floor overhead signaled me to stop yelling for her to get out of bed.

Now, only weeks before she leaves for college, her favorite spot is on the living room sofa, surrounded by book-lined walls and the fruits of her artistic endeavors over the years. I've already packed her bust of a pensive man in blue ceramic, but I'm waiting until the last minute to bubble-wrap her first-grade painting. It's titled *My Masterpiece,* a glorious reminder that there was a time when she was just that sure of herself.

Soon, a moving van will pull up in front of the address sign my daughter helped make in the summer of 1996. Burly movers will trudge up and down the front walkway where she used to draw giant chalk faces and bouquets of flowers and the occasional I-love-you heart for her mom.

They'll step on the porch and won't give a moment's notice to the rusty swing holding Cait's old Winnie-the-Pooh comforter folded just right, or the Amish rocker a friend carried up the day I turned forty. They won't know that this is the very porch where we used to paint our nails and cuddle during rainstorms and listen to my grown son play guitar on his visits home.

They won't know any of that, but I do. I remember it all.

I love my new life, but I am grateful for the tug of memory that reminds me of the life I am leaving behind. For a long while, we were just a mother and a daughter in a place we called home.

To my surprise, I'm a little sad to see it go.

That makes me happier than I could ever have known.

STORIES TO MAKE US STOP AND WONDER

hose who care for the dying are full of stories that fill the rest of us with wonder.

My friend Diana, for example, loves to share this story from a hospice volunteer who was assigned to care for a Vietnamese man. The volunteer had visited his country the year before and offered to bring in photos from her trip.

"You can imagine their surprise," Diana said, "when he recognized people in her photos, for she had visited the village where he grew up."

Sometimes the word "coincidence" is just too limp.

Someone describes an experience that defies our idea of reality, or we're suddenly reeling from our own mystical moment, and we are forced to think about what we do and do not believe in. After we catch our breath, that is, and our scalps stop tingling.

Often, there's a frankness to these stories that makes them hard to dismiss. Hospice workers often talk about the spirits dying patients say they see in their rooms. Once, a nine-year-old boy told me his mother, who was in a coma, had visited him in a dream to tell him it was time for her to go, but she would always love him. She died as he dreamed.

Recently on National Public Radio, one of Unabomber Ted Kaczynski's victims described the explosion and his certainty that he would die.

Then he heard a voice: "You're going to be fine."

"I will never forget that," he said.

Diana calls these moments blessings, reminders of a force much greater than our own and willfully trying to comfort us if we'd just stop thinking so hard.

Most who experience such moments want to talk about it, as if saying it out loud will somehow make it more real. We're cautious, though, fearing the doubtful face, the dismissive scoff. Diana is a gentle, soft-spoken woman, a safe place in this world of clamor and haste, and so people spill their stories to her as if prodded from behind with an invisible poke.

Last month, she decided to share her bounty. She wrote down some of the stories in hand-sewn books for friends and relatives for Christmas.

She's always loved people's stories about their childhoods and their lives, she wrote in the introduction. "Just as intriguing to me are mysterious stories that may involve encounters with animals or visits from someone who has died. Sometimes the story is about what seems like an extraordinary coincidence. I started recording these stories so I won't forget them. I like to retell them. I love how they make me feel."

A friend described a stork with a broken wing that lived for years in her parents' Florida neighborhood. Other storks regularly visited him. When he died, they visited one last time, forming a circle around the stork's body and stretching their wings wide. They stood there a long time before flying away.

Diana coaxed the following story out of an aging tailor, Greg, she met at a fabric store in Maine, where she lives. He told her he worked for a tailor and his wife, both Polish immigrants, in Brooklyn in the 1970s.

Even in the hottest weather, Greg said, the couple wore long sleeves. One day the wife, Rose, reached for a shelf and her sleeve fell, revealing the numbers tattooed on her arm. She lost twenty-nine family members in the Holocaust, she told him. She was imprisoned in the same camp Greg's father helped to liberate in 1945.

Years later, Rose visited Greg in California. While she was there, Greg introduced her to another woman from Poland, who told her a woman from Rose's village lived only a mile away. Greg took Rose to meet her. He knocked on the door as Rose stood behind him. When the door opened, Rose fainted.

"It was her sister," Diana wrote.

Diana left blank pages, urging us to record our own stories.

Here is one of mine.

Soon after my mother died, I was driving and listening to NPR like I always do when, inexplicably, I reached down and switched the radio station. "I know you're watching over me from heaven," the singer crooned.

Still raw with grief, I sighed and said out loud, "I miss you, Ma."

Then I looked at the license plate on the car straight ahead:

MISS U2.

SNOW TESTS THE MUSCLE
OF A BOOKISH FAMILY

When *your car is* wedged in a frozen mound of snow tighter than the rusty lid on an ancient jar of Vicks VapoRub, you don't want a bunch of bookworms offering to push you to freedom.

You want brute strength. You want muscles, lots of muscles. You want big, strapping young men marching down the middle of the road singing beer songs until they hear your desperate yoo-hoo over the whirl of spinning tires, at which point they rush to your side yelling, "We'll save you."

That's what you want. It's not what you get, though, in our family.

We read books. That's what we do. We bond not through rounds of Ping-Pong and touch football, but by reading aloud favorite passages that leave everyone feeling a tad unworthy in the presence of such genius. Some of us even have the annoying habit of correcting others' grammar, prompting competitions rivaling the fiercest Foosball.

You don't build up biceps turning pages no matter how big the book. Even when a book has a preface, a foreword, an introduction, a pound of footnotes, four appendices, an index, and a bibliography of every book the author has read since preschool, it doesn't pump up your physical prowess unless you lift it in rapid repetitions over your head. We don't do that.

This never stops us, though, from thinking we're mighty. Who needs upper body strength when you can outsmart the problem, we tell ourselves. And so, when my stepdaughter Emily found her car stuck in the snow, we tossed aside our memoirs and novels and even my husband's brand-new two-volume edition of the *Oxford English Dictionary*— *A* through *M* goes on his side of the bed, *N* through *Z* on mine—and set out to outwit the snow.

But only after serious discussion.

Emily's car was around the corner, so we didn't know right away that she was stuck. Emily's dad, wearing seven-year-old sneakers and a large fur hat shaped like a mobile home, trudged off to retrieve his daughter's car so she could leave. He soon trudged back.

"The car," he said, "is stuck."

Silence.

"We're going to have to push it out," he said.

We let that "we" sink in a bit.

Emily cleared her throat. "I have a plane to catch."

Emily was headed for Key Largo.

That's Key Largo. As in Florida.

After a brief discussion, we decided to help her anyway.

My husband asked if we had any boards of wood sitting around to slide under the tires. His scowl suggested he was actually serious, so I stopped laughing and suggested he check the basement because I've heard that's where other families keep things like wood and nails and all sorts of tools. And wouldn't you know, he reappeared carrying two fiberboards from a discarded bookshelf.

"You threw away a *bookshelf*?" he screeched.

Emily cleared her throat. "I have a *plane* to catch."

Off we trudged—a mother and a son, a daughter and a dad—stamping bravely into the snow Emily was about to leave behind.

Once we reached the car, decisions had to be made. First, we debated who should be behind the steering wheel and who should push. That took a while.

Then, we debated exactly how the fiberboards should be positioned under the tires. That took even longer.

Finally, the moment was upon us. We grunted and pushed. We growled and pushed. One of us swore and then we pushed some more.

Nothing.

More debate. Then a switch in drivers. Then a lecture on how front-wheel drive isn't what it's cracked up to be.

Just when it seemed as if brains don't matter at all in pushing a car out of the snow, I said, and I quote: "Maybe the fiberboards under the wheels aren't working."

More discussion, then a vote. We pulled out all the broken pieces of fiberboard, my son took the wheel, and then we heaved every last ounce of our beings into the front of that tiny little car until it practically flew to freedom.

We cheered. We clapped. We high-fived and yelled, "And we *read,* too!"

It's going to be a great new year.

A FATHER'S GIFT GIVES HIM AWAY

Only he can give this gift to his daughter on her wedding day.

It has been years in the making, and it is almost finished. The deadline looms.

Night after night, he sits in the ratty stuffed chair in the corner, his tongue poking his cheek as he peers through his reading glasses. He glances to his left at the open page of the old book, then copies it word for word into the new book on his lap.

He glances again to his left, writes some more. Over and over, until sleep insists on having its way.

These are his memories, the ones he wrote in the book he bought a few months after his divorce.

Emily was five then, Elizabeth was only two. He was a divorced dad who refused to be forced to the periphery. The artificial boundaries of scheduled parenting seemed to sharpen his senses when his daughters were with him.

He hung on their every word, their slightest gesture. Sometimes, he stared at them in wonder. They were as mysterious as they were beloved, and he was afraid that, over time, the miles of living would wear down his memory of all the small moments together that enlarge a life and give it meaning.

So he started writing down their exchanges, an entry or two at a time, for the next nine years of their childhood. At some point, the girls started calling it *The Funny Book.* There was only one rule: If you tried to be funny, it wouldn't make it in.

Now he was copying the book, in his own hand, to give to twenty-four-year-old Emily on her wedding day. He will do the same thing one day for Elizabeth, who is twenty-one.

New rule for *The Funny Book:* No editing, no changes. Copy it, word for word.

May 1987: "Emily clearly had the holidays on her mind when she prayed tonight: 'Dear God, I know you are Santa Claus and the Easter Bunny and you were just dressed up.' "

August 1988: "I called Emily the night before her first day of school.

"Dad: 'Well, Emily, tomorrow's the big day.'

"Emily: 'It's the same size as any other day.' "

September 1988: "Emily was lying on the bed one morning, complaining about being tired and refusing to get ready for school.

"Dad: 'Emily, if you would go to bed earlier, you wouldn't be so tired.'

"Emily: 'It's the weight of my years.' "

October 1988: "Dad: 'Elizabeth, you're a piece of work.'

"Elizabeth: 'You're a piece of wood, too, Daddy.' "

He writes for a while, pauses, sometimes looks off into the distance for a moment. Then writes some more.

Sometimes, *The Funny Book* is not so funny.

October 1988: "Elizabeth drew two pictures and gave them to me. 'The first picture, Daddy, is all four of us, when you and Mommy were undivorced. The other one is just you. See the tears?' "

He writes about seven-year-old Emily's reaction to a friend's explanation at a Cleveland Indians game: "You mean they make their *living* doing this?"

He records five-year-old Elizabeth trying to outshout a boisterous family. "When I say, 'Please pass the grandmother,' it means I want some attention."

He copies the passages from their many train trips across the Midwest, their adventures in New York with Uncle Bob. He writes the lyrics to the song they wrote about their life together, describes how he played it on the guitar.

All last week, my husband wrote in the new *Funny Book* for the little girl who isn't little anymore, for his daughter who is about to become a wife.

He wrote, and I read.

My favorite passage, the one that forced the air into my lungs, is the story about nine-year-old Emily as a flower girl in a friend's wedding.

That day, she walked down the aisle—back straight, face forward—until she reached the pew where her father was sitting. She turned toward him, paused for just a moment and gave him the biggest smile.

He wrote in *The Funny Book* what she said to him later that day.

June 1990: "Emily said to me, 'Dad, I saw you crying. What are you going to do when I get married?' "

A DIRE WARNING FROM A GRIEVING DAD

Jeff Williams sat a few feet away from his fourteen-year-old son's open casket on Monday and talked about saving other children's lives.

Most parents can't focus beyond their own grief in the wake of such loss, but Williams is not like most parents. He's an East Cleveland police officer, and he's seen too many kids die too many ways. This is how he copes, pulling threads of hope from unraveling lives.

At 11:45 on March 2, Kyle Williams's mother, Kathy, kissed him good night in their Painesville Township home. She returned to his room about 5:45 the next morning to wake him for school. When he refused to respond, she thought he was joking.

"He's impossible to wake," Jeff said, unaware of his present tense. "He can sleep through anything."

Kathy pulled back the covers and found Kyle lying motionless. Next to his face lay a can of Dust-Off, a common computer cleaner. The nurse in her could see that he was dead. The mother in her tried to revive him.

Jeff was on duty when he got the call. He and another officer sped all the way to Painesville Township. "He's going to be fine," Jeff told himself. "He's going to be fine."

Several Lake County Sheriff's Office squad cars were clustered around his house when he arrived.

Jeff ran straight for his son's bedroom. He took one look at his oldest boy and knew he was dead. The coroner said he died between midnight and one A.M.

Kyle died after inhaling the propellant from a can of Dust-Off. There are similar spray cleaners on the market, and they are the latest in a long list of chemical inhalants some teenagers abuse—it's usually called "huffing"—for a quick high. When they use the computer cleaner, they call it "dusting."

You can find these cans next to home computers and in classrooms across the country. No one knows for sure how many times Kyle inhaled it before his young heart suddenly stopped. It could have been the third time. Could have been the twelfth. For some kids, it only takes once.

In the days between Kyle's death and his funeral, Jeff did what good cops do: He interviewed friends of the victim. Kyle had inhaled Dust-Off before. He thought it was safe, as did the friends who taught him how to use it. Jeff wants those kids to know he does not blame them for his son's death, and he doesn't want anyone else blaming them, either.

Kyle's calling hours reminded me of something I wish I'd never had to learn. I've attended enough services for dead children to know that adults behave differently when there's a young person in the casket. There isn't the usual milling near the body, the clusters of conversation and occasional laughter. It's just too much for us grown-ups to bear.

Most adults paid quick respects at Kyle's side, then drifted to the back of the room or spilled into the hall where he was out of sight.

The children, though, hovered and stared. Jeff prays they learned something from the sight of his dead son.

"I have to stop this from happening to anyone else," Jeff said. "I'll hurt and I'll hurt and I'll hurt, but I'll make sure there isn't a parent out there who doesn't know."

The thing is, there's a part of Jeff that thinks he should have known. But "dusting" is different from sniffing other chemicals. The usual symptoms, like burn marks or chemical stains on kids' shirts, aren't there. Kyle threw up once in the week before he died. He complained once that his tongue was numb. That was all the warning Jeff and Kathy had, and they missed it.

"I'm a cop," Jeff said, his voice breaking. "Tell everyone. That's what I keep saying: 'Tell everyone.' "

Jeff Williams's mother, Barbara, took his plea to heart and is spreading the word. One of her friends said her grown daughter sat her children down to warn them of the dangers of dusting.

As the mother spoke about Kyle, her eleven-year-old daughter's face grew increasingly frightened.

"I'm sorry, honey," she said, "I didn't mean to scare you."

The girl looked at her mother with horror on her face.

"I already tried it, Mom," she said. "I tried it once."

Tell everyone.

TRYING TO REMEMBER HOW HAPPY WE ARE

We were in the middle of our usual dinnertime banter with family and friends when the conversation turned to the recent terrorist attack on the Russian school in Beslan.

Hundreds of students and teachers died. Hundreds more were injured. My sister-in-law, Catherine, quoted a woman who had talked to *New York Times* reporter C. J. Chivers as she rubbed medicine into the burns of her eleven-year-old nephew, Azamat Bekoyev.

"We never knew how happy we were," Zalina Basieyava said.

Our dinner table grew quiet.

We never knew how happy we were.

Quite a wallop.

Most of us learn the hard way that the boundaries of sorrow deepen the moment we recall what we failed to cherish. In an instant, we see what we took for granted and, with the startle reflex of a baby, we flail at our newly excavated grief.

How could we not have seen that this was as good as it gets? Why were we always so impatient, so hurried, so eager to set our sights on the other kind of happy we were sure would find us when.

When we made more money.

When the kids were out of diapers.

When we had the perfect whatever-we-don't-have-now: Spouse? House? Car? Career?

I've grown weary of the pat little admonitions to "stop and smell the roses" and "live for the moment." Fine philosophies, but they're too gentle a prod for someone like me.

I'm not proud of this, but sometimes I need to get scared, to shock myself into appreciating my life in the here and now. So I play a little game that I learned from a Buddhist author years ago. I don't remember his name or the book I read, but I have never forgotten his lesson for living right here, right now.

The best way to value what we have, he said, is to imagine we have lost it forever. It's not enough, he said, to pretend that this is your last day on earth. Child's play, that one. So you die tomorrow: People are sad for a while, but life goes on. Your misery, at least in this lifetime, is over.

Instead, imagine that you have just lost what or whom you love the most in this life.

The spouse you yelled at this morning? Gone.

The kid who left her stuff all over the house? Gone.

Your busy schedule you love to complain about? You just lost control of your car and your legs will never work again. No more rushing for you.

I know it sounds maudlin, but it works. And it's my hedge against the grief that comes with no warning and no reprieve. None of us can stop tragedy and pain from visiting our lives, and I, like most adults and too many children, have lived long enough to know the losses that bring you to your knees. I just don't want the anguish over a misspent life to keep me there.

I say that, and still, I need the reminders.

Obligingly, God provides.

One recent morning, I sat on our porch swing after my husband dashed off to work. Thumbing through the day's newspapers he'd left in a rumpled stack, I grew increasingly irritated when I couldn't find one of the front sections I wanted to read.

He knows how I hate that.

I looked across the porch to the empty rocking chair where he sat reading a short time earlier.

The first thing I noticed were his reading glasses. They were turned upside down on the nearby planter, just as he had left them on the half-folded napkin he used during breakfast. The front section I wanted was at the foot of the rocker, turned to the last page he read.

To anyone else, it would have looked like a spot in need of tidying. Nothing more. To me, though, in that moment, it was a reminder of what sudden loss might feel like. "Just this morning, he was sitting there reading the paper," I imagined starting my story of heartbreak. "I didn't know . . ."

I reached for the phone. He had no idea why I was rambling on, but he didn't seem to mind.

And for a moment, I knew exactly how happy we really are.

GETTING TO LIVE OUT EVERY GUY'S DREAM

t took me all these years but I finally found a way to make men light up like fireflies.

Without so much as a wave of my mascara wand, I can capture both their attention and the green glow of their inevitable envy by describing how I'm about to perform every man's fantasy.

I get to throw out the first pitch in a major-league baseball game.

That's right: Me. Undeserving, unqualified, so-not-a-guy me.

Monday, I will stand in the middle of Jacobs Field, home to our beloved Cleveland Indians. I shall wave to the thousands of fans ignoring me. Then I will throw a baseball in the direction of what I hope will be home plate, where I'm told a real live Cleveland Indians player will capture it in his padded little glove and then hand it back to me.

"No way!" said the handsome young waiter who overheard me telling my daughter over dinner.

"Way," I said, ignoring my daughter's rolling eyes.

"You are kidding me!" said my cousin Dan at Mother's Day brunch.

"So not," I said, coolly popping another chilled shrimp into my mouth.

Even Dad, good ol' never-gets-excited Dad, sounded on the verge of happy about this one.

"The first pitch?"

"Yup."

"This is big," he said.

"Yeah."

"Really something."

"Yeah."

"Don't throw it in the dirt," he said.

This is a pattern. Guys' eyes pop open wide in utter awe at my news, then immediately narrow as they launch into advice born of the desperate hope that I will not bring shame to whatever relationship we share.

"You gotta warm up," said Dad, who started teaching me how to throw right about the time I started to walk.

"I know that, Dad."

"Do you have someone to help you warm up? You need help. Who's helping you?"

The question would be, who isn't helping me?

"I'm going to mark off how far you'll have to throw," said my husband, a lifelong Indians fan. By the time he stopped and yelled, "Okay, throw it!" he looked smaller than the toy in a Happy Meal.

"Are you sure it's this far?" I yelled.

"Yup. Sixty feet, six inches."

It was nice the way he ran over and started fanning me with his glove when I collapsed on the grass.

The next day, my three buddies at work, Jim, Mike, and Bill, tried to reassure me.

"Don't worry," said Jim. "You won't have to stand on the mound."

"Yeah," Mike said. "They never make you stand on the mound."

"Right," Bill said. "Nobody stands on the mound."

To be certain, I called Bryan Hoffart in the Cleveland Indians' office.

"You have to stand on the mound," he said.

"On the mound?" I said loudly, scowling at the resident experts.

"Yeah, you toe the rubber. Unless . . ."

He hesitated.

"Well, unless you think you can't make it."

I quietly hung up the phone.

"You have to make it from the mound," said Jim.

"Yeah," said Bill. "You have to."

"For us, man," said Mike. "Don't throw it in the dirt."

"Oh, yeah," they all groaned. "Not the dirt. Bring the heat. . . . Pound the leather. . . . Give 'em the high, hard cheese. . . ."

I felt like the only English-speaking guest at a family reunion on Mars.

Wednesday, though, I had a fleeting moment of calm after Jim offered to help me work on my throw in the parking lot. After a few throws, he smiled.

"You'll do fine," he said over the din of heckling passersby.

I practically skipped to my desk.

Then Mike walked over.

"Here's how you throw a fastball," he said. "Grip the ball perpendic-ular to the seams, at their widest point, with your middle and index fin-gers spread one-half inch apart. Your thumb lies perpendicular to the seams on the underside. . . ."

Help.

Me.

2.

Love in the
Middle Ages

S*ometimes life happens* only if you get out of its way.

On a snowy night in January 2003, I sat crouched behind the steering wheel of my parked minivan and decided I could not bring myself to go into the restaurant to meet my future husband.

I didn't know he was my future husband, but I knew he was my future *something* because I felt like a forty-five-year-old teenager whenever he sent me an e-mail or called me on the phone.

Thus, my panic.

Understand, I had written off dating two years ago after too many outings with men who had no idea I was sitting there listening to them, wishing I were in bed with a good book instead. It wasn't their fault. I was just a longtime single mother who had reached the age to know exactly what she did not want. By my early forties, I could hear the gate of opportunity slam shut before we even parked the car.

None of this explains why I had agreed to meet Sherrod Brown for dinner.

Two months earlier, an e-mail popped up on the screen of my computer at *The Plain Dealer,* where I had been a columnist for exactly two weeks after working as a features writer for eight years.

It was a short letter. "Ms. Schultz," it began. "Where did *The Plain Dealer* find you? You are a breath of fresh air; your writing reminds me of that of Barbara Kingsolver, one of my favorite living writers."

He signed it simply,
Best Wishes,
Sherrod Brown
Lorain, Ohio

No mention that he was a member of Congress. That was nice.

Comparing me to one of my favorite writers? That was way nicer.

"He's really sucking up with that Barbara Kingsolver line," I told my friend Jackie later that day. She stood in my living room and laughed as she started waving Sherrod's printed e-mail in my face like a referee throwing the flag.

"Dolly, this is the one," she said. "This is *my* horse in the race, and he's going to win. This is the man you're going to marry."

This was *so* Jackie. She loves to make outrageous predictions. For years, she also insisted I would one day win the Pulitzer Prize.

Sherrod and I began exchanging e-mails that grew increasingly playful.

He invited me to lunch.

Then his scheduler called to change the date.

Then she called again to reschedule it again.

The third time Pat called (she and I were on a first-name basis by now) to reschedule yet again, I asked her if she had a pen.

"A pen?" she said. "Sure."

"Good," I said. "Write this down please: 'The Camp David Peace Accords were easier to schedule than lunch with the congressman, and I'm no longer interested.' "

She drew her breath. "Oh, I can't tell him that."

"Yes, Pat. Yes, you can. And you must."

Then I called Jackie.

"Oh, my God, you didn't," she said.

"I did."

"He'll be back," she said.

He was. We made plans for dinner on a night when even congressmen are guaranteed the day off.

"Don't tell Pat," he wrote in an e-mail to confirm our plans for New Year's Day. "She hates when I schedule stuff on my own."

And so, there I was, in the parking lot of a Cooker restaurant, dialing Jackie on my cell phone to tell her I was backing out.

"You're nervous?" she said sweetly.

"Yeah."

"You really think you can't do this?" she said, still sweetly.

"I really can't."

"Hmmm," she said. "Okay, listen to me."

I pressed the phone to my ear.

"You turn off that car and march yourself into that restaurant," she said, no longer sweet at all. "Call me when it's over."

Ten months and twenty-six days later, Sherrod asked me to marry him.

I said yes.

Jackie is gloating still.

JUST DON'T CALL ME MISS DIRECTION

What did I tell him before we even got in the car?

I am terrible with directions, I told him. My mind darts around like a plastic bag in a windstorm. Highway signs all look alike after the sixth mile or so.

Now, if I told you that, and we were on a trip from Connellsville in western Pennsylvania to Cleveland, wouldn't you want to glance up occasionally and make sure we weren't headed for Hoboken, say, or the place we left behind two hours ago?

More specifically, would you have been humming along to Beatles tunes as you rifled through the tape collection? Would you have whiled away the miles writing poetic little missives on fancy note cards? Would you have played with your tiny computerized handheld doojey that keeps you in touch with the entire world but not the signs directly above your speeding head?

Honestly.

We switched seats after he drove for about an hour, which I pointed out was nowhere near the halfway mark for our trip home even if it took three and a half hours, rather than the six it became. He loves numbers and knows I hate them, so I thought this particular numerical fun fact might interest him if for no other reason than that it was downright fascinating to me.

"If you drove, I could get some things done," he said sweetly.

Being the intuitive woman that I am, I sensed immediately that the things he wanted to get done had nothing to do with making conversation with me. This despite my own efforts over the last sixty-seven miles to hang on his every word when I wasn't entertaining him with my collection of life-altering anecdotes.

"Fine," I said. "But make sure you pay attention to where we're going, okay?"

"You'll do great," he said, flipping on his little computer. "Just follow the signs. How hard can that be?"

I could answer that very question about an hour-and-a-half later, right after I spotted the sign welcoming us back to Connellsville.

"Huh," I said.

"What?" he said as he tap-tap-tapped.

"What do you think the chances are that there are two towns in Pennsylvania called Connellsville?"

Silence.

I looked over at him and flashed my biggest you-da-man smile, which might have held sway if he hadn't just spotted the oncoming sign announcing our ever-diminishing distance from the one-and-only Connellsville, Pa.

He squinted at the road, then I think he squinted at me, only I'm not sure because no way was I looking at him. As if on cue, the Beatles picked that unfortunate moment to do their hee-hee-hee-ho-ho-ho thing from "I Am the Walrus."

"Hmm," he said in a low, calm voice. "How do you suppose this happened?"

I wanted to sit a little higher in my seat, throw back my hair and deliver a tirade that began, "How did it *happen*? I'll tell you how it happened."

Only I couldn't. I looked into his imploring eyes as another Connellsville sign whizzed by and started babbling like Lucy Ricardo whenever Ricky insisted she had some 'splaining to do.

"Maybe when I got back on the turnpike . . . or when the cell phone rang . . . or when George started singing 'Something' and you know how that makes me all squiggly-iggly. Or maybe?"

He leaned in, his raised eyebrows just a smidgen below his hairline.

"Maybe?" I squeaked again as I leaned against the door. "Maybe you should have been looking, too?"

The car was silent until Paul started singing. Big help he was: "The lonnnng and wiiiiiinding roooooad . . ."

"That'd be about right," he said, but he laughed as he pointed me in the right direction. "Well, it's not as if you didn't warn me."

"Right."

"You told me this could happen."

"That I did."

"Of course, I thought you were exaggerating."

"Yes. Well."

The next day he sent me an e-mail assuring me all was forgiven. "I especially enjoyed the side trip to Philly," he wrote.

For the record, we were not remotely near Philly.

At least, I don't think so.

RELATIONSHIP RAINS CATS AND DOGS

H*e is not* a cat person.

That's what he told me as soon as he found out we had two black felines. "I don't hate them," he said. "I'm just not a cat person."

We'll see, I thought.

One of our cats is your typical oh-it's-you-and-I'm-so-very-bored variety. Her name is Winnie, and her usual greeting for strangers is a flash of fang followed by a heart-stopping hiss.

Lovely.

Our other cat, however, is Reggie.

Reggie has a sordid past. He has crawled into burning fireplaces and repeatedly leapt into large tubs of bathwater when he cannot swim. He once needed $800 worth of emergency surgery just to pee. He is why our handyman hacked out a chunk of plaster the size of Buffalo to free Reggie from behind the closet wall where he had landed with a thud after climbing behind the attic insulation. Covered in dust and mute from crying by the time he was rescued, Reggie was still Reggie, purring for all the happy humans as he strutted around the room like a conquering hero.

"Everybody," I said, "loves Reggie."

He shook his head. "I'm a dog person. I like to get on the floor and wrestle with a dog. You know, a little growlin', a little rollin' around. That's what you do with dogs."

Then he met our dog, a neurotic, quivering mass of pug named Gracie. The only thing she would ever wrestle is a T-bone, preferably medium rare.

"That's not a dog," he said, staring down at the wall-eyed creature desperately whimpering to make his acquaintance. "I don't know what it is, but it's definitely not a dog."

Meanwhile, Reggie cast his net.

"Hi, cat," he said one afternoon. I turned from the kitchen counter and saw Reggie wrapping himself around his ankles.

"Reggie," I said. "His name is Reggie."

"What's he doing?" he asked as he stared at the slithering length of fur weaving in and out.

"He's saying 'Hi,' " I said.

Reggie leapt onto his lap. "Oh, no, buddy," he said, shoving Reggie to the floor. Reggie jumped back up. He shoved him off again.

Up. Down. Up. Down.

Finally, he laughed and then patted his lap. "Oh, all right then. Come on."

Thus, the romance began.

A few days later, Reggie pounced on the bed where the supposed dog lover was reading and wrapped himself around his neck like a woolen muffler.

"Whoa, there, buddy, whatcha doin'?"

He started to reach for Reggie's head.

"Don't touch his ears," I said. "Reggie hates that."

"Doooo you?" he said, rubbing Reggie's head from ear to ear. "Do you really, really hate that, buddy?"

I gasped. Reggie shook his head so hard, it sounded like a horse's whinny.

Then he purred.

It is a sobering moment when one realizes her pet is about as loyal as a hooker. Does he care that I was the one who fed him milk from an eye dropper when he was only five weeks old? Does he even remember my tearful embrace after the traumatic wall rescue? Does he, even for a moment, consider the tons of cat litter I have emptied for the benefit of his sorry little bottom?

Ho-no. Reggie has a new pal whose terms of endearment for him now outnumber the ones he has for me. When he walks through the door, he seldom yells, "Hi, honey!" anymore. Instead, it's "Rehhhhh-hhhgie. Where's my Rehhhhhhhhhgie?" Guess who comes galloping on his floppy feet no matter how sound asleep he was when I called him.

It was time for a little soul-searching, some truth-talking, if you will.

He was lying on the sofa with his book held high so as not to disturb Reggie, who was sprawled across his collarbone.

"You know," I said gently, tugging on his toes. "I think it's time to admit it. You are a cat person."

He looked at me as if I'd just asked him to sever a limb so I could use it to snake the drain.

"What are you talking about?" he said. "Reggie's not a cat."

He started rubbing Reggie's ears. "You're not a cat, are you, buddy? No, no, no. You're a dog. Yes, you are. You know you are."

Reggie just purred.

LEARNING TO DIG GARDENING

It was a gray day in winter when he leaned across the kitchen table, grabbed my hand and said, "Let's plant a garden this year."

A garden.

I considered the implications. We would be making plans. The time for planting, after all, was at least another two months away.

We would be making joint decisions, too, and I would have to depend on his experience. I am a flower gardener. I know nothing about his world. What vegetables would we plant? How many types? Where would we buy them?

We were talking about commitment, too. We'd have weeks of tending, watering, weeding. Harvest wouldn't come until summer, two whole seasons away.

I hesitated. "Would we plant tomatoes?"

He smiled. "Sure."

"What kind of tomatoes would we plant?"

"What kind would you like?"

"Cherry?"

"You got it."

I became bold. "I'd want big fat juicy ones, too," I said.

He nodded. "Whatever you want."

We agreed on peppers, too, and green beans.

The deal almost fell apart over the marigolds.

"I heard they keep the rabbits and squirrels away," I said.

He smiled, shook his head. "No, that's a myth. And they'll take up too much room."

We waited for spring.

In May, we went to a greenhouse run by a cheerful woman and her husband, who laughed and said his wife must be right if she told us marigolds keep the bunnies away. We bought three types of tomato plants, three kinds of peppers, too, and seeds for green beans.

He saw me glance at the marigolds. I shrugged my shoulders and said, "That's all right. We don't need them."

"Let's get some," he said. "Let's get a whole flat of marigolds, and you can plant them all around the border."

I resisted. He persisted.

"They're pretty," he said. "And they'll remind me of you."

Later that day, we stood over the small, overgrown garden he had tilled many times before. It looked old and weary. I saw in it what had been. He saw what if. One shovelful at a time, he turned over the soil, and with each *chuff* of his spade, another patch of weeds disappeared.

I pulled the stubborn growth sprouting from between the stones that outlined the square of dirt, which was becoming moist and black and full of wiggly worms stretched out like question marks. With each yank, the past gave way to now.

And so, here we were, a man and a woman steeped knee-high in tomato plants and middle age, clearing a path for something new. I dug holes for the tomato and pepper plants, then lined the garden with the marigolds coaxed into several shades of yellow.

When he began to drop little seeds into rows of trenches, I stood and stared. "Those will grow?"

He stopped humming, touched my cheek. "You'll be amazed," he said. "First, there's nothing. Then one day you'll suddenly see all these little sprouts shooting through the soil."

It's summer now.

The tomatoes steadily climb the wire cones, barely able to restrain their enthusiasm. The peppers are making promises I hope they can keep.

He does most of the watering, and the garden always looks a little sad afterward, when all the plants droop under the weight of what is good for them. "They'll spring back up," he said the first time.

A couple of hours later, sure enough, they were tall and straight again, as if renewed by a good cry.

Last Sunday morning, there were still no bean sprouts.

That same evening, he called to me. "Look! Look!" he said, beaming as he stood by the garden and pointed to dozens of little sprouts yawning from the trenches.

"They just needed some sun."

I stood at the edge of the garden, amazed. I smiled at this man so full of faith in what we are sowing.

"You were right," I said.

Silently, I cheered on the tiny sprouts.

Grow, I urged. *Grow.*

SIDESTEPPING MANURE
IN THE GARDEN OF LOVE

This gardening thing has gotten way out of hand.

At first, I was all for it. He invited me to plan a garden with him last winter, when the snow was flying and our love was newer than a baby's bottom. I was touched to high blush, and immediately saw his urging me to sow seeds together as a metaphor for the new love sprouting between us.

Here's how I imagined my life as a gardener:

My head would tilt just so beneath a wide-brimmed straw sea-grass hat as I strolled among the tomato plants in a silk peasant dress and plucked bright red Beefsteaks, dropping them ever so delicately into my hand-woven Longaberger basket. Butterflies would light upon my shoulder, their translucent wings flapping approval. Birds would not just sing, but serenade.

His version of gardening was a tad different. Visions of compost bins danced in his head, and we saved every table scrap for months before he found the perfect contraption. My most recurring memory of the long winter is of him with his hand down the disposal, saying, "I thought we talked about this."

In his garden, weeds have motives.

"Look at them," he'd growl, yanking them by their wicked little roots. "As soon as we pull out of the drive, they start growing."

No problem, I said, pulling on my brand-new Smith and Hawken French embroidered gardening gloves.

Then over the next two weeks, I plucked the same patch of soil forty-seven times.

"Okay," I said. "Problem."

No matter how many times I pulled those nasty things out of the ground, they returned two days later like old girlfriends with a hearing problem.

"This is no fun," I said.

He spread his fingers and started counting off the list. "Let me get this straight," he said.

"You want to plant the tomatoes. You want to pick the tomatoes. You want to eat the tomatoes. You just don't want to help grow the tomatoes."

Finally, a man who can read my mind. Am I the luckiest woman on the planet or what?

He wasn't nearly as impressed with this epiphany as I. In fact, I had an inkling of where this relationship was headed when he began talking about what, in my opinion, was a lot of cow dooey.

"I suppose this means you don't want to help me with the manure, either," he said.

In an instant, it all came back to me, snippets of his Farmer Joe stories he'd been telling me since last December:

Yup, worked on the family farm when I was a kid . . . Best stuff there is for the soil . . . I go down and get several bags of it every fall.

I looked at his disappointed face and thought: *Can I really let this man down? Can I really break his heart and refuse to help bag cow manure? Do I risk losing his respect by revealing myself to be a pathetic, spoiled city girl?*

"Ple-he-he-he-he-eeeese," I said, my hands clasped in prayer. "Don't make me do this."

Well, his response was awful, just awful. Something about how of course it's up to me and he'll love me no matter what. How he just thought digging up manure would be one of those little adventures that brings us closer. How it'd be another funny story to tell our children and our children's children but never mind, that's okay. He'd do it alone.

When we went to the farm, he wore his oldest blue jeans and a grin wider than a strip mall. I brought running shoes and a prayer for rain. God in his wisdom showered us with the brightest patch of sun we'd had all fall.

It wasn't so bad until I stepped into a cow pie the size of Delaware. It got worse when he let out a spasm of laughter and then slapped his hands over his mouth like a ten-year-old who'd just said the f-word in front of his mother.

"Oh, geez, honey, I'm so sorry," he said, pat-pat-patting my back as if he were putting out a campfire. "Nobody'll notice, and you look so cute . . ."

It was right about then that I considered his chosen profession and saw a new metaphor for our relationship.

It involves a politician, a shovel, and manure.

Lots and lots of manure.

WHEN YOUR HEART KNOWS HE'S THE ONE

Even when I make him madder than a swatted bee he still calls me honey.

The first time I realized that, I took a deep breath in the middle of our heated discussion and thought: *Oh, my. He could be the one.*

Then I quickly perished the thought. I was too old for such daydreams.

But still.

It will come as a surprise to no one, I suspect, that I can frustrate the most patient of men. It's a gift, but I try not to brag. Over the years men have told me, usually through inexplicably gritted teeth, that the issue is my in-de-PEN-dence, always pronounced as if it were a diagnosis of eczema.

In retrospect, my "as God is my witness" speech about how I could take care of myself probably was overreacting a bit to their offer to buy lunch, but I was terrified of ever depending on anyone again. I spent years as a single parent figuring out how to be happy on my own. As anyone who's scaled that cliff knows, it's a climb full of scrapes and bruises, and the last thing most of us want to do after we finally heal is to open ourselves to the risk of new injury.

Fortunately, love is stubborn that way. It seeps through the thickest of scars and takes hold of the very heart we thought was beyond its reach. For me, that two-fisted grab came with a jolt of caffeine.

We had been dating for a couple of months when it became clear I was breaking all kinds of rules I'd set for myself. For one thing, I was dating, which I'd sworn off quite some time ago. I was also making plans with him, marking dates on a calendar even. Shocking.

Friends noticed. They tittered and teetered and performed hilarious imitations of me denying that this could be anything serious.

Every time the phone rang, though, I jumped. This worried me.

One cold winter day, I took a bold step to reassert my independence. The first time he offered to make me coffee, I refused.

I can do it myself, I insisted, and headed for the coffee beans.

Instead of backing off, though, he put his hands on my shoulders and asked me to sit down at the table. Leaning within an inch of my nose, he calmly but firmly said, "This is going to have to stop. You are not surrendering your right to vote and own property if you let me do something nice for you."

"I don't need you to—"

"I know you don't need me to," he said. "But I want to."

When a woman who's paid to give her opinion can't wrap her tongue around a single vowel, progress is made.

Ten months and a hundred cups of coffee later, I think back to that moment and recall my favorite William Blake drawing titled *I want. I want.* In it, a child stands at the foot of a ladder that reaches all the way to the moon. A friend gave it to me when my long-troubled marriage started to crumble.

"Try to believe in something better," she wrote. "It's there, waiting for you to find it."

She had it almost right. Nine years later, something better found me when I wasn't even looking.

Falling in love when you're knee-deep in middle age takes some getting used to. For one thing, you feel mighty silly giggling all the time, especially in front of your grown kids. You don't know how to introduce each other either, and I for one was sure getting sick of "My very, very good friend, Connie." And there's all that speculation from colleagues in our chosen professions—congressman and columnist—who've carved out second careers for themselves wondering how long this could possibly last.

We've finally come up with a ballpark figure for them: We're thinking 'til death do us part. Considering I'm already forty-six and he's fifty-one, we figure the odds are in our favor on that one.

Just before midnight on the eve of Thanksgiving, Sherrod asked me to marry him. Actually, he started talking about how great our life is and how we ought to commit to spending the rest of our days together and finally I realized we had a Venus-Mars thing going on and, of course, I just had to interrupt.

"Are you asking me to marry you?"

"That's what I want," he said.

That's what I want, too.

Funny how that works.

EVERYONE'S ASKING: HIS NAME OR MINE?

In the two months since my engagement, I've answered the same question more times than I've tied my shoes.

Strangers ask. Colleagues ask. Longtime friends who should know better ask. Even my daughter asked:

Are you going to change your name?

Most are just curious; some, I suspect, are toying with me. But occasionally the question feels more like a test: How much do you love him?

Not enough, they may conclude, because I am keeping my name.

I am well into my forties, entrenched in a career where my name is my currency. I am marrying a man whose life is a public one in a world where many view the spouse only as a prop or a problem. I was reminded of this last weekend, when Howard Dean's wife—who newspapers constantly note is Dr. Judith Steinberg in her day job—walked to the microphone and immediately assured the crowd, "For those of you who might not know, my name is Judy Dean."

Oh, my.

Twenty years ago, I wore a married name for what I believed were all the right reasons. My new stepson, who lived with us full-time, already had a white-knuckled hold on my heart. Having the same name would solidify us as a family, I thought, render us traditional. Normal, even.

There was an underlying assumption to my decision, though, as troubling as it was imperceptible to me at the time. At twenty-six, I felt I'd accomplished virtually nothing under my own name that merited preserving. I wrote many stories under my maiden name, but that was in college and my early twenties—a lifetime ago, it seemed, before I dropped out of law school and ended up a part-time bookkeeper for a temporary employment agency.

I was adrift and embarrassed, eager to say good-bye to my failed self. I would box her up and take on a new life, a new name. A new me.

Our families, by the way, heaved a collective sigh of relief.

The new me was an awkward fit. It took me nearly two years to get used to her, in part because it took everyone else no time at all. I was Mrs. now, an extension of the man who was carving out his place in the world while eclipsing mine. Five years into our marriage, our son brought home the family directory for the school where I volunteered at least ten hours a week. In it, we were listed as Mr. and Mrs. His Name. Next to it was my first name. In parentheses.

My old self started to stir. From inside the box I heard the softest tap-tap-tapping on the lid.

The following spring, my daughter was born. Her middle name, I decided, would be Schultz.

Then I started writing again, wedging my maiden name between my first and last. When I became a single mother, I left the married name behind.

Soon, I will be a wife again. For the record, he doesn't care what I do with my name. "She's not changing her name," he tells those who ask, "and I'm not changing mine."

Some women who wear their husbands' names see my decision as a judgment, an indictment of their choice. They're mistaken. I am an old-fashioned feminist. To me, we are all sisters, united not just by what we have in common but by our differences, too, because that's what the women's movement was all about: choice.

Whenever eyebrows raise in response to my assurance that I will keep my name, I fight the urge to prove my affection. I want to tell them I make him peanut-butter-and-jelly sandwiches when he has no lunch meeting, that I stay up for his middle-of-the-night calls when he has to work late and exchange e-mails with him all day long. It is absurd, this need I feel to convince others that keeping my name is about me, not him.

What I really want to tell them is that ten years ago I pulled the woman I once was out of storage. I dusted her off, forced her to stand upright, and told her she was on her own. I was a little scared for her, but I was also eager to see what she could do.

God knows she's a handful, and far from perfect. She's still upright, though, and the only dust on her now is the stuff she kicks up on her own.

And she's the only me I really know.

WE'RE GIVEN LICENSE
TO LET GO OF THE PAST

He drove. I sat in the seat next to him, the evidence of our past failures piled on my lap.

The poker-faced guard told us we were in the wrong building. My own face crumpled like a used coffee filter.

"Just kidding, just kidding," the guard said, grinning. I rolled up the documents in my hand and smacked him.

"Good luck, guys," he said, still chuckling as we walked through the electronic scanner and then across the shiny marble floors of the echoing atrium.

A court official had told us that, because it was Friday, we probably would be in for a wait. "Everyone rushes to get it done before the weekend," he said.

There was no line at all, though, on this afternoon. The three clerks at the counter—Brenda, Barbara, and Anne—smiled at us.

"What can I do for you?" Barbara said. As if she didn't know.

We told her anyway. She nodded her head, grabbed a form, and began the rite of passage that millions of Americans perform every year.

"Name?"

We told her. Mine, then his.

"Have you been married before?"

We both nodded our heads.

"How many times?"

"Once," he said. "Once each."

"I'll need to see your decrees."

I plopped the pile of papers in front of her, drew a deep breath. It isn't often you have to prove you failed before you are allowed to try again.

I winced as she flip-flip-flipped through the pages. Such a little stack for so great a burden. His divorce is sixteen years old. Mine is eight, and the paper trail of my marital demise is curled and dog-eared from years of worried use.

> Child custody, support and visitation were further ordered, adjudged and decreed on page 2. (Exhibit B)
> Divisions of property were further ordered, adjudged and decreed on page 7. (Exhibit D)

On page 9, the judge further ordered, adjudged, and decreed that I be "restored" to my former birth name. "Restored," as if my previous self were within reach. Or would be ever again.

I was divorced in this same building. Three floors up, the wooden benches are smooth from decades of cradling the anxious and the angry, the frightened and the ferocious. I know those benches well, particularly the one outside courtroom 1-A. There I sat, through pretrial this and pretrial that, as attorneys duked it out in the judge's chambers.

Most of my memories of that time have melded into one enduring image: I sit alone, wedged against the left arm rail, my stomach in knots and my right hand curled around wooden prayer beads. One bead, two beads, three beads—round and round, praying to keep the panic at bay.

Once, a husband and wife fought two feet away. He screamed at her, but she could only sputter between sobs. "You disgust me," he hissed, stomping off.

She turned to me, and, with tears streaming down her face, she asked about my beads.

"They're Buddhist prayer beads," I said. "A gift from a friend."

She stared at my moving fingers. "Would you say a prayer for me?"

"I already have," I said. She thanked me and walked away.

If walls could talk, they say. I imagine those at 1 Lakeside Avenue in Cleveland would wail.

And yet, here we were, on the first floor, full of hope that makes us giddy and new promises we intend to keep. I expected to dread being in this building where so much fell apart, but I found myself grateful for the reminder. If we can't remember the wrong turns, we're bound to get lost again.

Anne, fresh out of college and full of her own dreams, typed our driver's license information into the computer. She smiled when we told her our children will walk us down the aisle. "This is yours," she said, handing us a white envelope labeled MARRIAGE LICENSE in bold, fancy letters.

We walked back through the atrium, we joked with the guard, then we headed for our car.

He drove. I sat in the seat next to him.

I threw the evidence of our failures into the backseat.

The marriage license rested on my lap all the way home.

CAKE AND FLOWERS ON MOM'S BIRTHDAY

he anniversary of my mother's death is not the day that derails me.

Granted, there are memories of that crisp, autumn morning I'll never purge: the astonishing shift in the air when Mom's heart stopped. The assault of sunshine. The kind attendant in the hospital parking lot, who quietly lifted the gate as I dug and dug for my parking ticket then started babbling through tears that I was so sorry I couldn't find it but I was here all night and my mom just died and Mom always knew where her ticket was because she worried about things like that.

"You go home now," the woman said. "Just go home."

So, yes, I remember that day, but its anniversary has no choke hold on me. That maneuver of memory is reserved for her birthday.

My mother loved birthdays because she cherished surprises. She was so much fun to give a present to, giggling and squealing whenever a bundle of ribbon and bows was plopped on her lap.

Her hoots and hollers made others laugh, and who doesn't want to do that? Her birthday week was one long parade of friends and family bearing everything from ghastly animal figurines and crocheted toilet paper covers to French perfume.

"It's exactly what I wanted," she crowed every single time, shooting a scowl at me whenever my own gaping mouth suggested otherwise. "Ma," I'd say later, "a guitar-playing pig?"

"You never know when you might need one," she'd say, turning the plump little guy round and round in her tiny hands.

This Saturday, my mom would have turned sixty-seven. That's one of my newer traditions, I guess. Every birthday since she died four years ago, I wake up and think, "Mom would have been sixty-three . . . sixty-four . . . sixty-five. . . ." I still mark her birthday in my calendar, for no good reason except I can't bring myself not to. It leads to nothing but sadness, and that would have disappointed my mom. Birthdays, she said, are for celebrating.

A few days before she died, Mom grabbed my hand and told me, yet again, how she wished I'd meet "some nice man." She hated to see me take on so much alone, and the same independence she counted on sometimes made her worry.

"You'll know he's the one when he ignores all your protests and pays for the dinner," she said, wagging her finger. "But just in case you're not sure, I'll let you know."

I rolled my eyes and said, "Okay, Ma."

Four years later, I woke up one morning and wondered what she would have thought of the man I agreed to marry, and not just because he bought that first dinner. There was that familiar knot of questions wrapped around no answers and tucked just so, making it impossible for me to draw a deep breath. "Oh, Ma," I said out loud. I busied myself with the morning's activities, headed to work.

The first person I ran into that morning was one of my closest friends, who beamed at the sight of me. "I was just thinking how happy your mother would be for you now," she said, her eyes misting. "I just know she'd love him."

Breathe, I told myself.

Soon after, I decided Mom was right: Birthdays, including hers, should be joyful. And just because she's not here anymore doesn't mean I can't give her a present. It's a whopper, too.

On Saturday, I will wake up and remember Mom would have turned sixty-seven. I'll probably feel that usual pang, but it won't last, for do I have a surprise for her.

Our home will bustle with the antics and one-liners of grown kids who have far too much fun teasing their parents, the bride and groom. We'll dart over and around one another as we eat and shower and wriggle into costumes designed to lend credibility. We'll pile into various cars punctuated with an assortment of dings to drive to the church where family and friends will meet us in a sanctuary brimming with lilies.

We'll laugh and sing and pray together, maybe cry a little too, and after we say "I do," one of the pastors is going to haul herself up to the belfry and ring the church bells so even the sparrows know the celebration is on.

I think Mom would have loved that.

In fact, I'm sure she will.

EXCHANGING SWEET NOTHINGS

"*Listen to this,*" he said.

I looked over the top of the newspaper section in my hands to where my husband sat across the kitchen table with his part of the paper. My reading glasses were perched on the tip of my nose but, curiously, that did not alert him to my endeavor.

"You weren't in the middle of reading something, were you?" he asked.

"Well, there's this essay by this woman whose dad was lifelong friends with Grace Kelly—"

"Oh, good," he said. "Listen to this. You're not going to believe this."

Actually, I will believe it. In fact, I could probably recite the story by heart because my dear husband was about to read aloud the four-millionth story written so far about the presidential race.

But I listened. I nodded. I winced, scowled, and even booed at all the appropriate places. When he finished, he pulled off his reading glasses.

"Can you believe that?" he said.

"Well."

He looked stunned. "I'll tell you what," he said, "I sure don't believe it."

He flipped the page; I returned to Grace Kelly. For about five sentences.

"Oh, my God," he said. "I didn't even see this. Listen to this."

He can't help himself. For my husband, every factoid, every anecdote, every quotable quote is a discovery meant to be shared with the world. Or, in the absence of the entire world, me. Lucky, lucky me.

It only starts with the morning newspapers. There are all those health advisories we get, the special-interest magazines with the latest poll results, and newsletters from nonprofit groups whose letters from volunteers in the field always make me feel like a self-indulgent slug unworthy of the gasoline it takes to get me to work every day.

And then there are the books. His recent treasure trove was Bill Bryson's *A Short History of Nearly Everything.* Emphasis on everything. "Did you know Einstein's very first paper was on the physics of fluids in drinking straws?" he asked.

"Huh," I said.

"Did you know that, left unmolested, lobsters can live as long as seventy years and never stop growing?"

"Huh."

"Oh, get this," he said, right after I complained that my entire face has shifted south. "Your skin cells are all dead. You are lugging around five pounds of dead skin which sloughs off several billion tiny fragments every day. Run a finger along a dusty shelf, and you are drawing a pattern very largely in old skin."

"Oh, you sweet talker, you," I grumbled.

It's not that I mind when he reads to me. It's just that, like most men I know, he has limited interest in being read to.

He denies this.

"I'm listening, I'm listening," he'll yell over the roar of the garbage disposal he flicks on the moment I start reading. "I heard every word you said."

Our problem, I think, is content. He wants to share the Second Law of Thermodynamics (curse you, Bill Bryson), while I just as excitedly want to tell him what I've learned about mood rings in *The Encyclopedia of Bad Taste.*

"Inside their 'quartz' stones were heat-sensitive liquid crystals chemically synthesized out of grease extracted from sheep's wool," I read. "Just like what they used in hospital thermometers."

He gave me that look. I hate that look. You know the look I'm talking about, where he's staring at you and you just know he's thinking, *Wow. Sure wish I'd known that about her.*

Now, in fairness, he did try listening to me recently when I announced—and I do mean announced—that I wanted to read to him a poem by Grace Paley.

"The whole poem?" he said. Smart man that he is, he took the set of my jaw as a yes and put down his own book. "I'm ready," he said. "I'm listening."

The poem, titled "Here," is about an old woman sitting in her garden with a grandson on her lap as she watches her husband talk to the meter reader. At the end, she tells her grandson to fetch Grandpa because she is "suddenly exhausted by my desire to kiss his sweet explaining lips."

I looked up from my reading, on the verge of tears. I smiled at my husband.

"Huh," he said.

BASEBALL IS STILL HIS FIELD OF DREAMS

When I was a child, I spoke like a child, I thought like a child, I played like a child.

When I became an adult, I put away my childish ways.

Then I met the man I would marry.

One day early in our relationship, I opened a cupboard door in his kitchen and discovered enough plastic Cleveland Indians cups to meet the beverage needs of the entire population of Toledo. And he doesn't even drink beer.

"What are these?" I asked.

Reverently, he described them, one tower at a time. There are the 1994 Inaugural Season cups. The Playoffs cups. The World Series cups. The discarded cups he scooped up from under the seats on his way to the exit. There are also Detroit Tigers cups, Pittsburgh Pirates cups, Chicago Cubs cups. No Yankees cups, though. Never the Yankees. In fact, the word "Yankees" is never uttered in his presence unless to recite one of his e-mail addresses, which begins with "damnyankees."

He took one look at the horror on my face and wrapped his arms around the mountain of cups he'd stacked on the counter. "These stay," he said.

I married him anyway.

I used to think I was quite the baseball fan. I knew the basic rules of the game and sometimes even followed along by keeping score. Then I went to my first game with my husband.

"Stadiums always face the same way," he explained between innings at our first game. "They call left-handers 'southpaws' because the left hand of the pitcher always faces south."

Okay. I didn't know that. He's left-handed himself, so I figured he was just sharing a little part of himself. Sweet.

A few minutes later, he struck up a conversation about the foul pole.

"The foul pole and the foul line really should be called the fair pole and the fair line because if the ball hits the pole or the line it's a fair ball."

He looked at my blank face.

"Think about it," he said.

I flagged the beer guy.

Oh, what I have learned about baseball. Take hits, for example. Did you know they aren't just hits? Let's say the ball lands between the infielder and the outfielder. That's a blooper, which I found out when I mistakenly referred to a Baltimore chop as a blooper. But it also can be called a dying quail. Or a Texas leaguer.

"Why Texas?" I asked.

"I don't know. It just is."

"But there must be a reason it's Texas. Did it happen to a guy in Texas?"

"I don't know. It doesn't matter. It's baseball."

Doesn't matter? This is the same man who, upon finding out that the word "peruse" actually means to read thoroughly, now lobbies nearly everyone he knows to use it correctly. (For those of you who, like me, thought it meant to skim, think again. Please. At least before you run into my husband.)

But why is a hit called a Texas leaguer? Doesn't matter. It's baseball.

He also loves to play baseball. Every spring for about five weeks we go to the batting cages so that he can practice his swing for the office baseball game. I become the high school girlfriend he never had: I hold his car keys and cheer him on, and then afterward we go for ice cream.

One afternoon at the cages, a bunch of middle-school boys crowded around in awe as my fifty-one-year-old husband whacked one ball after another at sixty miles per hour. "Dang," one of them said. "Does he play for the Indians?"

Oh, Lord.

Last week, we were in Boston. A lot was going on there. Big convention. Lots of celebrities and important people and media from around the world. All of that, though, was a big so-what after the once-in-a-lifetime invitation arrived.

At high noon on a hot, sunny day in Boston, my husband walked up to home plate in Fenway Park for the chance to hit three whole pitches. He adjusted his cap, dug his toe in the dirt, then looked at me with a smile bigger than a triple before smacking a line drive to center and then a Texas leaguer.

I still don't know why they're called that. But right then, I didn't care. I just cheered and cheered for my baseball-whacking boyfriend, grateful for the chance at this second childhood.

LOVE HIM, LOVE HIS DOGS?

They taunt me, these dogs playing poker in our family room.

Or are they in the living room right now? Maybe in the kitchen? I can't remember. My mind is still reeling from the sight of them shuffling cards and puffing cigars in our bedroom.

Our *bedroom.*

This is what happens when two people in defiance of middle age fall in love and marry. Eventually, households must merge. And then they collide.

My husband and I married about a year and a half ago. Until this month, we lived in two homes because I was afraid that forcing my daughter to move across town in the middle of her high school years would inspire her own dark memoir by middle age. I imagined it having "Mother" in the title and hitting bookstores just as I was starting to make friends in the assisted-living center.

She has just graduated, and now here we are, husband and wife, nose to nose as we debate the final resting place of two framed paintings of dogs playing poker.

Let me just say that, so far, most men are not on my side.

With women, I can barely say "dogs playing poker" before they nod sympathetically and respond with their own three little words: Hefty Cinch Sak.

Men, however, hear that my husband has reproductions of artist Cassius Marcellus Coolidge's 1903 paintings titled *Waterloo* and *A Bold Bluff* and practically beg for a private viewing.

The original paintings were part of Coolidge's work for an advertising company in Minnesota. He painted sixteen in all, nine of them depicting card-playing canines.

Our two paintings, which I am forever stressing are on cardboard, capture four dogs getting duped by a St. Bernard. It's your usual poker scene, if you don't count the most unusual sight of dogs swilling beer and chewing on stogies. Spilled chips, spilled drinks, spilled pipe—your basic housecleaning nightmare whenever the menfolk gather.

My husband does not recall when or how he got these framed prints, only that they once hung in his daughters' room. I unearthed them from their childhood closet during packing.

It didn't help that his daughters, now grown, lighted up like snow globes on recent visits when they spotted the paintings temporarily—emphasis on not permanently—perched on my piano. Elizabeth, ignoring me as I waved wildly behind her father's back, proceeded to help him name all the dogs in the painting. Now they're family.

Then, earlier this year, the originals went up for auction and sold for $590,400. No, really.

"Yup," my husband brayed. "More than half a million!"

All this happened before we moved. Surely, I thought, he understood that what may have worked in a child's room or on a piano surrounded by moving boxes simply wasn't appropriate for our new grown-up house.

To illustrate this obvious point, I propped them up on the fireplace mantel the day after we moved and waited for him to come home.

Oh, the joy, the jubilation, the tremble, even, in his gravelly voice the moment he beheld the sight of his beloved poker pals.

"Perfect!" he said, hugging me tight. "Just perfect!"

Since then, the dogs have played poker in nearly every room of the house as we debate where they might fit in with our decor. Shamefully, we lobby friends, neighbors, and even innocent deliverymen with the zeal of pharmaceutical reps.

With heterosexual couples, it's almost always a tie vote.

"Oh, my," said our friend Emily.

"Oh, wow!" said her husband, John.

Gay couples just laugh and laugh and then kiss each other in gratitude that they found each other.

My friend Bill may have the solution. He took one look at the paintings and said, "Well, you know where they have to go."

I stared at him, expecting the worst.

"The bathroom," he said.

"Hmm," I said. "Never thought of that."

"Sure," he said, shrugging his shoulders. "It's the only domain we have left."

And as viewings go, it doesn't get more private than that.

3.

You've Got to
Be Kidding

There is a certain kind of column that comes so fast and easy that I'm not sure I should get paid for writing it.

I mean it, like manna from heaven, it just lands with a thud right there in front of my laptop and my fingers can't even stop themselves from tap-tap-tapping away.

This kind of column is the irrepressible giggle at a funeral, the raised eyebrow at the pregnant bride. I listen to a phone message, read a story buried on page 13, or chat with a colleague who's just called me over with a wave of the arm, shouting, "Oh, Connieeee, I think I've got something here for you. . . ."

And there it is: an easy day's pay.

This section covers the head-shaking part of life. You know what I mean. You hear something or see it with your own eyes and you can't help but think somebody has got to be kidding. But there they are, life's little absurdities sprouting like milkweeds on a tidy lawn. You can't miss them, and you can't ignore them, either. Well, I can't anyway, so I yank them out of the ground and yell, "Lookee, lookee, what I just found."

Who couldn't find a column in stories like these:

A young mother calls me and leaves this message: We went to a Cleveland Browns game, and they made us buy a $37 ticket for our five-month-old son—who was strapped to a Baby Bjorn on my husband's chest.

A *New York Times* story declares that friends and entire families—from beloved grandparents to cousins you can't stand—are now showing up in hospital delivery rooms for the big event. Sometimes more than one father-to-be shows up, too, and that's a duel you can't hee-hee-who your way through no matter how many gold Mommy Stars you earned in Lamaze.

Ohio lawmakers—do I even need to say these are all men?—want to ban breast-feeding in public places because such acts of nature might rob grown men of their last ounce of common sense and force them to gawk.

Honestly.

And I get paid to write about this stuff.

Granted, I am the butt of some of my own jokes in this section, but let me just say in my defense that I really thought I had turned off my cell phone before church and I'm sure I can't be the only one worrying about how many of my fellow airline passengers have been underestimating the weight of their baggage, so to speak.

And when are choir directors going to stop giving sopranos all the fun parts? I'm telling you, a lifetime of droning rum-pum-pum-pum does things to you.

A RINGING CELL PHONE HAS MY NUMBER

I *wanted to crawl* into the floorboards and live there for the next six months.

We were sitting in church during a sermon about our limitations as human beings. The room was still, as it often is when Pastor Woody weaves his stories.

Then the cell phone rang.

Not just any cell phone. My cell phone—and it pealed like the sirens of a British bobby. REE-ner, REE-ner, REE-ner.

I grabbed my purse and started rummaging as thoughts tumbled through my head like loose change in a dryer:

Where, oh where, is the phone?

REE-ner, REE-ner, REE-ner.

How did I forget to turn it off?

REE-ner, REE-ner, REE-ner.

I sure do wish I wasn't wearing bright pink right now.

REE-ner, REE-ner, REE-ner.

Finally, I found the phone and turned it off.

I took a deep breath and slowly raised my head. The minister was looking right at me. Fortunately, it was Pastor Woody, a man as benevolent and kind as his name suggests.

He smiled at me and gracefully segued into an anecdote about a woman who answered her cell phone in an inappropriate setting and actually began holding a conversation. Gesturing toward me, he said, "I'm not talking about when we forget to turn off our phones. That can happen to anyone. We all make mistakes."

Over the next few minutes, I felt the scarlet blush slowly creep back into my pores as I considered this one painful truth: Pastor Woody was kinder than I would have been.

I'm typically annoyed when someone's cell phone rings. *Why didn't they turn it off?* I wonder. *Why don't they have better manners?* (Translation: *Why are they not more like perfect little me?*)

Now I was one of the very people I was so sure I wasn't. I was embarrassed by my forgetfulness, mortified by my rudeness, and humbled by my past bad behavior in judging others. Chances are they simply forgot to turn off their phones. Chances are, they were just like me.

Once again my own bungling taught me a lesson in compassion. I'm all for enlightenment, but I sure do wish I'd figure out a different way to bring it on.

Well into my forties, I still seem hell-bent on learning the hard way. Just when I think I deserve something new and expensive as a reward for my own rectitude, I act like a complete fool and come face to face with irrefutable evidence that I am practically kin with the exact folks who drive me crazy.

I suppose this is true of most of us. Our mistakes and failures connect us to others in profound ways that our successes and conquests never will. It's in the moments of humility, when we have no choice but to see our own foibles and missteps, that the seed of compassion takes root in our hearts. The more we stumble, the more our capacity for compassion grows like graceful willows.

By now I should have a whole forest of compassion taking seed in my own thumping heart. I recoil, for example, when I think of how many funerals I skipped until my mother died. And I regret how often I hurt others when I was so sure some wrongs were beyond forgiving—until I committed them myself.

Fortunately, I often seem to have someone kinder and more thoughtful just a whisper away to pick me up, brush me off, and plant another seed. Those grow sturdy trees, let me tell you.

No one was better at that than Lisa Hearey, who was frail and dying five years ago when we set off for one of her last chemotherapy visits.

I was driving, which always made me a little nervous because she was so fragile. At the end of her life she weighed only eighty-seven pounds, and every bump in the road made her wince. I always drove slowly, carefully, constantly checking her face to make sure I was not compounding her pain.

On this particular morning, though, we were running late, and, sure enough, ended up behind someone driving fifteen in a thirty-five-mile-per-hour zone.

"Why is he going so slowly?" I said, pounding the steering wheel.

Lisa reached over and gently laid her tiny hand on my arm. "Well, we don't know why, do we?"

Down I stumbled. And another willow took root.

Well, this is definitely news I cannot use.

I had just reached the point where I could board an airplane without doing a mental list of who would attend my funeral later that week when the Federal Aviation Administration dropped this little bomb:

We're much fatter than they thought we were.

For the last eight years, the government has operated under the assumption that the average flier weighs 180 pounds in summer and 185 in winter, including clothes and carry-on items. Unfortunately, a steady diet of cheeseburgers and French—oops, I mean freedom—fries has rendered a third of all Americans over the age of twenty obese under federal guidelines.

As a result, the FAA's Flight Standards Office is now recommending airlines add at least ten more pounds to the estimated weight of every passenger.

Just to be sure, they say. Especially on the little planes.

I'm trying not to overreact here. I've been a white-knuckle flier ever since I gave birth and imagined my distraught children being raised by a twenty-two-year-old stepmom named Muffy. Reading how airplanes actually work has done nothing to ease my fear that we remain in the air only as long as God pays attention. And seeing the oversized bags some people claim as carry-ons makes me worry that God's just gonna smack us out of the sky for our lying ways.

Now they're telling us we might be too fat to fly? As in we might not stay up in the air? Bring in the scales, the fat calipers, the tape measures. I already willingly stand like a murder suspect with my feet apart and my arms straight out every time I enter the gate.

For years, I avoided flying, opting for buses, trains, and cars whenever possible. I figured, hey, Aretha Franklin hates to fly, too. And how cool is *she*?

Lately, though, I've been in the air more than a migrating goose. I've had plenty of opportunities to think about what all can go wrong on an airplane.

Two weeks ago, for example, I saw an airline attendant look sympathetically at the pilot standing outside the cockpit as we boarded.

"What's wrong?" she purred.

"Oh, nothing," he said, his face longer than a tube sock. "It's just one of those days."

One of those days? One of those *days*?

What kind of a day are we talking here? Feeling-a-little-tired day? Sure-wish-I-hadn't-had-that-last-scotch-and-soda day? I-have-no-reason-to-live day?

I gave him my best I-am-nothing-without-you smile and prayed all the way to Boston.

Which brings me back to God. It has come to my attention that airline passengers are calling him when they don't really need him. And we all know the story of the boy who cried wolf, don't we?

So, since the FAA folks are in the mood for change, I suggest they add this to their recommendations:

Under no circumstances should an airline passenger be allowed to shout, "Oh, my God!" unless they've just seen a wing fall off or their baby got sucked out an open window.

Twice on one flight I witnessed an unjustified use of "Oh, my God!" And both times my heart started pounding like a steel drum in a calypso band as that annoying little voice in my head (who is that guy, anyway?) screamed, "You'll never finish that novel now!"

The first time, a woman screeched, "Oh, my God!" I immediately felt for the flotation device under my seat and then turned to discover that her toddler had just thrown a tumbler of Cheerios into the aisle.

The second time, it was a young man who yelled, "Oh, my God!" I spun around as best I could within the confines of my seat belt—not disobeying that rule, not me, nosiree—to find a college kid grabbing the shoulder of the young woman next to him.

"I know, I know," she said, as she nodded her head. "Can you, like, belieeeeeeve he said that to me?"

Overweight airline passengers. Carry-on bags the size of Volkswagens. People wasting his precious time. All this on a single flight.

And I've got four more trips in the next few days.

Oh, my God.

BROWNS POLICY NEEDS A CHANGE

Jacob Marvin Greene tried to pull a fast one on the Cleveland Browns.

He almost got away with it. For starters, he looks pretty harmless, what with his thinning hair and large, hazel eyes that practically scream, "I'm innocent." He's a wiry fellow, too, one who's used to slipping in and out of places without official notice, especially since he's never alone. In fact, he uses his own parents as accomplices.

In the past, Jacob managed to slip right through airline checks and the Cleveland Indians' turnstiles without paying. He does it at the movies, too, and will do the same thing at Cleveland Cavaliers games.

But at the Cleveland Browns' home opener this month, Jacob got nailed. The Browns' employee at the gate took one look at his benign little face peering out from beneath his oversize cap and said, Uh-uh. No way.

"Where's the ticket for him?" he asked, pointing to Jacob.

Jacob's parents, Heather and Bradley Greene, were incredulous.

He's a baby, his mother said.

He's five months old, said his father, wrapping his arms around all thirteen pounds of his son nestled in the Baby Bjorn strapped to Dad's chest. Heather assured the ticket taker that Jacob would sit on her lap the entire game.

Doesn't matter, he said. Laptop Baby or not, Jacob had to pay.

The Greenes knew that the Cleveland Indians don't charge for children under two, which is also the Cavaliers' policy. Surely, they thought, this was a mistake.

But still another Browns official told them they had to pay.

"He said, 'Just go buy the cheapest ticket you can get in any section, and we'll let you in,' " Bradley said.

Disapproval rumbled through the crowd. "Can you believe it?" the Greenes heard over and over. "They're making them buy that baby a ticket."

Bradley went to the ticket window and asked for the cheapest seat he could buy. Only single seats were available, so he paid $37 for seat 11 in row 13, section 346. That was quite a hike from his parents' seats, which were numbers 20 and 21 in row 16, section 533. Jacob can't actually sit on his own, though, so that was hardly the issue.

When I called the Browns, some in their corporate office questioned the parents' judgment. "Who would bring a baby to a football game?" they grumbled.

Those die-hard fans the Browns woo, that's who.

The Greenes have loved the Browns their entire lives. And they trusted the Browns' repeated assurances that they cracked down on tailgate parties and alcohol abuse in the stands. They wanted little Jacob's baby book to include photos of him at his very first game for their beloved team, wearing his official Cleveland Browns onesie with a football on the butt and matching booties.

Attempting to turn the issue into an indictment of their parenting is nothing but a common courtroom tactic meant to distract the jury from the real issue.

When I called the Browns, they first said charging admission for babies was NFL policy. The NFL, however, told me that isn't true, that the teams set their own policy.

"Well," said Browns spokeswoman Amy Palcic. "It's been a longtime policy here." Translation: We've gotten away with it until now.

Browns spokeswoman Lisa Levine said charging for babies "isn't about the money."

"This is about the babies' safety," she said.

Hmmm. So the babies are safer after they pay $37? I'm no football expert, but I'm going to go out on a limb here and say no. If safety is the issue, then ban babies from the game.

Levine told me Wednesday they are reviewing their policy. For guidance, they might look to the Cleveland Indians and the Cleveland Cavaliers. They could also watch their own television ad airing this week in parents' homes across northeast Ohio.

In it, a hospital nursery brims with newborns wearing Cleveland Browns caps on their precious little heads.

So, as ticket buyers or commercial currency, the little guys are real moneymakers for the home team.

That's some bottom line, baby.

PEDOMETER CRAZE IS TAKEN IN STRIDE

Today I *will log* between 5,708 and 5,980 steps on my pedometer before noon.

I share this because I am in search of anyone who might care.

You don't care. I realize that—really I do—but now that I'm counting my every footfall, I need you to try.

Before a pedometer dug into my waistband, I would not have expected you to care. You have bills to pay, dinners to plan, and a slew of questions about the future of Social Security. Why would you care about the number of times my pendulum mechanism registered the g-shock of my foot strike?

G-shock, by the way, is pedometer parlance for gravity-shock. To paraphrase writer David Sedaris: Me talk so pretty these days.

All those fitness gurus who encourage you to clamp a pedometer to your waist never warn you about the way it changes you. Oh, they crow about all the burned calories, the plummeting cholesterol counts, the thrill of indoor mileage. But they never mention that you inevitably will succumb to that most annoying of human afflictions:

You will want to brag. A lot. And this bad habit creeps up on you like the mile-a-minute vine of Georgia kudzu.

You e-mail your spouse every hour with your latest trot tally because he, too, wears a pedometer, and what started out as something fun to do has become Marital Olympics.

Then you map out the longest route to the office washroom and feel the need to explain exactly why to every colleague you run into along the way. You dismiss their rolled eyes and exchanged glances as g-shock envy of the sedentary.

Before you know it, you are lifting the hem of your sweater in front of total strangers in the checkout line so you can glance down at your pedometer and say with a chuckle, "Well, whaddya know, I just walked another 412 steps in this here grocery store."

You learn things about people after they take to wearing a pedometer. One of my friends is as even-tempered as they come, or so I
thought until she started wearing a high-tech digital pedometer that's
about as big as a minicam. I ran into her on my new route to the ladies'
room and asked her how many steps she'd logged so far. She raised her
arm and reached for her hip like Matt Dillon on *Gunsmoke*.

"Let's see," she said, pressing a button, "I have walked . . ."

She gasped.

"Oh, no."

"What?"

"Oh, I didn't."

"Didn't what?"

She looked at me as if I had just handed her a ransom note demanding a wad of unmarked tens and twenties if she ever wanted to see her
children again.

"I just deleted how many steps I've walked today."

It was late afternoon, so I figured she must have already checked her
pedometer about forty-two times that day.

"Can't you estimate based on what it was five minutes ago?"

She shook her head. "That would be cheating."

That hit a nerve, I must say, as I've devised quite the system for rack-
ing up steps here and there without ever lifting my foot from the floor,
and I refuse to call that cheating.

My U-turn on the road to self-deception started after I hit a pothole
on Chester Avenue and felt a little blip of movement at my waist. Sure
enough, I checked my pedometer, and its nice, big numbers said I'd
walked two more steps. Just like that.

When I laughed, it blipped again. Another step! In all, I logged fourteen steps from home to downtown without even setting my two-toned
pumps on solid ground.

Ah, there's nothing like the swell of superiority that renders you
light-headed when your pedometer clicks as you pass someone sitting at
a computer in a workplace just brimming with such moments of im-
mobility. And I just found out that some pedometers can talk.

I don't know what they say, but you can bet I'm going to find out.

I'm hoping for something that coos, "Look at your fine self step-
step-stepping your way to fitness. One step, two steps, three steps, look
at you go . . ."

Finally, someone will care.

WE WILL REVEAL THOSE WHO CONCEAL

See *what happens* when you tell a guy he can hide a gun under his sport coat?

Right away, he starts strutting as if he were Matt Dillon kicking up dirt after a little coochy-coo with Miss Kitty. Threatening this, threatening that—it's embarrassing, really, especially when the fellow playing shoot-'em-up is a state official.

State Representative Jim Aslanides is just full of spit and swagger now that his concealed-weapon bill has passed. Thanks to Cowboy Jim and his posse, your average citizen—not to mention your not-so-average raging ex-spouse and disgruntled employee—can carry a hidden weapon around any street in the state.

Cowboy Jim was one of the first to take aim, firing away at any journalist armed with the silly notion that each and every resident in this fine state of Texas, I mean Ohio, has a right to know who's carrying a loaded weapon in their neighborhood.

This little showdown came about because one of the new law's provisions prohibits the general public—that would be you—from finding out who is purchasing a permit to carry a concealed weapon.

Only journalists are allowed to get that information. So that is exactly what we intend to do. We will find out who bought the permits to carry concealed weapons and then let you know, too.

That gets Cowboy Jim's spurs to spinnin': "I want the journalists in the room to know that if they abuse this access, they can lose the privilege."

I'm sure he meant "right": we'll lose the *right,* as provided by *law.* Some folks get a little jittery when their finger's on the trigger.

His sidekick from the state senate, Tag-along Steve Austria, fired the second shot. He said publishing the names of permit holders would be the exact kind of abuse they're talkin' about. Why, he said, the whole idea behind concealed carry is that the rest of us aren't supposed to know who's carrying 'em. Publishing their names would threaten the safety of the very men and women who don't want you to know they're packin' in the first place.

Hmm.

It seems to me the ones who need protecting aren't the folks who tuck a Glock under their armpit every time they step out to walk the dog or buy a quart of milk. I hate to make assumptions here, but I can't help thinking that folks who carry concealed weapons aren't the ones quoting Gandhi. And if I'm in a store that's about to be robbed, the last place I want to be is between a robber and the Dirty Harry wannabe who's decided to take the perp down.

As a parent, I want to know who's armed in my neighborhood. This is entirely consistent with my family policy of long standing. Whenever my kids were invited to a new family's house, I asked the parents whether they had firearms in the house and, if so, how and where they stored them. Did they have a child safety lock, which is not required in Ohio? Was the gun loaded?

If that sounds excessive, keep in mind that, according to the most recent stats, in 2001 alone, eighty-seven children and teenagers in Ohio died from gunfire.

That's eighty-seven children too many. And, so far, children can't buy guns. Money buys guns.

Money drove this legislation, too. And only money can stop it, says Lori O'Neill, president of the Million Mom March, Cleveland chapter.

"This was special-interest legislation passed solely for a handful of people incredibly well funded. Poll after poll shows that 70 percent of Ohioans oppose the concealed-weapon law. But our legislature passed it anyway."

The only way to fight it, she says, is to collect the 193,000 signatures needed in ninety days to put a referendum on the ballot. "We'd need at least a half-million dollars to do that, and we don't have it."

So, what can you do to keep your family out of firing range?

Not much, if you're the average Ohio citizen. You can't even find out who in your neighborhood, your office, or your school district has bought a permit to carry a hidden weapon.

So, we journalists will find out for you.

That's not a threat.

That's the law.

AN UNSUNG ALTO'S SOPRANO ENVY

his is the week of weeks for church choirs.

From the tiniest chapels to the most cavernous cathedrals, choir members who've been rehearsing in anonymity for weeks will pull on their long flowing robes and strut into sanctuaries like preening peacocks.

And why not? They've earned it, almost as much as the choir directors who've managed not to physically harm any of them on the road to Bethlehem.

The choir members performing this Christmas Eve gave up precious family time and countless episodes of *CSI* for evening rehearsals. They stoically weathered simmering resentments of the musically challenged who (a) think they should be the soloists and (b) can't quite believe their ears that you-know-who got it instead. They've endured the tyranny of those who read music versus those who do not.

And, if they're the altos in the choir, they've spent endless hours as background instruments droning rum-pum-pum-pum while the sopranos send pigeons flying with their soaring descants performed on tippy-toe.

Yes. I admit it. I suffer from that dreaded affliction.

I have soprano envy.

I am an alto. I didn't want to be an alto. I wanted to be frilly and feminine and hit something higher than middle C without sounding like a mating rooster, but alas, God took one look at me and said, "Nah."

My soprano envy started when I was in the high school choir. I'd look longingly at the soprano section way over there, where the girls always sang melodies—easy, nonchallenging, already-known-to-everybody melodies—while we learned eighteen different ways to hum. Sometimes we sang *wooooo*.

The only time I didn't sing alto was when Mr. Allshouse needed an extra tenor.

"You," he'd say, pointing at me, always at me, ignoring my hands folded in prayer. "You can go lower."

There I was, wedged between the hulking shoulders of Micky Dean and Gerry Allen—brothers all—belting out "Lida Rose, I'm home again Rose, without a sweetheart to my name." The sopranos, of course, giggled in high C.

I thought I'd outgrown soprano envy until I joined the volunteer choir for the Cleveland Rape Crisis Center fund-raiser earlier this year. No sooner were we into the first verse of "Ain't No Mountain High Enough" than I found myself muttering, "Apparently not."

There they were, the show-off sopranos, warbling up in the clouds somewhere over the mountaintop while I rooted around the ravine in search of a key no one cared if I found anyway. I've learned this much as an alto: When the audience thunders with applause, it ain't because they couldn't get enough of that *wooooo*.

Now, I don't want to give all my fellow altos a bad name. Most of them are much nicer than I am about sopranos.

My friend Jackie, for example, is a perfectly sweet alto when it comes to dealing with sopranos. No, Jackie only becomes a raging alto when someone mentions White Christmas Marie. That's what she calls her, White Christmas Marie, every time I make the mistake of mentioning her days in the high school choir.

"She was plucked from obscurity," Jackie says in a low, guttural drawl. "No good reason whatsoever. They still favor her. Her face is all over the alumni magazines. Marie this. Marie that. Always Mahhhhh-reee."

Man, those choir memories. They haunt you.

On behalf of altos, I must say the one thing we have over the sopranos is we do sultry. Sopranos twitter and chirp. Not us. We purr. Sometimes we even growl. Think Bonnie Raitt. Carly Simon. Ethel Merman.

Okay, maybe not Ethel Merman. Never Ethel Merman. But when Carly Simon flaunted her indisputably braless self on the cover of her *No Secrets* album in 1972, she did it for altos everywhere. Quite a year, that one.

Christmas Eve service is almost here. Most people will oooh and ahhh over the sopranos hitting notes over the steeple. But don't you worry, altos, I'm there for you. I'll be listening for every one of those *wooooos*.

NO OTHER CAPITALIST
WOULD SELL AS SWEET

he cookies taunt me from our kitchen counter.

"Cohhhh-neee, Cohhhh-neee!" they call as I stare down at my boring bowl of oatmeal and feel my willpower wilt. Pinpricks of dread crawl up my arms. I feel like Shelley Duvall in *The Shining*, right after she runs into the ghosts of those murdered twin girls slowly calling to her like zombies, "Come plaaaaay with me."

How is it that I once again succumbed to the Girls Scouts of America marketing muscle? Worthy cause be damned. I vowed I would not be swayed by the harmless-sounding Do-Si-Dos, Lemon Coolers, and Tagalongs. I know the partially hydrogenated oils they're packing, the invert sugar they're hiding, the coconut and/or palm kernel they've buried deep in their sweet little innards.

I know all that, but here I am anyway, on the verge of convincing myself that an entire column of peanut butter creme cookies wrapped in cellophane is actually a single serving no matter what the box says.

This is all Ellen's fault.

I can resist the grown-ups, all those well-meaning moms and dads, uncles and aunts, who peddle cookies, candies, and raffle tickets for children who've already decided that they're management. Ellen, though, is eleven years old, and her mom has this radical notion that it is the children who should be selling the stuff to make money for the children's troop, team, choir, band—you name it. I'm a sucker for positive parenting. Besides, it's Ellen. Smart, funny, gotcha-wrapped-around-my-little-finger Ellen.

I've known Ellen since she was three seconds old. I watched that headstrong wiggler right after she was born and thought, *Oh, my, that there's a child entrepreneur just waiting to add pounds to my inches.*

Sure enough, come first grade, the newly anointed member of Girl Scout Troop No. 1311 called. Nervously, she asked, "How many boxes would you like?"

I thought about all those calories and grams of fat and decided that, cute as she was, I would order only one box. Then Ellen cleared her throat and added, "You're the first one I called 'cuz I knew you'd be nice."

"I'll take eight," I said.

Thus began Ellen's career as top seller.

She's good at reminding me what I bought the year before and coaxing me to raise my sights a bit. "You really ought to think about something different," she always says. "Not that there's anything wrong with having favorites."

She has honed her skills over the years. With every passing grade, she grows more confident—and more persuasive. The first year, she said she was nervous about calling. By second grade, she said it was easier because some of the people she called were repeat customers. Nowadays, she doesn't feel timid at all. "I prefer to sell them myself," she said. "It feels really good to know I can do this."

Ellen was her typically kind self when I asked her how she felt about the girls whose parents do the selling for them. "Well, my dad has sold a few for me, so I understand. But Mom? No way. And that's okay, because it really should be the Girl Scout who does it. The whole point is that we have the stuff in us, and one of the ways we honor the Girl Scout promise is to show it."

The stuff?

"You know, the independence, the courage—all those things that make you strong and stand up for yourself."

When the phone rang last month, I glanced at the caller ID and said, "Uh-oh, it's Ellen."

"Don't get any for me," my fiancé said. "I mean it. I can't be eating that stuff."

Ellen was her usual chirpy self. "How many would you like?"

I gave her the usual rundown of favorites, then noticed a hand waving in front of my face. "What are those things with the chocolate stripes?" he asked.

No way would I be party to his downfall. I handed him the phone and watched another grown-up succumb to Miss Ellen's charms.

"Yeah, it's round," he said. "And it has that—right! That's it. Yeah, sure. Okay."

He avoided my stare as he handed back the phone.

"He'll take two," said Ellen, giggling.

Of course he will.

GIVING BIRTH TO A DINOSAUR

When it comes to today's trends in childbirth, I am a dinosaur.

Conniesaurus rex here.

Take the whole notion of birthing arenas, for example. Granted, they don't call them that, but they may as well because the only things missing from this sporting event are the bleachers and a guy shouting, "Beer here!"

An increasing number of expectant mothers are inviting everyone from their best friends' moms to the in-laws to their bosses—their *bosses*—to watch them pop out babies and anything else the body wants to spurt like a trumpet during labor and delivery.

Hear my primeval cry: Ew, ew, ew.

I'm sorry. I don't get why anyone would want her father-in-law to see that.

Expectant dads? Yes, they should be there. This is, after all, their baby, too, and every couple should experience that magical moment when Mr. Empathy leans in a little too close to coo, "Honey, I feel your pain," and she starts screaming for a hammer.

Talk about the warm fuzzies.

Surrounding a woman writhing in pain with a gaggle of relatives bickering over who was supposed to bring batteries for the video camera strikes me as a dubious way to grow new memories worth keeping. And watching the nurse monitoring your epidural suddenly abandon you for the grandfather who just passed out on the floor could affect Thanksgivings for years to come.

Then there are the uninvited guests.

Whenever there's an invitation-only party, there's always someone trying to talk himself through the gate. Only in this case, he's called a labor crasher.

That's right.

You read it here first.

Unless, of course, you, too, read *The New York Times,* which is how my morning oatmeal grew cold last week as I held my hand over my mouth and devoured instead the story about the laboring mother in full splay who looked over her freshly raised gown to find a male cousin she could barely stand.

In the same story, staff members at Bellevue Hospital Center in New York described their astonishment when two men in the same delivery room started arguing over who was the father of the child about to be born.

People, people, people, let's get control of ourselves and keep the circus where it belongs—at funerals where grieving sons find out they're adopted and weddings brimming with multiple stepparents.

As if this news weren't enough to force me into orthopedic shoes, I found out last Friday that many of today's expectant mothers are whining about the book that got most of my generation through pregnancy: *What to Expect When You're Expecting.*

It's too scary, they complain. Too negative. Too much information.

Oh, this is just too much.

That book was the bible of my pregnancy in 1987. I'm the kind of optimist who can only be an optimist after she's prepared for every worst-case scenario imaginable. This book was absolutely perfect for that, if you don't count its lapse in not warning us on how to thwart the advances of panting strangers on elevators who confess that your bulging belly turns them on.

Well, hey, no book is perfect, and the police later assured me they caught the guy on the twenty-first floor.

I checked out some of the reader reviews of *What to Expect* on Amazon.com, and it appears that too many expectant parents don't want to think about how that baby's getting here.

J. Radley complained that the book must be read "cover to cover." Another woman who called herself "Secret Squirrel" returned the book after reading only a few pages. "I became worried that what I was carrying was not an embryo but a dead blob of cells," wrote Squirrel.

Morocco Mole was unavailable for comment.

"If you plan on being neurotic and scared out of your mind your whole pregnancy, then this is the book for you!" wrote E. Simmons.

Neurotic? Scared? Worked for me, worked for my whole generation.

And now I'm sounding exactly like my mother when she used to complain that her generation never used car seats and isn't it amazing we all survived.

BARING THE INJUSTICE OF
A BREAST-FEEDING BAN

The *first time my* daughter poked a hole bigger than Texas right through my logic was when we talked about sex.

Actually, it wasn't about sex, not really, or at least it didn't start out that way. But the issue of men came up. Then it was about sex, even though it still wasn't about sex as far as we were concerned, but you know how that goes.

She was nine years old, and we were playing catch on one of the hottest days in July. We're talking the mind-wilting, energy-sapping kind of heat that makes you want to shave your head just to lighten the load you're dragging around. Cait's own hair was plastered to her face, which was redder than a squirt of ketchup, and she'd finally had enough.

"Mom," she said, pulling off her glove. "Can I take off my shirt?"

We were playing on the sidewalk right in front of our house, and as much as I wanted to say, "Sure, go ahead," I shook my head.

"Not a good idea."

"Why not?" she said. "Boys do."

"Well, yes," I said slowly. "But girls don't."

"Why not?"

"Laws," I said. "There are laws."

"What kind of laws?"

I stared at my pint-size little jock and started babbling something about public standards for decency and how they differ for men and women and how the sight of women's breasts apparently excites a lot of men beyond their control and that's not a good thing at a soccer game, say, or at the grocery store.

It was the first time I ever got that withering stare my daughter has since perfected. "So I have to wear a shirt because men can't control their urges?"

"Not all men," I stammered, wishing I could come up with a name or two.

She put her hands on her hips and shouted, "Not! Fair!" and stomped into the house.

I couldn't help but think about that little talk with my daughter when I learned that, once again, our esteemed state legislators are considering whether Ohio should finally let mothers nurse their babies in public. State Representative Patricia Clancy, from Cincinnati, introduced the bill after the Sixth U.S. Circuit Court of Appeals ruled in July that Wal-Mart could prohibit mothers from breast-feeding in public areas of the store. (Wal-Mart, ever the clever retailer with an eye to who buys, changed its policy anyway.)

"In this day and age, it's just ridiculous to prohibit busy mothers from feeding their babies," Clancy said. "And 99.9 percent of them are very discreet. Most of us walk right past a nursing mother and never even know it."

A similar bill never saw the light of day five years ago, after then–State Senator Rhine McLin and State Representative Dixie Allen tried to change the law that makes the public showing of a nipple—only a woman's nipple, that is—a fourth-degree misdemeanor.

"It never got out of committee," said McLin, who is now mayor of Dayton. "And it was because of the men. They were very concerned about 'exposure.' They were a bunch of prudes, and I could have followed a lot of them straight out the building and right down the street into a girlie bar."

Yes, well. There's the rub.

Any woman who's nursed can tell you that having a hungry critter attached to your breast has nothing to do with sex, at least not when he's the size of summer squash and needs you to wipe his bottom eight times a day. And anyone, man or woman, who feels uncomfortable watching a mother breast-feed ought to stop watching. That's a whole lot of none of your business anyway. If you find it titillating, then you've got problems I can't solve in 16.6 inches of copy.

McLin summed up the problem nicely when she gave me a little history lesson this week. "Listen," she said, "when men didn't like pumps and implants for penile dysfunction, they got Viagra. When they didn't like that little wiggle-wiggle finger test for prostate cancer, they got a blood test. But they want us to feed our babies in a bathroom. The only way this bill will ever pass, I'm afraid, is if a man introduces it."

Once again, I am reminded of the wise words of a nine-year-old girl who had to bear more than her share of the heat:

Not. Fair.

"REFUGEE" TAG ADDS INSULT TO INJURY

L *ate into the third* night of the horrifying television coverage, it hit Frances White.

"Wait a minute," she said, staring at the screen. "Something is wrong. Why are we calling them 'refugees'?"

For three days, the Cleveland-area resident had watched the images of Hurricane Katrina.

People stranded on rooftops screamed with outstretched arms.

Thousands of ravaged adults and frightened children packed into the Louisiana Superdome, many of them so hungry and thirsty they were talking out of their heads.

White shook her own head in disbelief at the images of bloated bodies floating facedown in flooded streets.

"I cried so hard my heart hurt," she said.

On the third night, she grew angry.

"It's 'refugee' this, and 'refugee' that. Those are poor people, poor people who are citizens of the United States. They aren't refugees, they aren't running from their government. They had no means to get out. No car. No money."

Her voice fell soft and sad. "I'm a black woman, but this isn't about race. This is about poverty. There are poor white people there, too. And it is not respectful to call any of them refugees in their own country. Not in a place like this. Not in America."

For some Americans, the word "refugee" is just that, a word, and a fitting one to describe the hundreds of thousands from Louisiana, Alabama, and Mississippi who were displaced.

Many Americans, though, including the Reverend Jesse Jackson and members of the Congressional Black Caucus, have denounced the depiction as racist.

The United Nations describes a refugee as someone who has fled across an international border to escape violence or persecution. *Web-*

ster's New World College Dictionary defines it as "a person who flees from home or country to seek refuge elsewhere, as in a time of war or of political or religious persecution."

To understand why "refugee" is a loaded word, consider who was left behind in the hurricane. An Associated Press analysis showed that about 60 percent of the 700,000 in the three dozen neighborhoods hardest hit were minorities. Nearly 25 percent of them were below the poverty line, almost double the national average.

Consider, too, the appalling disconnect between the federal government and the people who desperately needed its help.

While the storm raged, the president attended a fund-raiser and played golf. Secretary of State Condoleezza Rice went shoe shopping in New York.

Three and a half days after Katrina hit the ground, Michael Brown, the head of the Federal Emergency Management Agency, told CNN that he didn't know until that very day that tens of thousands of New Orleans residents and tourists were holed up at the city's convention center.

Earlier this week, the president's mother, Barbara Bush, visited the Houston Astrodome, where tens of thousands of the poor who lost everything in the hurricane now wait.

They're fine, she said. Just fine.

"So many of the people in the arena here, you know, were underprivileged anyway, so this is working very well for them," she said.

Define "well."

"Refugee" no longer feels like a word, but a way to distance ourselves emotionally from what we can't quite believe is happening to citizens in our own country. To many, it sounds like an attempt to excuse the inexcusable.

The American Red Cross has instructed all its chapters not to use the word "refugee." *The Washington Post, The Miami Herald,* and *The Boston Globe* also are not using it.

As of today, *The Plain Dealer* also will no longer refer to the hurricane victims as refugees.

This may strike some as just too politically correct, but to others it's a small gesture with a huge embrace. In the weeks and months ahead, we will have plenty of chances to show support and concern for survivors we've never met but feel we know by now.

Let's not start by calling them refugees.

They are Americans, and it's time we take care of our own.

4.

Family Values

Every year, *a personal* Social Security statement arrives in the mailbox of those of us over twenty-five to let us know the future benefits we have accrued so far from working in America. And every year, mothers around the country who chose to stay home to raise their children have the chance to see in hard, cold facts what their dedication to their families is worth in this time of so-called family values: not one penny.

I used to be one of those mothers, and every time my statement comes in the mail, I stare at the numbers that represent the amount of Social Security I accrued for the years I stayed home to raise my children.

1985: $0.
1986: $0.
1987: $0.

And so on.

It's quite a statement, that sheet of paper, for those of us who did what some politicians and religious leaders, usually men, insist is the most important job a woman can ever do. These would be the same people who blame working mothers for single-handedly bringing down America as we once knew it, when men were men and women were making soap from bacon grease, or something like that.

America is mighty conflicted when it comes to defining what it means to be a family.

When I was a kid, no one talked about family values. We just lived them, one day at a time, as best we could. In our working-class neighborhood, we had married parents, widowed parents, divorced parents, and neighbors who never married but acted like surrogate parents to every kid on the street. When my mom went to work as a nurse's aide, no one suggested she was abandoning her children. Maybe it's because they knew she was trying to make it possible for her children to do what she never got to do, which is go to college. Maybe they just thought it was none of their business. Either way, they were right.

These days, it seems that everyone has an opinion on what it means to be a family, who qualifies and who doesn't. But just like the families on the streets of my childhood, most homes are filled with people doing the best they can.

I went from being a stay-at-home mother to a single mom with a full-time job in the time it took me to rip open a certified letter. It arrived at my home right before Mother's Day in 1994. There wasn't a lot of time to think about what that mushroom cloud of divorce would do to my family values. Like most parents I know and so many I've never met, I did the best that I could, one day at a time.

After I became a columnist, I wrote frequently about life as a single parent. I wanted America-at-large to know that there are plenty of mothers and fathers who no longer love each other but would throw themselves across train tracks for their children. Over time, family values crept into my columns at every crossroad of American life. Kids showed grown-ups how to mourn after a beloved cat in the neighborhood died. A grown daughter forgave a whole childhood of hurt to take care of the aging mother who never took care of her. My own daughter did what I could never do when it came to issues of race.

At every turn, this notion of family is more than a value. It is the map we use to navigate our lives.

NOTHING BROKEN HERE;
THIS IS A WHOLE FAMILY

M*y son, Andy,* is coming home for Thanksgiving.

News of his impending arrival, his very existence, may surprise those who know only my teenage daughter. Some may relish doing that annoying little calculation in their heads, raising their eyebrows the moment they realize I was only seventeen when Andy was born. I have been on the receiving end of that math exercise many times: the step backward, the "Oh, I didn't know," as if I had just confessed some deep, dark secret.

My friends, the ones who've been around for decades and those who populate my daily orbit, suffer no such tremors of disillusion. They know that I did not give birth to Andy. They know I never adopted him, either. But no way do they doubt he is my son, and they would be surprised only if he were not at our table today.

As a family, we may not be typical, but we are hardly unique in today's America. Or here in Cleveland. If we could sneak a peak today into dining rooms across the country, we would find families headed by married parents, gay parents, divorced parents, remarried parents, single parents, biracial parents. There are couples without children, couples raising other people's children, couples with grown children, and couples who are still children themselves. Thanksgiving belongs to us all.

My story is unique only in the particulars. Andy was seven when I met him, barely nine when I married his father. That marriage dissolved thirteen years later, but there is one photo from that day I still treasure. I am in my wedding dress, and Andy is wearing his very first sport coat, tan corduroy with suede patches on the elbows. In the photo, we are collapsed on the church floor, laughing because his full-growl hug had just toppled us both.

By that day, our relationship needed no name, no official designation, to be real. We already had spent a great deal of time together. His mother, who would soon move out of state, had surrendered custody, so he lived full-time with his father. I taught Andy how to needlepoint and throw a ball. He taught me Donkey Kong and how to rub his feet just right. Together, we had memorized nearly a dozen Shel Silverstein poems. Andy and I were both moon-faced chatterboxes, and most strangers who saw us together thought he was my son. By the time I married his father, I thought so, too.

Much has happened in the nineteen years since that wedding photo was taken, just as much happens in the life of any other family. In some ways, the changes have rendered us far from the traditional configuration of family, where two parents produce two or more children and live happily ever after.

Instead, we are divorced mom with used-to-be stepson and teenage daughter living ever so happily. Most of the time, anyway. We've had our share of stumbling, standard fare in what writer Lillian Hellman called "the daily mess of life." In that way, we are quite normal, indeed.

There are those who bemoan the many configurations of family as evidence of the decline of American society. Theirs is a voice of despair born of their own pinched view of what is normal, what is right. I look at my two children and the family we've nurtured and know they are the most right thing I've ever done. No one will ever convince me otherwise, and I wonder why anyone would even try.

When I was married, my relationship with Andy at least had a legal name. I was his stepmother, he was my stepson. Of course, that also telegraphed whatever else others wanted to hear: Broken home. Second wife. Younger wife. Ex-wife. I learned early to ignore the labels. I taught my kids to do the same, and I knew the lesson took the day we sat around the table with friends, and someone brought up the term "half-brother." My kids all but spat on the floor. There is nothing halfway about their love.

Eight years ago, when my divorce was just under way, some friends asked me, "What will you do about Andy?" He was already in college, so their question wasn't about custody. It was about contact. To me, it was about love, and that was nonnegotiable. I could no more sever ties with that kid than I could part with my own beating heart.

To abandon children, any children, after divorce is to teach them that love is not only conditional, but also circumstantial. Some legacy that is. Divorce is hard enough on children, our own and the ones we come to love once we share a family member and the same bathroom.

Shutting them out means shutting off a part of ourselves, not just to them, but to anyone else we may try to love in the future. Not much of a plan.

Any parent of grown children, biological or otherwise, knows that how we treated them when they were young determines how much we will see of them once they have control over their comings and goings. We disregard that truth at our peril. There is no loneliness more hollow and dark than the emptiness that comes when we are abandoned by those we loved but mistreated. I've known people like that, and the bitterness of their daily lives scares me. I never want to be one of them.

Children can be painful reminders during divorce, but only sometimes, and only for a little while. Turning away from Andy would have cast dark clouds over my head that never would have lifted. And I would have missed so much in the last eight years if Andy had not been in them.

I would have missed the chance to buy him his first guitar, to hear the beautiful songs he writes and watch him sing, head swaying, eyes closed, softly smiling. I would have missed reading the love story he wrote after touring France, the stretch of his arm across my back during the prayer at my mother's grave, his goofy imitations of me when I'm in cleaning mode.

I would not have witnessed the childlike delight in his adult face every Christmas morning as he empties the stocking I made for him when he was eight years old.

The list is endless, and with every memory I see another part of me that wouldn't exist were it not for Andy. These are some of my best parts, and I thank him for helping me find them.

It's time to baste the bird and make the biscuits, uncork the wine and add two leaves to the table. I need to rouse my daughter from the sofa and set her to sorting the good spoons from the jagged ones snared by the disposal. I'll put up another pot of coffee, too, and make sure the guitar is tuned and ready.

Because this is a day for family.

And my son is coming home.

MOST DIVORCED DADS DESERVE
TO SEE THEIR KIDS

D*ivorce seems to suck* every drop of common sense right out of us.

How else to explain the latest child-custody arrangement—called "birdnesting"—reported by *The Wall Street Journal*?

Birdnesting allows the kids to live in one house all the time while the parents take turns sleeping over. That way, say the few who support it, it's the parents who suffer, not the kids.

Granted, there are those who feel that all divorcing parents should suffer. And suffer. And suffer.

These are often the same married folks who inexplicably are drawn to murder mysteries where the spouses are chopped into chunks and then sold as shrink-wrapped Spam, but who am I to suggest hidden motives? Besides, as a single mother myself, I've been far too busy ripping apart the fabric of American family life; I haven't got time to worry about which unraveling threads the unhappily married ones are pulling.

Birdnesting forces two adults who can no longer stand the sight of each other to share a household and live their lives in suspended animation.

Imagine trying to get on with your life when you are still sharing a bathroom and cat-litter duty with the person who brings out the worst in you. Your children are teased into stoking their most heartbreaking fantasy—that Mom and Dad will get back together. And, inevitably, they decide it is their castle, breeding in the little darlings a sense of entitlement to rival Richard Grasso.

Who, I wondered, would support this? I read on and found my answer:

Fathers, that's who.

In their relentless effort to matter in their kids' lives, some fathers would willingly sacrifice their privacy and any semblance of independence for the chance to be regularly involved in their children's lives.

I know fathers like this, men who are divorced but desperate to be steeped in the daily mess of life with their kids. They want to help their children with their math homework, remind them that even Spider-Man changes his underwear, and promise that tomorrow morning they'll not only serve Pop-Tarts, but the ones with frosting. Oftentimes, the only impediment to forging this kind of relationship is the bitterness of divorce.

We hear a lot about deadbeat dads, the ones who fail to support their children financially, and those who drop out of their kids' lives. We talk—and write—a lot less about the fathers who are jerked around by bitter ex-wives who feel the only power they have left is their ability to manipulate visitation.

Talk about a loaded word: visitation. The first time I used that word with one divorced friend, his face fell.

"I do not *visit* my daughters," he said. "I don't babysit them, either. I drive two and a half hours one-way so that I can bring them home to our house, our home, the one they share with me."

When I apologized, he shook his head sadly. "I hate the word 'visitation.' I hate what it suggests about me as a father, and my relationship with my daughters. And I hate what it communicates to them."

Divorce under the best of circumstances is the hardest thing many of us will ever go through until it comes time for us to die. Even when it's best for the children that parents part, the pain is searing.

Wounds can heal, though, if they aren't constantly ripped open, which is what happens every time a child's time with a parent becomes a tool for revenge. While most courts now favor shared parenting arrangements, the mother remains the primary caregiver in the majority of divorces. Mom's the one with the power, and it is heartbreaking to watch children suffer when she decides the only way to make her ex-husband pay is to steal away their time with him.

A man's failure as a husband does not automatically disqualify him for fatherhood. If he is not a physical or emotional threat, then he has the right to spend time with his kids. And they have the right, the need, to know him as someone other than the man Mom loves to hate.

We should always keep in mind that kids grow up. When they do, they figure out for themselves if their relationship with their father failed—and why.

There's not a mother alive who wants to be on the receiving end of that blame.

NEIGHBORHOOD KIDS MOURN A FRIEND

S*ome called him Chester.*

Others called him Copper. He answered to Tangerine and Orangie, too.

His real name was Tim-Tom, but he didn't make a fuss about that. If it was a child who beckoned, the red-haired cat padded down his owners' driveway and greeted him with a purr. Like clockwork, there he'd be, waiting for his little friends on their way to school. He was there again on their way home.

For the ten years he lived there, Tim-Tom stood sentry for the students at Onaway Elementary School in Shaker Heights.

Marianne and Paul Carey got Tim-Tom eighteen years ago when their son was eight and needed help falling asleep. Tim-Tom was the perfect nanny. At bedtime, he cuddled with the boy until his breathing grew slow and steady. When the cat walked downstairs, the parents knew their son was asleep.

But by Saturday, October 16, the Careys knew Tim-Tom was sick. They knew it was time.

So Paul wrapped their beloved cat in a towel and carried him outside for the heartbreaking drive to the veterinarian, who would end his suffering.

Tim-Tom, though, pushed his paws against Paul's chest once they were in the driveway. Paul set him down on the ground.

Tim-Tom laid down his head. Marianne sat next to him in the driveway and gently placed her hand on him until she felt his heart stop. They buried him in their garden and spent much of the day in tears.

The next school day, they noticed children at the end of the drive. They were looking for their friend.

Marianne and Paul decided to post a notice on the lamppost. Tim-Tom was, after all, a public servant. And his public had a right to know.

They hung the obituary at kindergarten height:

"We would sadly like to let the neighborhood know that our dutiful Tim-Tom passed away on Sat. at age 18 years and 2 months. He is peacefully resting in our garden."

The letters of condolence started arriving a few hours later, left on the grass beneath Tim-Tom's picture. One girl drew Tim-Tom's face and circled it with a string of tiny hearts. Another drew a variety of Tim-Tom's poses as best she could recall. He was an active fellow.

Some of the children left a coin or two so the Careys could buy another cat.

"Dear Tim-Tom owner," wrote one boy. "We are sorry tim-tom died. We used to call him copper. We loved copper/Tim-tom dearly. I would pet him when he was out, he would pur like crazy. We hope this dollar will help buy a new cat/kitten. From, josh. p.s. my friend and I wrote this together." At the bottom was a tiny drawing of a cat.

In some notes, a mom or dad helped out. "We are so sad about chester DYING," Chloe wrote. "He was a sweet cat." She asked her father to draw a picture of Tim-Tom. A postscript from her father added, "Note: my daughter called your cat 'Chester.' She will not believe that wasn't his name. He'll be missed!"

For days now, children have poured out their grief in pictures and letters to the Careys. It has eased their own sorrow, and the Careys wanted them to know.

Marianne typed thank-you notes, wrote the children's names on the envelopes, and slipped them into sandwich bags. Paul hung them on the lamppost.

"Dear Eileen, dear Llana," Marianne wrote. "Thank you very much for your kind letter. It makes us happy to know that you have fond memories about Tim-Tom. He was really special! We enclose two pictures for you."

The Careys also wanted the young mourners to know that Tim-Tom left behind a one-and-a-half-year-old buddy named Nibbles.

"We believe and we hope that you agree," Marianne wrote to Josh, "that the best investment of your dollar would be to buy some treat or a little toy for Nibbles to cheer her up."

The Careys plan to post Tim-Tom's obituary until Halloween. Until then, children may continue to touch his picture on their walk to school.

Every once in a while, one of them glances up the driveway, looking for the friend who is no longer there.

And then they move on.

BE THE PARENT, NOT THE BARTENDER

am bone weary of being the parent of a teenager.

It's not the kids who are wearing me out. It's the parents.

Teenagers are a handful, but that's their job. They push our buttons and our boundaries, and sometimes they don't have the good sense God gave a goose. That's frustrating, sometimes even frightening, but it's also normal. The part of the brain that helps us form sound judgment has not yet fully developed in theirs. That's why we're here for them. Or at least we're supposed to be.

The parents pushing me to the limits of my patience are the ones who don't want to be the grown-up in the room. It's hard enough to monitor what my daughter and her friends are doing when she is not at home, but the one thing I count on is the network of parents out there who, I hope, share my values. Short of that, I assume they would obey the law.

Well, you know the old saying about the word "assume." That bray you hear is mine.

A growing number of parents, I've discovered, are allowing under-age children and their friends to drink alcohol in their homes. I hear the stories from parents of my daughter's classmates. Readers write to complain about other kids' parents serving beer or wine to their teens without their knowledge or permission. And if you are tempted to delude yourself into thinking this is some other neighborhood's problem—some folks just love to blame our ills on the poor and uneducated—let me tell you about the Shaker Heights mother I met last week.

She approached me after a panel discussion on teens at risk. "I just found out that one of the parents of my kid's friends allows them to drink at home. He says that at least they'll be safe at his house, rather than out drinking somewhere else without supervision."

She shook her head. "And he's a pediatrician. But I just can't agree with this. I think it's wrong."

A weak smile crossed her face. "Do you think I'm overreacting?"

I imagined for a moment my state of mind if I found out my daughter drank with the blessing of another parent. I pictured the storm clouds and howling winds gathering 'round me as I marched up their front walkway, pounded on their front door with both fists and yelled over my shoulder, "Right here, Officer! This is where they live!"

"No," I said to the mother. "I don't think you're overreacting."

The law is clear. It is illegal in Ohio for anyone under twenty-one to possess or consume alcohol. If you are an adult who knowingly allows someone else's underage kid to possess or consume alcohol, you can be fined $1,000 and sentenced to a six-month jail term.

But that's only the start of why parents should never allow kids to drink.

Study after study shows that alcohol is the illegal drug of choice for teens, over all other drugs combined.

Most of us already know about the car accidents. Across the nation and here in Ohio, car crashes are the leading cause of teenage deaths. One-third of those crashes are alcohol-related.

"So we keep the kids at home," argue the parents who allow teens to drink. "They're going to drink anyway; at least this way they won't be on the road."

Parents who allow underage drinking in their homes willingly put their children—and ours—at greater risk for all sorts of problems that could devastate their lives and those who love them.

Here are a few salient stats from child-advocacy groups:

The median age at which kids start drinking is 15.7 years old.

The brain keeps developing until about age twenty-one. Alcohol consumption not only interferes with that development but can cause permanent damage.

Drinking puts teens at greater risk for drug abuse, violence, dropping out of school, and suicide.

A child who starts drinking before age fifteen is four times more likely to become an alcoholic in adulthood.

I've heard too many parents dismiss teen drinking as just another rite of passage.

We're not supposed to punch their ticket. We're supposed to be the roadblocks. The only way we can do that is by saying no.

A TOT'S BEST FRIEND IS HER BLANKIE

It was a plea for help that parents throughout the neighborhood wished they could answer.

LOST BLANKET read the large black letters above a photo that telegraphed all we parents needed to know about why this was a family emergency.

The photo showed a blanket—clearly hand-knitted in panels of pink, blue, and green—draped over two little bodies caught in mid-squirm. Tiny feet stuck out from under it.

The blanket had a name.

But, of course.

This one was called "Ba," because when Sheila Scanlon was really little that was the only way she could say "blanket." She's six and a half now, and she can say "blanket" and all kinds of other words but a name is a name and this blanket's name was Ba.

Ba was lost near the high school's track last week, where Sheila and her two younger siblings played with their dad until the sky said it was time for bed. Sheila didn't even realize it was missing until her mother, Jackie, asked: "Where's Ba?"

They made posters, twenty-five of them, and Jackie taped them up all over the neighborhood the next day. Strangers walked up to her and shared stories of their own children's cherished blankets.

We're sorry for your loss, they said.

Jackie went home and waited. And waited.

Two teenagers called in low, menacing voices, pretending they were making ransom calls.

Not funny, guys.

By Friday morning, Jackie found out the awful truth. The school's custodian, a kind man who once helped her retrieve a scooter, had found Ba tossed over one of the football team's blocking sleds, right where Sheila had left it. He took one look at the ratty blanket and threw it away.

It was long gone, on its way to a dump in Pennsylvania.

"It had holes in it," the custodian said.

You have no idea how important those holes are, she wanted to say.

The blanket had a loose weave because it was knitted by Sheila's Aunt Ann, who has cerebral palsy. She painstakingly knitted Ba, one slow stitch at a time.

Her labor was rewarded when baby Sheila anointed it The One.

It's instinct, really, that moves babies to such loyalty, and they do it in their own good time. Oh, relatives will lobby, shamelessly so, foisting any number of stuffed animals and family heirlooms on newborns in the hope that they will wedge a special place for themselves in family history.

But babies are headstrong about such things, and they decide for themselves what can still their shudders and chase the ghosts away. Then it becomes a who, for how long nobody knows for sure. Woe to the child whose parents think they set that deadline.

That's a puzzle, really. At what age do we stop needing such comfort? Judging from all the booze, food, and pills in the grown-up world, it's a safe bet to say never. Let's let those innocent blankies be.

Baby Sheila picked Ba because she could poke her fingers through its holes when she nursed. As she grew, Sheila discovered she could see straight through Ba, even when it was over her head and made her invisible. Sometimes Ba was Sheila's cape, sometimes a boa. Always, Ba was Sheila's sturdiest companion, which is why she took it with her when she went outside to play last week.

Ba was always alive, Jackie says.

Now Ba is gone.

Or is it?

Aunt Ann has some yarn left over from the very threads she wove into Ba. This time she will teach Sheila how to knit a new blanket. Ba Junior, maybe.

In the meantime, Sheila insists on growing up.

"That's okay, Mommy," Sheila said. "Every time I walk into the house, I see Ba."

She pointed to the family portrait she painted when she was only three. In it, there are the usual stick figures that populate every pre-schooler's home life, but there's someone else in the picture, too.

Next to Sheila, a blur of stripes in pink, blue, and green hovers just so. Sheila looked at it and smiled.

Long live the magic of Ba.

A MOMENT OF JOY IN A HOUSE DIVIDED

This can be a real tough time for children of divorce, particularly the young ones.

Traditional Christmas stories brim with nuclear families. Tiny Tim has a daddy who carries him home every night to his mother. Rudolph's parents brainstorm how to protect him from all the other reindeer who laugh and call him names. Cindy-Lou Who not only has two parents but a village full of relatives in a town that bears the family name.

The geography of divorce is painful and inevitable: Mom lives one place, Dad lives somewhere else. Some holiday traditions necessarily die, but there's one ritual that every child deserves to keep no matter how bitter the divorce: Every kid should be able to give a present to both Mom and Dad.

I learned the importance of this the hard way when my daughter was only eight years old. It was a few days before Christmas, our first since her father and I had separated, and we were singing Christmas songs as we wrapped presents at our dining room table.

Suddenly, I was singing alone. "Hey, what happened to the soprano?" I said. When she didn't answer, I looked over and found her in tears.

"I don't have a present for you," she said, sobbing.

I tried to assure her that it didn't matter, but she was inconsolable. From the time she was two, she always gave each parent a little present at Christmas. My offer to take her shopping only made her cry harder.

"But then you'll see it," she said. "It's supposed to be a surprise."

The next day, I told a friend who was also a single mother what happened. She didn't hesitate. That evening, she called and asked for my daughter, whose chin raised in self-importance as she walked toward the phone. She spoke in whispers through a cupped hand,

and after she hung up she told me she would be late from school tomorrow.

"I have an errand to run," she said, grinning.

In a perfect world, divorced parents shove aside feelings of hurt and resentment toward their ex-spouse and support their children's relationship with them. They don't interfere with visitation, and they help them pay tribute to the other parent on special occasions. They remind them of birthdays, for example, and take them holiday shopping.

Alas, this is not a perfect world. Many of us can't bring ourselves to commit even an indirect act of kindness toward someone who has hurt us deeply. So, we lead with our injuries, and our children inherit the wounds. They want to love us both, but we constantly telegraph: *Choose.*

If I could, I would stick this little reminder in every single parent's Christmas stocking: Whenever we thwart our children's efforts to show love, we dishonor them and diminish ourselves.

This is a time of year when friends and relatives really can make a difference in such a child's life. We all know single parents; most of us know at least one with a young child. A simple phone call will let us know if we can help.

We're not talking DVD players here. A handmade ornament, a little bar of scented soap, a cardboard frame plastered with Elmer's glue and glitter to hold this year's school picture—it doesn't take much to honor a child's heart. As for what you've given them, well, that gift is priceless. You've just taught them they don't have to choose.

The night my daughter returned from Christmas shopping with my friend, she looked like a pregnant second-grader as she held the bulging gift under her coat and ran to her bedroom.

"Mom!" she yelled. "Where's the wrapping paper?"

"In the closet," I yelled back.

"Mom! Where's the tape?"

"With the paper."

"Mom!"

"The name tags are in the bottom of the bag."

Almost an hour later, she emerged, carrying the package as if it were a gift of the Magi. I took one look at it and made a mental note: *Buy more tape.*

Dropping to her hands and knees, she slid my gift under the tree, right next to the one she had wrapped for her dad. With her head still buried under the evergreen, she started singing.

"Christmas is coming . . ."

This time, it was I who could not sing.

As I read the thirty-eight-year-old mother's blog entry, I could almost see a younger version of myself float by, like the Ghost of Mommy Past.

"There's a cacophony of voices inside my head today that are causing me to lose sleep, focus and patience, and not necessarily in that order," wrote freelance writer Wendy Hoke on her blog at www.creativeink.blogspot.com.

"Slept so fitfully last night and actually felt as if I were jumping out of my skin, all twitchy and itchy and restless."

She rattled off the to-do list that hammered her days and too many of her nights:

"Did I send this follow-up?

"Did I get this billing out?

"Have I paid this bill?

"Did I miss my volunteer time at school?

"Did I confirm speaking engagement?

"Did the boys have homework this weekend?

"Did I update the checkbook?

"Have I called the orthodontist?

"Is Tylenol PM addictive?

"Am I losing my mind?

"When was the last bloody time I exercised or did anything for me?"

I read this entry and took a deep breath, batting away at my own complicated memories of that time in my life when everyone got a piece of me but me.

I am only ten years older than Wendy, but it feels like an entire lifetime when I think of how hard I was on myself as I tried to be the perfect mother to my children and superwoman to everyone else. I look back on those days and marvel that I'm still upright.

No two mothers are exactly alike, of course. Unlike Wendy, my carefully constructed world had already started to crumble by the time I was her age. I had left the world of freelancing for full-time work. My son was grown, and my young daughter and I had begun a life out on our own.

Everything was unfamiliar: our tiny apartment, our silverware, even the pot holders hanging over the stove.

Like Wendy, though, I was constantly worried about my kids and my work and about a hundred other things over which I had no control. At the end of the day, all I could see was where I had failed. The mere thought of setting aside any time for myself struck me as a deranged fantasy of the narcissistic.

Grace arrived in the form of my friend Buffy, a successful business-woman who had become family over the years. She took one look at me spinning like an unfurled spool and yanked hard to stop the unraveling.

"Listen to me," she said one evening, pointing for me to sit at the kitchen table.

"When you fly on an airplane and the flight attendant demonstrates how to use the oxygen mask, what does she say to do if you are sitting next to a child or someone else who needs your help?"

I stared at her, shook my head.

"Put your own oxygen on first," she said, reaching for my hand.

Then she repeated it: "You have to put your own oxygen on first. If you don't take care of yourself, you will never have what it takes to really take care of the ones you love."

Ah, now she had me. Over time, I got a little bit of me back.

Mothers often feel such urgency about the rest of their lives, particularly stay-at-home moms or those who choose to work part-time. While they are fairly certain of their choices, they wonder if they've sabotaged the rest of who they were meant to be.

I read Wendy's list, and hear what she doesn't say.

Why isn't parenting enough for me?

What's wrong with me that I can't juggle career and family better than this?

Will there be any me left by the time the kids are grown?

Am I just too selfish to want more?

Some dismiss such angst as the luxury of suburban moms too steeped in their own privilege to see how the rest of the world has to live. A handy put-down, but it does nothing to resolve the conflicts created by a culture that insists young women build careers to support society and their own upkeep but also warns them never to neglect their families.

All these years later, I still cannot watch a flight attendant demonstrate how to use that oxygen mask without thinking of Buffy's advice.

Every time, I'm reminded to breathe.

5.

Blue-Collar Blues

The first time I visited my father at his job, I did not recognize him.

I was a nineteen-year-old college sophomore home on break and Dad was working a second shift at the electric company to pay for my schooling, which fueled his dreams as much as my own. He had a wife and three kids still at home, and while my mother's job as a nurse's aide helped pay the bills, it didn't come close to covering tuition, too.

Mom had many rituals around my father's work devoted to his consumption of food. For the day shift, she packed his lunch pail with sandwiches and surprise desserts. When he worked overtime, she carefully arranged a heaping plate of food because she knew that, without it, he would miss dinner.

This time, though, she would not be the one to make the ten-minute drive to the power plant on Lake Erie's shore.

"I want you to take this to Dad," she said as she pinched a sheet of tin foil over the rim of the steaming plate. "And don't talk to any of the other men when you get there."

She caught me rolling my eyes and frowned. "In fact," she said, wiping her hands on her apron, "take the dog with you."

This line of defense might have made sense if our dog had been a German shepherd, say, or at least bigger than a snow boot. Our dog, though, was a nervous, wiry little thing named Shiloh who routinely got her front paw stuck in her collar and then hobbled around like an amputee until someone yanked it out. Hardly a beast.

I don't remember the drive that evening, but my memory of what happened after we arrived steers my own work still. I pulled through a gated cinder drive just as my mother had instructed, then walked out to the front of the car with Shiloh and waited for my father to show up.

A few moments later, a man appeared from behind another gate and started walking toward me. He was large and lumbering, his face blackened with grease and soot. His filthy clothes hung like rags, and I felt my throat tighten as he headed straight for me. Shiloh, frightened by the stranger, began barking her fool head off.

"Shut up, Shiloh," he said.

"Dad?"

My father grinned, reached down to calm the dog.

I stood there and stared at my father, who always took such pride in his appearance. At home, he usually wore freshly ironed shirts and cotton pants, never jeans. I had never seen these clothes before. The only dirt I'd even seen on his face came from the dust of the softball field after one of his league games. This guy, this man, couldn't have been a stranger version of my dad if he'd shown up in a suit and tie.

Until that night, it had never occurred to me that my dad was one of those men who showered after work, that his clothes from his job at the plant were so black they had to be washed separately from the rest of the family laundry.

Until that night, I never thought about how my dad earned the money that bought the new school clothes he insisted we have each year.

Until that night, I'd never thought about his job at all.

He reached for the plate in my hand, told me to tell Mom he'd be home after midnight.

"Schultz!" a man growled as he walked out from the dark doorway of the factory. He was small and clean, and he squinted as he took a look at me and decided I didn't matter.

"Schultz!" he yelled again.

I stopped breathing. In our family, my dad was the mighty force that scattered us like dry leaves caught in a gale. I loved and feared him with equal measure. Nobody talks to my dad that way, I wanted to yell. Nobody.

But I was frozen in place, afraid of what my father was going to do.

He swore softly under his breath, then sighed.

"Well," he said, shrugging his shoulders. "Gotta go."

"Dad."

He rolled his eyes, pointed over his shoulder. "Tell your mother it's going to be a late one tonight."

I stood there in front of the car, the heat from the running engine warming the back of my legs as I watched my father walk away. Any other time, Shiloh would have run after him, but she just sat on my foot and stared.

Thirty years later, the memory of that night still has a choke hold on my heart and on my conscience. So often, I see this country, this world, through the eyes of that college kid whose own world changed the moment she realized that, to those in power, her beloved father and workers like him were worse than unimportant. They were invisible.

Over time, the memory has squeezed ever harder, loosening its grip only when I tell the stories of working Americans like my dad. They are everywhere even if we refuse to see them, and their stories—about their jobs and their lives—generate more reader response than anything else I write.

Some managers skim servers' tips and swipe the cash left for coat check clerks. Customers abuse valet parkers just because they can. Airport workers making $3.50 an hour must rely on tips that never come to make minimum wage. Every day, more hourly wage earners join the ranks of the working poor, who rely on emergency rooms and free clinics for primary care. I tell their stories.

A PROMISE IN A LUNCH PAIL

want Dad's lunch pail.

I imagine it on my desk, right next to my computer, holding all my pens, notebooks, and stick-'em pads. A reminder of a promise made, and a promise kept.

So I pester him. "Have you found it yet?"

"I don't even know if I have it anymore," he told me last week. "I may have thrown it out when I left the plant."

Please, no.

My father does not understand why his lunch pail matters to me, probably because he never thought his job mattered, either.

For thirty-six years, my dad worked in maintenance for the Cleveland Electric Illuminating Company. He was twenty, already married and the father of two-month-old me when he walked through the doors of the power plant carrying a union card and a brand-new black metal lunch pail. He never replaced it. By the time he retired, there were holes on the bottom corners where metal nubs used to be.

That lunch pail is my most enduring childhood memory of life with Dad, who was big and burly and not much for small talk or late-night tucks into bed. Most evenings, it lay open on the kitchen counter until my mother filled the Thermos with milk and made four sandwiches wrapped in wax paper. Sometimes she drew a funny picture on his paper napkin, or scribbled a little note.

"I love you," she would write in her loopy backhand. "Meatloaf for dinner!"

When I was little, I didn't understand what Dad did for a living. His job was simply the thing that kept him away. He worked a lot of overtime, and even when he came home on time, he had little to say about his day. Little good, anyway.

"You could teach a monkey to do what I do," he said some evenings to no one in particular, staring straight ahead as he nursed his Stroh's. At six-foot-one, 220 pounds, my father was a giant to me, and I could not bear to imagine him any other way. I would scurry off, unwilling to meet his gaze.

Once I started working for a living, I occasionally prodded my father to tell me about his work. I wanted the reality check, the reminder that no matter how hard I thought I was working, I would never come close to the hard labor he knew.

"What did you do there?" I would ask. "Tell me about the equipment you used. Who did you talk to all day long?"

He was never interested in the conversation. "It was a job," he'd say. "Not a career."

That's probably why he can't understand why I want his lunch pail, but he's promised to keep looking for it. To Dad, it is a daily reminder of the job he hated. To me, it is an enduring symbol of the promise he made to his four young children.

"You kids are never going to carry one of these to work," he'd tell us, over and over. "You kids are going to college."

He made good on his promise. I am the oldest, so I was the first to go. Whenever I came home for a weekend, my dad would take me with him to run errands and, inevitably, we'd end up at one of his favorite taverns. His buddies always said the same thing when we walked through the door: Here comes the college kid.

Dad would beam. "Yup, she's never going to carry a lunch pail, by God." A dozen glasses would rise in the air.

My story is as old as the bricks under Cleveland's earliest streets. I am the child of working-class parents determined they would be the last of their kind. And there was the same unspoken deal in thousands of households: We'll send you kids away, but don't you ever forget where you came from.

As if we could.

I went to college, and so the heaviest piece of equipment I have to lift is a laptop. I became a writer. That is what I do.

My home is now in a neighborhood where the railroad tracks groan under the weight of the commuter train, instead of the freight trains of my childhood. That is where I live.

But I am also the girl whose father carried a lunch pail for thirty-six years.

And that is who I am.

BALANCE IS LOST IN A WIRELESS WORLD

t was one of those moments when you try to tell yourself that most people don't mean to be so rude.

As theories go, it was a hard sell.

I was next in line at the checkout counter, and I watched the customer in front of me. The woman never so much as glanced in the cashier's direction as she talked nonstop into her cell phone.

"I know," the customer said, nodding her head to no one in the room as she ignored the cashier's greeting. "Well, yeah, and then she said . . ."

She furrowed her brow in annoyance when the teenage bagger whispered "Paper or plastic?" Rolling her eyes, she pointed to the plastic and then said into the phone, "Sorry about that. Where was I?"

Behind me, another customer also was yakking away on a cell, and I noticed that she, too, never acknowledged the cashier's greeting.

I leaned in to the clerk and motioned to the dueling cell phones. "Does this happen a lot?" I asked.

She nodded. "All the time. It's worse when they're wearing a headset, and you think they're talking to you."

I've been on the receiving end of that one, walking down the grocery aisle or through a department store when a stranger suddenly appears to be talking to me and I attempt to answer. My favorite so far was the woman who pointed to her headset, shook her head at me and snapped, "Not *you.*"

We've lost the battle over how to stop others, and sometimes ourselves, from talking on cell phones in public. Annoying conversation devolves into something more troubling, though, when we use cell phones to whittle away at others' dignity.

Maybe I was so worked up in the checkout line because this was happening at my grocery store, the one I've been going to for more than a decade. Many of the cashiers are the familiar faces of my daily world, where relationships evolve from the details.

I know that one is married to a retired firefighter and why another collects angel pins.

I've had long chats with the Cleveland Indians fan who talks with equal passion about politics and why she still wears her hair long after forty.

These women are the same ones who used to grin when my daughter stood on tiptoes to press the buttons on the bank machine and now shake their heads at how time marches on whenever she shows up next to me, shoulder to shoulder. And yet, increasingly, these same women are invisible to customers who consider them nothing more than downtime.

This supposed era of new moral values sure makes for curious times. We hyperventilate over who's kissing whom and what constitutes a viable human being even as we ignore the human being standing right in front of us. Parents with cell phones plastered to their heads push strollers loaded with state-of-the-art technology but are oblivious to their own work of art nestled in the poufy biweave baby cushion with optional cold-weather foot muff.

Last week alone, I saw three such parents in animated conversations with the invisible other as they shepherded their small children.

We all need breaks from high-alert parenting, but that's what walks in the stroller used to give us. Our little ones could point to a bush, and we'd say, "That's a bush." They'd look at a bobbing robin, and we'd say, "That's a robin." Sure beat chasing them away from the radiator or walking the floor with them as they screamed into our necks.

I never thought I'd long for the days when the only person with the emergency phone was the president while the rest of us had to find a pay phone or wait until we got home.

Nowadays, we all get to feel important. We're wired like Secret Service agents, all but talking into our cuff links so that everyone, everywhere knows that we are far more important than the life we appear to be stuck in at the moment.

Shutting off cell phones to pay attention to the people actually with us has its risks.

We might, for example, feel less important in the world at large.

But think what we'd bring to the world unfolding right before our eyes.

SERVERS DESERVE OUR RESPECT— AND TIPS

My *first waitressing job* was my last.

I was a brand-new high school grad with three months to kill before I started college and left the small town I vowed would never claim me as one of its own. My parents were hourly wage earners saving every dime they could for my tuition. Spending money was up to me to earn, and so I worked the busy three-to-eleven P.M. shift at a local restaurant.

Thirty years later, I still say waitressing was the hardest job I ever had.

I was only seventeen, but by the end of the night my back throbbed and my feet screamed. I once made the mistake of kicking off my shoes during break and could barely squeeze back into them. My hands grew red and cracked from steamy dishwater, and my face sometimes ached from all that obsequious smiling to pry loose change from folks who could afford the restaurant dining that my own family went without.

The minimum hourly wage in 1975 was $2.10. Because we got tips, we made less than a buck an hour. We paid for our own uniforms. Any dish we broke, we bought.

I was one of only two college-bound students working there. Everyone else was decades older; some had worked at the restaurant for years. They never begrudged me my big dreams or snubbed me because I couldn't keep my mouth shut about my career. Sometimes, they'd grill me: Where are you going to go? What are you going to study? How much money are you gonna make?

The day I left, the hostess cried. "This is your chance, kid," she said, tugging at my collar. "Now you get out of here, and don't you dare come back."

She didn't have to tell me twice. Nothing kept me in college like those memories of waitressing.

Restaurant work still breaks backs and bruises egos, but in 1975 waitresses could make ends meet on tips and a prayer. That's a rarity now, which *Plain Dealer* reporter Leila Atassi eloquently chronicles in her two-part series, "Just Getting By." It starts, appropriately, today—Labor Day.

Leila and I talked a lot during her reporting because the job started to get to her. Not her job as a reporter, but the one that forced her to get to know the individuals who would still work at Bob Evans restaurant long after Leila went back to her journalism career.

They were the problem. Try as she might, Leila couldn't help but care about them. They were no longer anonymous. They were real people with real lives, and Leila struggled to make sense of a world that allows so many to work so hard for so little. It's the mantra of the working class: the harder the work, the lower the pay.

Many days, the only thing the working poor can lay claim to is their dignity, and that's a threadbare wrap for too many of them because of the bad behavior of too many of us. Even if we surrender to the tired adage that life is unfair, that doesn't mean we have to be unfair to one another. How we treat those who can't force us to be kind says everything about who we are as a people.

Nearly every time we eat out, we meet someone barely getting by. I've written a lot about tip policies this year, and the response has been heartening. Servers throughout the region tell me more customers now ask if servers keep the tips and whether management deducts service charges from tips left on credit cards.

Almost as important as the tips is the conversation, the willingness to treat servers as fellow human beings. We've all seen customers abuse hired help as if they were invisible or, worse, discardable. Treating another person badly because we can diminishes us as a culture and a country.

We can do better. If our server identifies his or her name, we should offer ours. We should thank them for every refill of our coffee cup or water glass. And we should leave a 20 percent tip for good service, in cash. Remember, most servers only make $2.13 an hour.

A community help-line director told me that people dependent on tips are often the ones now pleading for groceries to feed their children. They crowd free clinics, too, seeking basic medical care for their families.

They aren't lazy, and they aren't con artists. They are fellow human beings who can't quite believe what has happened to their American dream.

DON'T DISMISS TRAILER PARKS

I *am descended* from trailer trash.

Mind you, I never thought of them that way. They were just my beloved grandmothers, who spent their last years in compact homes set up on cinder blocks and nestled among the weeping willows of rural Ohio. Their trailers were tidy and clean and always smelled like something good on the stove, and we never called them anything but "Grandma's home."

I was in college the first time I ever heard the term "trailer trash," and it made my eyes sting. Nowadays, people don't throw that slur around with the same sloppy ease, but the stereotypes of those who choose to live in trailers endure.

I was reminded of that this week when I strolled through the abbreviated streets of Euclid Beach Mobile Home Park on Cleveland's East Side. The trailer park has been in the news recently because of a dispute over what should be done with the abandoned Humphrey Mansion, which is tucked away in a corner of the park and overlooks Lake Erie.

The developer who owns the house wants to replace it with more trailers. Preservationists and neighborhood activists, including Cleveland city councilman Mike Polensek, want to restore the house and create more green space along the lake.

"The last thing we need is more trailer homes," Polensek told me. "I'm not saying we should force any of them to leave, but the next logical step for the city would be to buy the trailer park and lose the trailers through attrition. When someone dies or moves away, we wouldn't replace them."

No one would argue that a trailer park is a boon to lakefront property. Silent in this debate, though, are the voices of the trailer-park residents, some of whom have lived there for decades.

They don't tend to speak up, activists tell me, out of fear of losing what they have. They also know how many feel about their choice of homestead, as if trailer parks and the people who live in them are just the tumbled discards in life's junk drawer.

"People say 'trailer park' and make that face," said sixty-nine-year-old Katherine Cole, who's lived at the park since 1986. "I say, 'Listen, we have a good life here.' And we take care of one another. We are as much of a community as any other neighborhood."

She points to the lake a short walk away. "Oh, my, I've spent so many evenings down there. We all do. It's the prettiest thing you'd ever want to see."

You have to really like people to live in a trailer park, because that's what you find three steps away from you in any direction.

Just about everyone I ran into at the park offered a friendly hello and stopped to chat, eager to share good-natured stories about their neighbors and why they love living there.

"This is the most integrated neighborhood I've lived in," Debra Hall told me. She takes care of other people's children during the day, and three of them clustered around her like chirping baby chicks. "We're all in it together here."

The trailer park brims with the quirks typical of a neighborhood that hasn't had the life zoned out of it. For every lot that needs tending, several others telegraph the pride of their owners, from the wooden lattices waiting for another summer of roses to the cheerful Easter banners flapping in the breeze.

As in most neighborhoods, there are SUPPORT OUR TROOPS magnets stuck to the backs of trucks and tattered American flags waving from porch railings and car antennae.

Feral cats dart in and out like ghosts.

"People drop them off here when they don't want them anymore," Mrs. Cole said, shaking her head. "We feed them, take care of them as best we can."

She was gardening Tuesday, and when I asked what vegetables she plants, she gushed about her tomatoes. Biggest things you'd ever want to see, she said, especially that two-pounder she had last year.

She smiled at my raised eyebrows.

"You wait right there," she said. She ran into the trailer and brought out a photo of a tomato big as a pumpkin.

"You want fried green tomatoes, you come back here in the summer," she said. "I make 'em every year, and you're always welcome."

THE REAL GIFT OF DOING UNTO OTHERS

My mother didn't have a lot of advice for her three daughters when it came to men, but her one cautionary note rang with the clarity of church bells:

Don't marry him until you see how he treats the waitress.

I think she was worried less about who we dated than about who we might become if the bad behavior rubbed off. Her own formal education ended with high school, and all of her working life, as a nurse's aide and then as a hospice worker, was in service to others. She loved her work, but she imagined another life for her girls.

We would go to college and meet a different caliber of boy from the ones in our blue-collar neighborhood. College life would introduce us to wealthier, more sophisticated men who already led lives steeped in rank and privilege.

That's what worried her. How they wore those advantages, she said, would reveal their character. Anyone who mistreated subordinates was a bully and a bore.

"Everyone has a name," she'd say. "Everybody has someone who loves them. Everyone deserves to feel they matter."

So, she raised us to do our bit in her campaign to convince everyone we met that, yes, indeed, they mattered.

We were expected to use our best manners with every waitress, housekeeper, bellhop, parking lot attendant, mechanic, salesclerk—anybody who waited on us or someone else for a living.

If we dared to groan under the weight of this responsibility, she was quick with the wagging finger: "Many of those people could be your relatives."

Her rules were simple and intractable: Make eye contact. Smile at them and call them "ma'am" and "sir." Thank them for their help. If they're grumpy, don't yell at them. Instead, tilt your head just so and say, "You must be having a bad day."

And never, ever rob them of their dignity.

Author Robert Fuller, the former president of Oberlin College, calls the abuse of subordinates "rankism." In his recent book on that topic, *Somebodies and Nobodies,* he offers this example: An executive pulls up to valet parking, furious that no one immediately takes his keys. He yells at the approaching teenage valet, "Where the hell were you? I haven't got all day." Then he throws the keys at the kid's feet.

When the boy asks how long he'll be, the man yells, "You'll know when you see me, won't you?" The valet winces but remains silent.

We can all add examples from our own experiences: A customer berates a store clerk because she has to take time to change the register tape. A working mother turns to the stay-at-home mom and says, "What do you *do* all day?" A surgeon calls his patients by their first names but insists they call him "Doctor."

The harder list to compile is the one detailing our own missteps. Do we know the names of the servers in our company cafeteria, the person who keeps the washrooms clean, the security guard who nods hello to us day in and day out? When is the last time we asked the clerk at the dry cleaners how her family is doing? Have we ever? How often do we greet a weary cashier with a loud, disgusted sigh?

Christmas is one of the busiest weeks of the year for many of us. We'll dart in and out of stores for that last-minute gift, the film we forgot to pick up last night, groceries to feed all those guests. We'll have plenty of opportunities to be kind, or not, to the harried folks who have already had to put up with God knows what by the time we show up.

We won't change the world by smiling and asking how they're holding up, but if you doubt for a moment your kindness makes a difference, let me tell you one more story about my mom.

She never held elected office, was never a company president or in charge of anyone other than her own four kids. But when she died, more than eight hundred people showed up for her calling hours.

I heard tender stories about my mom from almost all of them.

I met the hairdresser who teased up her beehive, the clerk who sold her olive loaf at the corner market, the man who rotated her tires, the seamstress who hemmed her pants. . . .

HERE'S A LITTLE TIP ABOUT GRATUITIES

If *you've ever used* a coat check, you probably noticed a tip jar on the counter at evening's end.

You might stick a bill or two into that jar without even thinking about who is getting the tip. You probably assume the person behind the counter, usually a woman, is getting the money.

That's certainly what I always assumed. From now on, I'm going to ask.

In the last year, I have attended three charity events at Windows on the River, a banquet hall at the Powerhouse in the Flats here in Cleveland. At the end of each dinner, I picked up my wrap at the coat-check counter.

One of those times, I pointed to the large tip jar bulging with bills and said to the weary clerk, "Well, at least you get a decent amount of tips for standing here."

She shook her head and said, "Oh, we don't get to keep those."

I thought I misheard her. "What?"

"We don't keep the tips."

"Who does?" I asked.

"Management."

When I asked her how that made her feel, she sighed. "They say they use it to give us a Christmas party."

Nowhere was there a sign indicating that the pile of bills in the tip jar was going, not to the clerk, but to management.

Recently, I attended another dinner at Windows on the River. This time, the tips were stuffed into a large, opaque box. I watched as one person after another shoved bills into the slot on the top.

"Who gets these tips?" I asked the coat-check clerk.

She resisted telling me, but I pressed. "Management," she said softly.

"How does that make you feel?" I asked.

She shrugged her shoulders. "Life isn't fair, right?"

This week, I called Kristine Jones, the general manager for Windows.

"Why are you asking about this?" she said. "Why do you care?"

The "girls," she insisted, are happy with the current arrangement. "It's not like they're standing there all night. The girls check the coats and then wait on tables until the last hour. And they're already paid an hourly wage."

Later that same day, two vice presidents—Dave Grunenwald and Pat McKinley—called on speakerphone from Jacobs International Management Company, which owns Windows.

"We're confused," Grunenwald said. "This is newsworthy?"

They were brimming with assurances. Their thirty or so employees—some of the kindest, most professional servers I've ever encountered—are paid more than the minimum wage. How much more, they wouldn't say. The company matches any 401(k) contribution they can make but offers no health insurance because they're all part-time.

And they get a free meal. "Some places charge their employees for food," McKinley said.

Grunenwald and McKinley say they collect only $800 a year in that tip jar. Hard to believe, judging from the amount stuffed into the box last Friday night. "We match it for their Christmas party," Grunenwald said.

When I asked if they'd ever let the employees decide between keeping the tips and having a party, they fell silent.

That would be a "no."

"Why does this matter?" they asked.

Dignity is nonnegotiable, writes scholar Vartan Gregorian. It is also every human's birthright, and management's blatant rankism at Windows is an assault on the dignity of all involved.

Generous patrons are misled. Hardworking employees must stand silently by as they watch management walk off with hundreds, perhaps thousands, of dollars intended for them.

"Maybe we need to rethink this," Grunenwald said. "Maybe we do," echoed McKinley.

There's no maybe about it. Both union and industry officials say keeping the coat-check tips is unacceptable.

General manager Jones was unrepentant. "I don't ever think about who's getting the tip when I use a coat check," she said. "I don't care."

Then she added, "I don't think anyone else cares who gets the tip, either."

I think she's wrong.

What do you think?

AN UNFAIR BURDEN

Ohio is balking at paying Michael Green money owed him for thirteen years of imprisonment for a rape he didn't commit.

Michael Green has not received one red cent of the money Ohio owes him for the thirteen years he should never have spent in prison.

Before I delve into that outrage, though, I want to describe two sets of police photographs from the time of Green's arrest. Even a cursory glance at them suggests the magnitude of the injustice committed against Michael Green.

Green is a skinny kid looking downward. The photograph was used by police as part of their investigation to convict him for a rape at the Cleveland Clinic Hotel that he did not commit.

Another photo shows Rodney Rhines, the real rapist. Green's lawyer, Alphonse Gerhardstein, says these photos were available at the time of the police investigation, as were photos of other current and former Clinic employees. Rhines's photo was never shown, however, to the rape victim in the photo lineup presented by police as they built their case against Green.

Green and Rhines look remarkably different in profile, particularly in their jawlines. Rhines's skin is dramatically darker than Green's, and his face is square, while Green's is long and narrow.

Both Green and Rhines are black men, and there the similarities end.

That didn't stop the victim, a white woman from West Virginia who had virtually no contact with blacks before she was raped by a black man, from identifying Green as her assailant.

It didn't stop police from overlooking evidence exonerating Green after he voluntarily turned himself in and offered blood, hair, and urine samples to prove his innocence.

It didn't stop the Cuyahoga County prosecutor's office from charging him with rape.

It didn't stop the grand jury from indicting him.

It didn't stop the jury from convicting him.

And it didn't stop the judge from sentencing him to twenty-five years in prison.

Now, a year and a half after Green was exonerated and released from prison, his innocence hasn't stopped the state of Ohio from compounding the injustices that already have robbed him of his youth, his health, and his freedom.

Former Ohio attorney general Betty Montgomery and her successor, Jim Petro, have ignored Ohio law, which stipulates that Green is owed at least $40,330 for every year he was in prison. (The statutory amount was $25,000 at the time of Green's release, but the Ohio legislature increased it last year.)

The law also stipulates that Green be compensated for his lost wages and his attorney fees.

This is the law, and everyone involved knows it. Court documents filed by the attorney general's minions, however, insist that Green's case be dismissed in its entirety and that Green be ordered to pay court costs.

That Ohio law requires Green to hire an attorney and sue the state for the money owed to him is outrageous enough. That the state is now fighting restitution for Green is reprehensible and brings shame upon every fair-minded Ohio citizen who believes justice should be swift and color-blind.

Here is a particularly interesting sentence from the state's response on behalf of the Ohio Department of Rehabilitation and Correction:

"Defendant [Ohio] is without knowledge or information sufficient to enable it to admit or deny [Green's] allegations."

The specific allegations the state is referring to are documented in an entry filed last November by the Common Pleas Court of Cuyahoga County stipulating that Green "is a wrongfully imprisoned individual." The court entry also declares, "Michael Green is hereby informed that he is entitled to commence a civil action for damages against the State of Ohio."

For the record, that court entry itself was more than a year in the making because of repeated delays and quibbling over language by the Cuyahoga County prosecutor's office.

Since the state says it "is without knowledge or information sufficient to enable it to admit or deny" Green's claim to retribution, perhaps I can help.

I chronicled Green's story in the *Plain Dealer* series "The Burden of Innocence," which ran in October 2002. Over five days, the series detailed the rape, Green's false conviction, his years in prison, and the difficulties during his first year of freedom.

Rhines read the series and, a week after it ran, confessed to the crime. A DNA test confirmed that Rhines was the rapist.

The story made national headlines, none of which apparently was noticed by the attorney general's office.

Not to worry. Reprints of the series are in the mail to Petro's office.

Earlier this week, the attorney general's spokeswoman, Kim Norris, said Petro was "on the road" and unavailable for comment.

"This is in negotiation," she said yesterday. "We certainly don't dispute that he is entitled to the $40,330 for each year of his incarceration. Everything else is still being decided."

She was momentarily speechless, however, when told that, in fact, state attorneys had argued that Michael deserved nothing.

"I guess I have to go back and talk to the attorneys," she said. "No one told me that."

If, as Norris said, everyone agrees that Green is owed, at the minimum, more than $524,000, why is he still waiting for it? Why not, as Gerhardstein suggests, separate that amount from the damages in dispute and pay him now?

"Well, it generally doesn't proceed that way," she said.

Soon after that conversation, Petro agreed to take my call.

"There's no doubt Michael is entitled to the $524,000," he said. "But to give it to him now means we would lose leverage on the lost wages argument."

Leverage? The state needs leverage against an innocent man it kept in prison for thirteen years?

"What if he [Green] said, 'I was going to become a classical concert musician'?" Petro said.

When I asked if he honestly thought Green would make such an argument, Petro answered, "No."

Recently, Ethel Kennedy became interested in Green's case. I met her at a reception in Washington, and she told me she had read the series. She said she was moved by his lack of bitterness and his courage and then asked me how he was doing. When I told her Green still had not received any of the money the state owed him, she was incredulous.

"How can that be?" she said.

She since has contacted an Ohio politician, urging him to get involved on Michael's behalf.

You can help, too.

There are three ways you can contact Ohio attorney general Jim Petro and insist on justice for Michael Green.

You can write to:

Ohio Attorney General Jim Petro
State Office Tower 30
30 E. Broad Street, 17th Floor
Columbus, OH 43215-3428

Or you can send an e-mail at http://www.ag.state.oh.us/contact/inquiry.asp.

Yesterday, Petro told me he will meet with his staff attorneys and urge them to initiate settlement discussions with Gerhardstein. Their original pleadings, which insist they owe Michael nothing, "is just boilerplate," he said. "Everyone does that."

A half hour later, Norris told me a letter was on its way to Gerhardstein.

In the meantime, Michael is barely getting by. "I had to work up a lot of debt just to get credit," Michael told me yesterday. "Now, I'm working just to pay bills."

Petro is still unwilling to let the state pay Green the amount now that, by law, it owes him for his false incarceration.

"It would be a very unique thing within the civil justice system to separate damage awards in that way," he said.

It also would be the right thing to do.

Epilogue: After this column appeared, hundreds of readers called and wrote Attoney General Petro's office, and the State of Ohio abruptly reversed its position and paid Michael Green.

"WORKING CLASS" BECOMES A STYLE

*O**h, for the days*** when the only guys driving trucks were the ones who actually needed them.

They were the Earls, Duanes, and LeRoys of my youth, the guys whose plain white T-shirts stretched two threads from splitting with muscles born of hard labor instead of workouts on the Nautilus NS 700 with Dual Pivoting Pulleys. They had big ol' trucks caked with mud and peppered with the inevitable dings of a life lived far from the bankers, doctors, and lawyers across town.

In those neighborhoods, the sofas only landed on the front porch twice: on their brand-new way in and then on their tattered trip out to the Goodwill, which is when their owners would give a holler to the guys with the trucks.

"Could you do us a favor?" they'd ask, and inevitably the guy with the Ford pickup would say sure. He'd get twenty bucks and one helluva funny story about the wheezer with the loosened tie grunting like a birthing heifer as he heaved his end of the sofa to the truck bed, chanting oh-jezus-oh-jezus-oh-jezus.

Those were the days, when the men who drove trucks looked like they ought to and everyone else stayed where they belonged, low to the ground in their Chevy Novas and Ford Fairlanes.

Nowadays, bankers, doctors, and lawyers are tumbling out of shiny new trucks big enough to tow their summer homes. Forgive me, but there's something a little too silly about a guy in aviator frames and a Brooks Brothers suit hopping down from his Ford F-150 Heritage XL maximum torque capacity pickup truck like a cowboy at the end of a posse run.

Turns out, though, that this truck thing is just part of a new trend to emulate the common folk. *New York Times* columnist David Brooks wrote this week that the privileged few, whose only working-class experience consists of the biweekly checks they write for the maid, now feel a deep need—an insatiable hunger, if you will—to emulate the working class.

Apparently, they're afraid they've become boring, wimpy even. So they're plowing through city streets with monster trucks and Harley bikes, sporting fresh tattoos on flaccid limbs and buying denim shirts and John Deere baseball caps in boutiques that share a street address with meatpackers.

Get this: They're drinking beer, too. Not Busch, mind you, but Stella Artois, the beer of the Belgian working class.

All this is generating considerable chortling among those of us who grew up in the working class, similar to our eye-rolling whenever wealthy white people who grew up in the suburbs tell us that Bruce Springsteen speaks to them.

Show of hands, please: How many could name at least one relative the first time you heard the Boss sing about how he got Mary pregnant and for his nineteenth birthday he got a union card and a wedding coat?

Greetings, brothers and sisters.

Now, there is a danger that those of us who grew up eating fried Spam and licking S&H green stamps until we thought our tongues would fall off could become a bit smug in the face of this new trend of blue-collar wannabes. One of our best-kept secrets, though, is that most of us were raised to have better manners than that.

Besides, we should not harden our hearts to their plight, especially considering how much cardiac distress we've already endured from spending our entire childhoods eating that aforementioned congealed meat product. These folks are working hard to romanticize the working class, and we ought to do our bit to feed the myth if we want to profit from our newfound celebrity.

So, forget those tiresome stories about digging change out of the couch cushions during labor strikes and working three jobs to get through college.

Bor. Ing.

And there's no point in going on and on about the other new trend that includes plant closings, blue-collar folks with no health insurance, and the ones who lost manufacturing jobs because the companies moved them overseas. Talk about a trend killer.

No, let's just keep all those silly stories to ourselves and let this craze for all things working class spread far and wide.

That is, after all, how fortunes are made.

SICK, UNINSURED,

AND DESPERATE FOR HELP

Immediately, Ione Freedman looked at the woman sitting across from her and noticed the blood oozing through her bra and T-shirt.

Then she looked at the woman's face and saw her terror.

She was in her mid-fifties, just like Freedman, and she was bleeding from the site of a breast biopsy performed that day at a local hospital.

You have cancer, the doctor had told her. You need surgery. We can do that for you. But you also have high blood pressure, and we can't operate on you until you get on medication to bring that down.

The woman worked part-time for a nursing home. She had no health insurance. No prescription drug coverage. And no money.

A government program would cover the surgery. But nothing else. The doctor wished her luck and sent her on her way.

That's how she ended up in the examining room with Freedman, a nurse practitioner at the Free Clinic of Greater Cleveland on Euclid Avenue.

"Please help me," she pleaded.

Freedman hugged her. Then she and her comrades did what they always do forty, fifty, sixty hours a week at the Free Clinic. They whirled into action. Within three weeks, the woman's blood pressure stabilized, and she was able to have the surgery needed to save her life.

This is just one of the thousands of stories of the uninsured in Cleveland. You'll note that the patient wasn't a drug addict. She wasn't unemployed, either. In fact, she wasn't a lot of the stereotypes some of us like to cuddle up to so that we don't have to think about who is showing up at the Free Clinic ill, frightened, and desperate.

This is Cover the Uninsured Week, as declared by health-care, faith, and community activists here and around the country. The Robert Wood Johnson Foundation spearheaded the nonpartisan campaign, blowing into town loaded with stories that make it impossible to indict the uninsured as just a bunch of mopes on the dole.

Here's what we're not doing for a growing number among us:

Almost 44 million people were uninsured in 2002; eight out of every ten of them are in working families. Yes, working. The U.S. Census says nearly 600,000 of the working people in Ohio are uninsured.

We know them by face, if not name. They wait on our tables in restaurants, deliver our pizzas at dinnertime, ring up our purchases at the local drugstore. They care for our babies in homes or in day care, supervise our children on playgrounds. They sell us gas for our cars and wipe them clean at car washes.

Our uninsured workers are everywhere, including the main lobby of the Free Clinic, where they wait at the end of a long day for help with often life-threatening illnesses such as diabetes, hypertension, and asthma. Many of them bring their children.

It's often standing room only at the clinic by four P.M., when unscheduled patients sign up for medical treatment. One in three patients is employed, often holding down more than one part-time job. These patients don't, however, qualify for their employers' health-care plans. Or they have preexisting conditions their insurance companies refuse to cover. Or they can't afford the co-payments.

So, they all end up at the Free Clinic, where the nights are long.

Freedman remembers one such evening not too long ago. The staff worked until eleven P.M., and still they had to turn people away.

She usually checks phone messages and e-mail before leaving, pulls out the files for tomorrow's follow-up patients. But this night had been too much. She shut off the light and headed home.

She cried as she drove, hammering herself with the unanswerables. How can this be? How can we have this many people sick on one night? What could I have done differently for this patient, for that patient?

So many decent human beings with nowhere else to go.

Her husband, Stuart, waited up for her. He looked up from the kitchen table when she walked through the door. Immediately, his face softened.

"What's wrong?" he asked.

She wiped her eyes and smiled. "This is the best job I've ever had."

FLUSHING TROUBLE DOWN THE DRAIN

I *met Superman last weekend.*

I'm telling you, I did.

Now, granted, he wasn't wearing blue tights, but considering how much I hate wriggling into pantyhose myself, I figured, hey, a superhero should be allowed his occasional blue jean moment.

There was no red cape either, but he was wearing a denim shirt—a definite uniform upgrade in my book. And, clever Man of Steel that he is, he didn't introduce himself as Clark.

"I'm Gary," he said, shaking my hand. "I understand you've got trouble here. Would you like to tell me about it?"

Would I.

It all started a week ago with the bathroom drain.

It was clogged. Real clogged. So clogged that it took a day and a half for the toothbrushing residue of a single swish-and-spit to make its way down the drain.

"This is not good," said the man of the house as we stood at his sink and stared at the drain.

After considerable discussion, we did what any two bookworms with absolutely no home maintenance skills would do.

We went shopping.

After another round of discussions in the household aisle of the grocery store, we agreed on a bottle of something so toxic its label guaranteed it would eat through decades of hair clumps, bobby pins, dental floss, and God-knows-what-else to unclog the drain. (I'm paraphrasing, of course.)

My father, by the way, would want you to know that I was raised better than this. He could fix anything with a wrench, some electrical tape, and a piece of rope.

But he was forever yelling up from the basement, "You kids are going to go to college!" So, we did. Which explains why none of us can fix so much as a jiggling toilet handle without union labor.

Back to my harrowing tale:

We brought the toxic chemical home. We poured it into the sink. We stood and stared at the drain with great expectations.

Nothing. Not so much as a gurgle.

"Hmm," said the man of the house. "I wonder what that stuff will do to the toothbrush down there."

Toothbrush?

"What toothbrush?"

He shrugged his shoulders. "I thought it would work. But then I dropped it."

Ever have one of those moments when it dawns on you that you must really be crazy about someone because no way will he ever make your life easier?

Later that night, the heavens brought forth a storm not seen since Dorothy's house landed due south of Oz. The following morning, a cold shower led to an inspection of the hot water tank in the flooded basement, which was at high tide by noon.

Clearly, we needed a hero.

"So, now," I told Gary, "there's no hot water, a clogged drain, and—aaaand—the disposal isn't working either."

Gary put his hands on his hips and slowly nodded his head. Then he smiled.

"Okay," he said softly. "Let's see what we can do."

That's when Superman took over.

At time and a half.

He was worth every penny.

"The disposal just needs a new switch," he said after spending thirty seconds under the sink.

"The water is gone from the basement and I relit the pilot light, so you now have hot water," he said after five minutes in the basement.

Then he went upstairs to the bathroom. Twenty minutes later, he came downstairs holding a two-pronged mass of something large, hairy, and black.

"Well, here's the toothbrush," he said. "It got tangled up with the pencil."

Pencil?

"What pencil?" I said.

Gary smiled. "Looks like it's been down there a while."

"I'm sure he thought it would work," I said.

Within two hours, Gary had righted every wrong. He even left the wastebasket cleaner than he found it.

"Well, I'm pretty much done here," he said, drying his hands on his own towel. "You have a nice day."

Then, in a flash, he was gone.

And that's when I knew for sure that, cape or no cape, I had just met Superman.

NO LIVING WAGE FOR AIRPORT AIDES

To *most of us,* they are invisible.

They are the wheelchair assistants at airports, the folks we rush past on our way to somewhere else.

They push elderly and disabled passengers through the concourses; sometimes, they lift them directly into their seats on the planes. Many of the assistants are elderly themselves; some have physical or mental disabilities.

Some are retirees just looking for fun money or a way to meet people. Others augment meager fixed incomes. For many, though, this is their only income, and they must rely on our tips to make minimum wage. Too often, they don't.

My friend Carol was volunteering at a homeless shelter last spring when she met one of these wheelchair assistants.

"She works full-time, and she's homeless," she told me. "She pushes wheelchairs for Continental at the airport and makes only $3.50 an hour."

Until recently, this worker and her husband of twenty-seven years had lived in their van. She worked for Flight Services and Systems Inc., which Continental hires to provide a variety of airport services, including wheelchair assistants.

"I like my job," she told me. "I meet a whole bunch of different people, and I get to walk, which is good for me."

When I asked about her wages, she hesitated, asking that I not identify her because she was afraid of losing her job.

"I make $3.50 an hour," she said. "The rest I'm supposed to make in tips. Some days, I can make between five and twenty dollars a day. Other days?" She shook her head. "Other days, not so good. Yesterday I had seven trips. Not all tipped. One tipped one dollar. Three tipped a total of fifteen dollars. Today, I had only three trips."

She showed me a recent two-week pay slip. For 86.75 hours of work, her take-home pay was $265.42, with $66 in tips declared as taxable income.

"Did you make sixty-six dollars in tips?"

She shook her head. "Not this time," she said. "Maybe next time?"

I since have talked to more than two dozen wheelchair assistants at various airports, including Cleveland Hopkins International Airport. Not one makes minimum wage. In Cleveland, they all make $3.50 an hour.

A few said they make decent tips. Most, though, said that, even with tips, their income doesn't meet the federal minimum wage of $5.15.

FSS insists that they can make up the difference in tips but also threatens reprimands if they solicit tips.

Company representatives offer the familiar defense for low wages: "It's the industry standard," Julia Omidpanah said.

Continental spokeswoman Julia King said the FSS employees' hourly wage was not the airline's concern.

"We contract [with FSS] for the service," she said. "We don't get specifically into wages."

Might Continental get specifically involved now?

"I'm not saying no one cares," said King, "but we understand that a lot of these positions are gratuity based and that this is the industry standard."

After learning this week about the wages at the airport, Mayor Jane Campbell said the city, which owns the airport, is investigating.

"I had no idea they were not making minimum wage at the airport," she said. "I'm sure patrons at the airport have no idea that there is an expectation that they should tip. I didn't even know."

Campbell said a Continental spokesperson claimed to know nothing about it, either.

"They are on the case," Campbell said. "Continental has agreed to work with the subcontractor and told them we have got to get this fixed."

The U.S. Department of Labor is also investigating, a spokesman said.

So far, FSS is unrepentant.

"It's a shame, really, to focus on the $3.50 people when most of our employees make more," general manager Mark Nichols said. "Some companies out there pay only $2.13 an hour."

For the record, their electric-cart drivers make a whopping $4.50 an hour.

Nichols insisted most airline passengers know to tip. When I told him that only 10 percent of more than two hundred passengers I interviewed said they knew this, he scoffed.

"I'd say seventy percent of passengers know to tip," he said.

Is he right? You tell me.

FREE TO CAST A BALLOT,
EVEN WHEN CONFINED

Molly *Wieser looked* into the eyes of the sixty-eight-year-old inmate sitting across the table and smiled.

"Will you be eighteen by November second?" she asked.

The bald black man laughed.

"Yeah, I'm going to be nineteen this year," he said.

"Good," Wieser said, writing on the voter registration form. "That means you'll be able to vote."

The inmate, a Clevelander serving a misdemeanor sentence in Cuyahoga County's workhouse in Highland Hills, leaned in and asked Wieser the question she is used to answering: "You sure I can vote?"

"Absolutely," said Wieser, a lawyer with the Ohio Free the Vote Coalition. "You're serving a misdemeanor, so you can vote even while you're in here."

She explained what too many lawyers, parole and probation officers, and ordinary citizens don't know: Anyone serving time in Ohio for a misdemeanor can vote. Once convicted felons are released from prison, they, too, have the right to vote in Ohio.

"The fact that people in prison can't vote has a disparate impact in the African-American community," she told him. "I really disagree with it. I think all people should be able to vote."

He nodded. "As far as I'm concerned, this is America. You should be able to vote no matter where you live."

Wieser nodded her head and handed him a printed card detailing his voting rights.

"If you know anyone with a felony conviction, you can tell them they have the right to vote," she said. "In the meantime, you'll be getting a card from the Board of Elections telling you where you can vote in your neighborhood. If you aren't out of here before then, we'll give you an absentee ballot."

"Yeah?"

"Yeah."

Molly Wieser is one of our quiet heroes. At thirty-six, she earns a fraction of the salary commanded by many of her fellow law-school graduates, but a partnership in a major firm was never her goal. She has built a career around advocating for those most of us choose to ignore.

For the last two and a half years, she has been director of the Racial Fairness Project, which led to her work registering inmates to vote. She and her volunteers registered 450 before last fall's general election. They have registered more than 250 for this year's election.

The daughter of an Austrian father and a Mexican-American mother, Wieser was raised to be an activist. She decided to go to Case Western Reserve University's law school after working in an Alaska salmon cannery.

"Most of the workers were white, but some were Latinos from Mexico," said Wieser, who speaks fluent Spanish. "They didn't speak English, and no one made any effort to find a translator, which was a real problem, because there were safety issues. Then two white college students who were deaf showed up, and everyone started learning sign language."

Wieser became the migrant workers' advocate.

"It was an important moment for me," she said. "They stood to lose something. I stood to lose nothing. So that made me think: law school."

She has been advocating for those who have a lot to lose ever since. For months, she has been leading the effort to register voters in the Cuyahoga County Jail. Last Friday, she loaded up her car with three young volunteers and the tools of voter registration—pens, forms, and phone books for checking zip codes—and headed for the county's workhouse.

She met with the usual obstacles. Her visit was scheduled, but it took additional haggling before guards allowed her to visit each pod to tell inmates about their voting rights. Then she was ushered into the stark visiting room and waited. And waited and waited.

Only about two dozen male inmates came in to register. Wieser questioned one of the corrections officers.

"This is it? What about the other units? And what about the women?"

The guard shrugged his shoulders. "Nope, that's it," he said.

Wieser shook her head, then took a deep breath as she packed up supplies to head for the annex, where she and the volunteers registered five more inmates, including the sixty-eight-year-old Cleveland man.

"Are you going to vote?" she asked him.

"Yes," he said. "Are you going to vote?"

She grinned. "Yes."

He pressed her to reveal her candidate in the presidential race, but she resisted.

"This is supposed to be a nonpartisan effort," she told him. "I haven't made up my mind."

"Okay," he said. "I can understand that."

Wieser leaned in. "You're going to vote, right?"

"I'm going to be like you," he said, grinning. "I'm going to think about it."

6.

Do Write Woman

A *woman I respect* a great deal, an editor in the newsroom where I work, scowled as I approached her one day. She pointed to a group of male editors huddled near the city desk.

"I'm trying to figure out why I'm not included in that meeting," she said.

I placed my hand on her shoulder and said as gently as I could, "I'm trying to figure out why you're waiting for the invitation."

If women always waited to be beckoned, we still wouldn't have the right to vote. Standing by hoping that someone else will recognize what we have to offer is a great way to end up an anonymous quote in someone else's life story.

When I give speeches, and the audience is full of women, I almost always ask for a question-and-answer period so that I can hear what's on their minds. So often, the conversation turns to the issue of power— who has it, who doesn't, and why are women always on the low end of the equation? Typically, the woman who asks this sort of question starts out tentative, but her voice grows in strength and timber as she notices the swell of camaraderie around her. You can feel it in the room. There's that telltale buzz, the nodding of heads as women lean over to whisper into sympathetic ears. At such moments, I am both humbled and inspired by the force of their collective intellect and their stubborn refusal to accept the status quo.

Many of the columns in this section are narratives of a few women's stories that illustrate how politics affects all women's lives. Some columns are meant to celebrate the female gender for all its strengths and silliness. And, sometimes, I just have a little fun poking the bear.

I'm paid to give my opinion, and so it's easier for me to speak out. It's also easy to find me if you don't like what I have to say, and women often ask if the vitriol of some readers ever gets to me.

I tell them the truth: Of course, it bothers me.

I just don't let it stop me.

And those women are the reason why.

THE LONG AND SHORT OF MY HAIRSTYLE

E*nough with the hair,* already.

Week in, week out, the unsolicited advice pours forth.

"I like your column," said a caller last Thursday, "but for God's sake, get a haircut."

Dozens of such readers have registered their disapproval with my shoulder-length hair in the last four months. Most of them insist a woman over forty should have short hair. Many of them say it's hard to take me seriously with "all that hair." Always they are anonymous. And every last one of them is a woman.

My goodness. In this space, we've talked about war against Iraq, the sexualization of young girls, abortion and racism and mental illness . . . and the best you can come up with is "Cut your hair"?

Not very sisterly, dear hearts.

When I first started writing my column in October 2003, I shared some worries with a trusted colleague. How soon should I take on controversy? I wondered aloud. How often should I mix up the serious with the lighthearted? What were readers expecting?

He smiled as I babbled on, then shook his head.

"You know what?" he said. "Don't worry about any of that. For the first six months or so, there will be a whole lot of people just wanting to tell you what to do with your bangs."

I thought he was joking.

Not anymore.

Who came up with this silly rule for hair, anyway? Almost from the minute I turned forty, I've elicited the disapproval of a certain kind of woman who thinks the length of one's hair is a measure of her willingness to be a grown-up. I thought raising children, holding down a job, and paying my gas bill on time proffered ample evidence, but apparently it doesn't count unless I also have a buzz cut.

And here's the really pathetic part: As I've inched my way through this decade of life, I've actually felt I should explain why I don't cut my hair short.

I have my list:

It's easier.

I like the wind in my hair.

Short hair would make me look like deposed columnist Bob Greene in his mid-length toupee.

Lately, I've started mentioning my American Indian roots. "I'm part Blackfoot," I say in a low, stern voice. "All my people had long hair." This works particularly well in Cleveland Heights, where people tend to wince and back away because the last thing they want to do is insult the Indian.

As of today, though, I'm done explaining anything about my hair because, intrepid reporter that I am, I have unearthed the reason for this silly over-forty hair rule. I got into my car and fought miles and miles of rush-hour traffic to find the one guy I knew could explain it all.

I went to my hairdresser, Kevin.

Kevin has tattoos winding all the way up his arms and two tiny green aliens affixed with nail glue to his workstation, which is only part of the reason I trust him. He's a man's man, happily married and crazy about women. He understands us in a way we don't even understand ourselves.

"It's our fault," said Kevin.

"I'm sorry?"

"Hairdressers. We tell women over forty to keep their hair short because short hair means they come in more often, which means we have more business, which means we make more money."

"Why don't you do that with women under forty?" I asked.

Kevin smiled and shrugged his shoulders. "Because younger women want to look different. But after forty, women get insecure. And insecure women always do what their hairdresser tells them to do."

You read it here first. We are pawns, my sisters, mere lemmings leaping without so much as a glance at the rocks below, where yards and yards of shorn tresses are strewn like a fishwife's laundry. All because someone who hates to blow-dry told us to jump.

Let's be done with this hair issue, shall we? I'm not cutting mine. Do what you want with yours.

Now, let's talk about something a tad more important.

That's a long list, I assure you.

AND YOU THINK IT'S A PAIN TO VOTE

he women were innocent and defenseless. And by the end of the night, they were barely alive.

Forty prison guards wielding clubs and their warden's blessing went on a rampage against the thirty-three helpless women wrongly convicted of "obstructing sidewalk traffic."

They beat Lucy Burn, chained her hands to the cell bars above her head and left her hanging for the night, bleeding and gasping for air.

They hurled Dora Lewis into a dark cell, smashed her head against an iron bed, and knocked her out cold. Her cell mate, Alice Cosu, thought Lewis was dead and suffered a heart attack.

Additional affidavits describe the guards grabbing, dragging, beating, choking, slamming, pinching, twisting, and kicking the women.

Thus unfolded the "Night of Terror" on November 15, 1917, when the warden at the Occoquan Workhouse in Virginia ordered his guards to teach a lesson to the suffragists imprisoned there because they dared to picket Woodrow Wilson's White House for the right to vote.

For weeks, the women's only water came from an open pail. Their food—all of it colorless slop—was infested with worms. When one of the leaders, Alice Paul, embarked on a hunger strike, they tied her to a chair, forced a tube down her throat, and poured liquid into her until she vomited. She was tortured like this for weeks until word was smuggled out to the press.

So, refresh my memory.

Some women won't vote this year because, why exactly? We have carpool duties? We have to get to work? Our vote doesn't matter? It's raining?

Last week, I went to a sparsely attended screening of HBO's new movie *Iron Jawed Angels*. It is a graphic depiction of the battle these women waged so that I could pull the curtain at the polling booth and have my say. I am ashamed to say I needed the reminder.

There was a time when I knew these women well. I met them in college—not in my required American history courses, which barely mentioned them, but in women's history class.

That's where I found the irrepressibly brave Alice Paul. Her large, brooding eyes seemed fixed on my own as she stared out from the page. *Remember,* she silently beckoned. *Remember.*

I thought I always would. I registered voters throughout college and law school, worked on congressional and presidential campaigns until I started writing for newspapers. When Geraldine Ferraro ran for vice president, I took my nine-year-old son to meet her.

"My knees are shaking," he whispered after shaking her hand. "I'm never going to wash this hand again."

All these years later, voter registration is still my passion. But the actual act of voting had become less personal for me, more rote. Frankly, voting often felt more like an obligation than a privilege. Sometimes, it was even inconvenient.

My friend Wendy, who is my age and studied women's history, saw the HBO movie, too. When she stopped by my desk to talk about it, she looked angry.

She was. With herself.

"One thought kept coming back to me as I watched that movie," she said. "What would those women think of the way I use—or don't use— my right to vote? All of us take it for granted now, not just younger women, but those of us who did seek to learn."

The right to vote, she said, had become valuable to her "all over again."

HBO will run the movie periodically before releasing it on video and DVD. I wish all history, social studies, and government teachers would include the movie in their curriculum.

I want it shown on Bunko night, too, and anywhere else women gather. I realize this isn't our usual idea of socializing, but we are not voting in the numbers that we should be, and I think a little shock therapy is in order. It is jarring to watch Woodrow Wilson and his cronies try to persuade a psychiatrist to declare Alice Paul insane so that she could be permanently institutionalized.

And it is inspiring to watch the doctor refuse. Alice Paul was strong, he said, and brave. That didn't make her crazy.

The doctor admonished the men: "Courage in women is often mistaken for insanity."

CARRYING THE TORCH FOR
WOMEN OF ALL AGES

The *young woman* sitting across the table was like a lot of young women I meet.

At twenty-eight, she's bright and interested and hell-bent on setting the world on fire. During our lunch, she was high theater, eyes wide and fork flying as she described her many projects and even more dreams.

Then I asked her the question that so often brings to a halt my conversations with women her age.

"How are women my age at work treating you?"

She looked down at her salad, then glanced up at me and shrugged her shoulders.

"Okay," she said.

"Are they reaching out to you? Have you found a mentor?"

She shook her head, and the stories that tumbled out were far too familiar.

The older women don't support the younger women in the office. They ignore them except when they can embarrass them in front of superiors or undermine them behind their backs. They don't talk to them unless they have to, won't ask them to lunch, and never seem interested in helping them get ahead.

"It's great with the other women around my age, and even the ones only four or five years older," she said. "But the older women? I don't know; they seem to be threatened by us. You get the sense that their attitude is, 'I didn't have these advantages when I was your age. Why should you?' "

Certainly, there are women who mentor younger women, but there are plenty who don't. Then again, I'd hate for young women to think we baby boomers have some major network in place for one another. There are far too many women who don't support other female colleagues no matter what their age.

Feminist scholar Phyllis Chesler, in her discouraging but necessary book, *Woman's Inhumanity to Woman,* summed up the problem with razor-sharp acuity: "Women are often quick to believe the worst about another woman."

There's not a woman alive who hasn't seen this animosity in action, and most of us have felt its sting.

All the more reason to reach out to the younger women who one day will replace us. True, many of us who've known success had few of the advantages our younger colleagues take for granted. Recently, for example, I met a woman in her thirties who works in a field over-whelmingly populated by men. When she admitted she was recruited for her gender, I asked her how she felt about that.

She chuckled. "I don't care about that," she said. "I'm no feminist."

I wanted to ask her, "How do you think you got here?" But I didn't, and I'm still not sure why, except that I felt such pride that she had that job. Maybe that's enough.

There are so many good reasons for the successful women among us to mentor the young ones. Today, I'll offer just one, courtesy of Mary Joyce Green, a wise seventy-something who is director of the Women's Comprehensive Program at Cleveland State University.

"Listen," she said, "this fight for women's rights is like dusting. We dust and dust and dust, and it keeps coming back. We can't take a break and we can't stop helping one another."

Then she gave me the reason.

"As long as my behavior is used to judge and evaluate other women, I have a responsibility to those who come after me," she said.

"Make sure you add that I know—I know—this isn't fair. But for the sake of a greater democracy, I have a responsibility."

She's right. It isn't fair. And it is our responsibility. I am reminded of another career woman I met recently. She is a retired black school-teacher, and her face beamed when she told a group of mostly white women about her college sorority.

"Our sorority motto was, 'Carry as you climb.' "

The room was silent.

"That's right," she said. "Even way back then, we figured it out."

Let's not envy our younger colleagues their youth and beauty, their early opportunities and breathtaking sense of entitlement.

They are the best proof we have that what we did mattered. And they are the women we wanted to be.

When I finally watched Sharon Reed's naked ploy for ratings last week on WOIO Channel 19, my own reaction surprised me.

I expected to be angry and appalled to watch this news anchorwoman wriggle free of her sexy lingerie for hundreds of thousands of television viewers.

Instead, I felt incredibly sad.

I was sad that local broadcast journalism had hit a new low.

I was sad that so many Clevelanders, including the media, fell for it.

Most of all, I was sad for Sharon Reed.

Reed is a beautiful, smart, highly educated black woman in a profession that would never have hired her thirty years ago. The daughter of two schoolteachers went to Georgetown University, then got her master's at the prestigious Medill School of Journalism at Northwestern University.

She had the talent and credentials to force open doors typically held ajar only for perky young blondes and men allowed to age until they're propped upright.

Instead, Reed chose to become, in her words, the first anchorwoman to appear nude on the news. She did this because her two bosses, both middle-aged white men, convinced her it would be great for the ratings.

Too bad they didn't care about her career.

Five months ago, news director Stephen Doerr and general manager Bill Applegate asked Reed if she'd agree to be filmed stripping for artist Spencer Tunick's nude group photo shoot here in Cleveland.

I called Doerr and Applegate to ask them why they approached Reed. I'll give Doerr credit for this: He didn't even attempt to mask their motives with praise for Reed's intellect or quick wit.

He said he adores her. "Sharon is a stunningly beautiful woman. We knew what this could do for our ratings."

Why this isn't sexual harassment, I'm not sure. If one of our bosses here called a woman in and asked her to strip for the job, she'd be screaming for a union rep and a good lawyer.

TV's different, Reed said. This is "art."

Applegate didn't return my call.

Reed said it took her about an hour to say yes, and she did it for Doerr.

"There is no one else I would have done this for," she told me. "I love Steve, I adore Steve, I truly trust him with my life and my career. You ask anyone who worked with him before he came here. They will tell you Steve is a god."

Reed actually was filmed at the shoot in June, but the station held the segment until November sweeps, when audience levels determine advertising rates. The station's racy promos paid off: The single broadcast last Monday drew the station its highest ratings ever. It also generated a great deal of national attention—and criticism—Doerr said the station neither expected nor wanted.

It also left its newsroom deeply divided.

None of the other editors, reporters, and anchors knew about Reed's segment until the week before it aired, and many of them were furious. Channel 19 later televised some of the staff criticism, but the worst never made the air. Some of it has made its way to me, though, and morale is in the tank.

"We should have sought out more opinions," Doerr conceded. "But you also have to understand what it's been like here for Sharon with other women in the newsroom. Some of the stuff they've done to her is the most vicious I've ever seen."

Well, yes, television newsrooms tend to be snake pits, especially when the emphasis is on youth and beauty, and smile lines can be fatal flaws. But it is the Doerrs of the world who insist on replacing veterans with an endless stream of youngsters. And it was this Doerr in particular who, during our interview, referred to a woman in their accounting department as "one of the girls."

Doerr and Reed both said he repeatedly asked her if she was sure about running the video.

"Right up to the day before we aired it, I told her we'd pull it if she wanted to," Doerr said.

"He kept asking, 'Are you okay? Are you okay?' " Reed said. "I kept saying, 'Yes. I trust your judgment.' "

That's an awful lot of hovering for a man who insists he knew what was best for the woman he adores.

RULE ON WIFE'S ROLE
BENDS ONLY FOR HIM

This business of preserving traditional marriage keeps getting messier and messier. Now, we've got to go after married people committing "deliberate childlessness."

Or so we are supposed to believe after an Associated Press story that ran in more than one hundred newspapers around the country, including this paper. The man behind the cause is Bryce Christensen, whom AP identified only as "a Southern Utah University professor who writes frequently about family issues."

The attack on couples who choose not to have children was a flash point for a lot of women, and for good reason. They intuited what the story did not report: Christensen's real target is women.

Christensen writes regularly for the Howard Center for Family, Religion and Society, a conservative organization whose chief grievance is that women have abandoned their biblically mandated roles as homemakers for the workforce. And blaming career women for the lack of "completed gestation" in their marriages is only the beginning of Christensen's rant.

Working mothers' children are "semi-orphans" languishing in day care and after-school programs. By middle school, they become adolescent criminals vandalizing malls.

Working wives are the reason two-income couples have bid home prices out of reach for single-income families.

They demean and humiliate their husbands, too, and rob other men of a "family wage" that could keep their wives at home.

In Christensen's view, working women aren't even very nice because their focus on jobs and careers has extinguished women's "traditionally feminine" virtues of "care and sensitivity."

I guess it was all so much better when we lived on farms and the womenfolk knew their place—in the home, performing a "score of productive skills" such as cooking, spinning thread and weaving cloth, and making their own candles, soap, and buttons.

If only Christensen were living the life he preaches. But like so many hell-bent on bending others to their version of hell, his rules worked until they didn't.

So he changed them. Just this once.

His wife, it turns out, works outside the home.

"She stayed at home with our three sons until our youngest was in sixth grade," he said, his voice halting. "She felt he didn't need her at home as much."

He bristled at the reminder that it was he who identified that as the age when "semi-orphaned" kids of working mothers begin committing crimes.

"I don't claim we're charting the ideal pattern for all couples," he said. "Our circumstances had changed."

What changed, said his wife, was that they needed more money.

Mary Christensen went back to teaching high school after it became clear that her husband's income would not "meet our expectations," she said. She worked part-time for one year, then went full-time.

As she spoke, at first, she parroted her husband.

"I resented that society put me in the position where I had to go back to work," she said. "I remember a time when cars were three thousand dollars, houses were twenty-seven thousand. But banks started taking second incomes as collateral, and that priced so many out of a home."

Then her voice softened.

"Did I want to go back to work? Yes. Yes I did." She talked about why.

She could finally buy a second car. She could help her husband maintain their current lifestyle. She loves to cook, and likes teaching cooking. And she didn't have to worry too much about her kids because they were in an after-school swimming program.

"That way they didn't come home to an empty house while I was at work," she said.

Just like the working moms her husband regularly attacks, Mary Christensen adapted. And her sons thrived.

When asked about her husband's rage toward working mothers, she sighed.

"One of the things you need to realize is that, if the wife goes back to work, there are problems that have to be dealt with. My house is still clean, for example, but it isn't neat the way I like it. You come down to choices."

She sighed again.

"I've decided I can live with it messy."

ANTIABORTION SERMONS

AND CATHOLIC WOMEN

This column is for the Catholic women who feel they cannot speak publicly about their feelings of anger, hurt, and betrayal with their beloved church.

For weeks, Catholic women have written and called me, often anonymously. They approach me in public, at meetings and after speeches, or politely interrupt me at the grocery store, in restaurants, even at sporting events.

These are heartbreaking conversations.

Almost always, they want me to know their faith is important to them, that they attend church regularly and want to remain active in their parishes. But they also want to talk about how painful it is to sit in church these days because their wombs, and what they do with them, have become fodder for sermon after sermon meant to influence how Catholics will vote in this election.

"It's not just what the priest says," one woman told me. "It's all the propaganda that comes with it. It's the leaflets at the back of the church, the parishioners who don't like your bumper sticker and tell you you're not a real Catholic if you support a woman's right to choose."

An Akron church has erected more than a hundred small crosses in its yard for babies who've been aborted. In the Cleveland area, several women described a troubling turn of events in their church parking lots.

"On every car, there was a brochure listing only candidates who oppose abortion," a mother of two told me. "I was so angry. I am smart enough to make my own decisions, and this is not why I go to church."

What upsets them the most is the church's assumption that a woman can't make this private decision by herself, for herself. The church argues that the life of the fetus trumps all else—including the life of the mother and victims of rape and incest—and that any argument about choice dehumanizes the fetus. Declaring that women are not stakeholders in decisions about their own bodies, however, dehumanizes them, especially when the person who declares you immoral is a man who will never have to face pregnancy or its consequences.

Peggy Driscoll, director of Pro Life for the Cleveland Catholic Diocese, says there is no official order for churches to step up antiabortion efforts in recent months.

"Those fliers in parking lots are not coming from the diocese," she said. "They are printed by secular organizations that sometimes adopt religious-sounding names so they seem to be from the Catholic Church, but they're not."

Sermons can vary, she said. If a priest regularly preaches against abortion, that's his agenda. Not all priests have taken up the cause against a woman's right to choose. They leave politics to the politicians.

The most painful conversations I've had about abortion are with Catholic women. They describe their horror as church leaders lectured that, should their own lives ever be threatened by an unplanned pregnancy, well, they've lived their lives. It's the baby's turn. And they cry over the guilt.

Heather Harrington, an abortion counselor at PreTerm, said many Catholic patients have told her, "I know I can't have this baby, but I'm going to go to hell now. I will not go to heaven."

"I feel so horribly sad for them," Harrington said. "They feel they can't receive any comfort or solace at their churches."

Catholics get abortions. A mother of two described hers to me this week. It was her first pregnancy, and her doctor said the fetus had a lethal genetic defect. She knew her baby would die, and so she made the difficult choice to abort. To this day, she tells no one.

"I certainly could not tell my priest, because he would say I should have carried the baby to term and let nature run its course. And we don't talk openly at church, so I have no idea who there would support my decision."

The antiabortion sermons at her church are turning her off, and possibly away. Recently, she resigned from a leadership post there.

"The priest is up there condemning women like me, and he has no idea what we go through when we make that choice. It's insulting, and it hurts. A lot of people tell me privately they disagree but just ignore it. I can't do that. I have to believe in the church, in my religion, and if I can't, then I'll have to leave."

INCITEFUL INSIGHT:
THE WISDOM OF A SIMPLE PHRASE
CHALLENGES AND INSPIRES WOMEN

At first, I thought the teacher hovering near my desk in the newsroom was taking pictures of the unmitigated mess she had just stumbled upon.

I imagined the poster-size photograph with a caption scrawled in black Magic Marker: DON'T LET THIS HAPPEN TO YOU.

Great, I thought. *I've become a cautionary tale.*

But then I saw her lean in and focus her camera on the bumper sticker hanging to the right of my computer, and I couldn't help but smile.

I should be used to this by now.

Her young students, all of them girls in plaid jumpers, giggled in a huddle as I approached their teacher, who was snapping away. I touched her elbow, and immediately she turned toward me and grinned.

"I love this quote," she said. "I wanted to photograph it so that I could hang it on our bulletin board."

She pointed to her fourth-graders. "It's a great one for them."

It's a great one for all of us:

WELL-BEHAVED WOMEN RARELY MAKE HISTORY.

The quote from historian Laurel Thatcher Ulrich has attracted a lot of attention in the three years it has hung on my cubicle wall.

Men sometimes smile, sometimes snicker. Some men, particularly those with daughters, stare at it with thoughtful faces. Others aren't so impressed. One man visiting my desk read the quote aloud, frowned, and then pointed to a photo of my friend with her newborn baby. "That's how women make history," he huffed, then walked away.

Women, though, usually have an *aha* response. They stop, read it once silently, then repeat it aloud as their eyes widen in recognition.

Some pull out a pen to write it down. Others want to talk about what it means to them.

These are usually long conversations. Women have a lot to say about the rules of conduct for our gender.

Most of us women over thirty were raised to be well behaved. First and foremost, we were to be ladies: Sit with your knees together, your hands on your lap, and your lips pursed tight against even the whisper of profanity. We knew how to set a table, baste a bird, and greet the man of the house with a drink and the newspaper after a long day at work.

The more subtle lessons of good behavior, the ones guiding us in our discourse with men, were the most disabling. Words of etiquette were code for "know your place." Considerate meant deferential. Respectful was obedient. Polite was silent.

"No one likes a know-it-all," we were told. And so we acted as if we knew nothing at all.

Hardly a recipe for success today—or any other time, for that matter. Think of the few women who forged their way onto the pages of American history and were reviled for having done so: birth-control activist Margaret Sanger, suffragist Elizabeth Cady Stanton, labor organizer Emma Goldman, feminists Gloria Steinem and Betty Friedan. Not a good girl among them. They insisted on being heard. They refused to be silent. And they were vilified.

The women of our history books are the few we know about. The quiet acts of rebellion by so many other women are unrecorded, unrecognized: the plantation owners' wives who defied their husbands and taught slaves to read; the midwives who safely delivered other women's babies into the world; the homemakers who quietly stitched their life stories into quilts made from the scraps of their families' worn-out clothes. As my friend Karen often tells her three children, "Anonymous was a woman."

It is this silent majority of women who speak to Laurel Thatcher Ulrich. A mother of five, she built her career as have so many women—course work wedged into a busy family life, studying when the kids were at school or asleep in their beds. She was hired for her first full-time faculty position at the University of New Hampshire when she was forty-two.

Now a grandmother, Ulrich is at Harvard University, a widely recognized feminist scholar, a MacArthur Fellow, and the author of several books, one of which won the Pulitzer Prize for history.

She is also, of course, the woman whose cautionary reminder about well-behaved women adorns thousands of bumper stickers, coffee mugs, buttons, and T-shirts.

My work took me recently to the Harvard campus, and I jumped at the chance to meet the woman whose six simple words relentlessly prod me to poke the bear of convention. In an e-mail to Ulrich, I told her how many have responded to the bumper sticker on my desk and said I'd like to learn more about the woman behind the quote.

Ulrich responded the next day. Turns out, she is writing a book about the vast appeal and marketing of her quotation.

"I have been puzzled, pleased, and entranced by the many uses to which this quotation has been put and have a small collection of T-shirts and stories about it," she wrote. "It would be fun to compare notes."

And it was. For a half hour or so, we met in her dimly lit office and talked about her quotation, which originally appeared in a slightly different form in a scholarly article in the 1970s titled "Vertuous [*sic*] Women Found: New England Ministerial Literature, 1668–1735."

Puritan women, she wrote, "prayed secretly, read the Bible through at least once a year, and went to hear the minister preach even when it snowed. Hoping for an eternal crown, they never asked to be remembered on earth. And they haven't been. Well-behaved women seldom make history."

Ulrich credits Jill Portugal, founder of www.oneangrygirl.net, for coming up with the idea of marketing the quotation on T-shirts, mugs, and bumper stickers. Portugal was twenty-three when she started her company in 1996. She found Ulrich's quote in a book of women's quotations—by then the word "seldom" had been changed to "rarely"—and asked Ulrich's permission to use it. Ulrich agreed.

"I didn't think anything would come of it," said Ulrich, laughing.

The T-shirt was Portugal's biggest seller that year. It still is. "I sell at least two thousand a year," she said. "I think it's like safe feminism. It appeals to reverends. Mothers want it for their babies' onesies. It's not in-your-face, but it's definitely a message of empowerment for women."

Ulrich agrees. "It really matters to feel you have an identity that extends beyond your lifetime," she said. "It's just a crime that girls and women do not have a sense of their own history."

Still, she is surprised at the quote's continued popularity. "There've been hundreds of sightings of it. It's on mugs and tote bags, it's been a crazy-quilt project. My favorite is the woman who painted the quote on her car and then covered it with names of women who didn't behave well."

Ulrich's quote was still fresh in my mind the following weekend when I visited Swarthmore College, where I had brunch with a group of young women from nineteen to twenty-two. They were an opinionated lot, and boisterously so. They criticized the layout of the dining hall and brainstormed other designs, discussed one woman's thesis on the Constitution's intent regarding slavery and needled one another about their choices in cereal, men, and literature. When I mentioned Ulrich's quotation, they laughed in recognition of what was already their battle cry.

"My mother has that quote," one of them chirped.

While my generation of women elbowed our way into the world, these women will fly at full wingspan. Emily, for example, plans to work as a bilingual union organizer on Wall Street, where thousands of workers, most of them immigrants, labor in office cafeterias without benefits or a living wage. When I asked her if it was sometimes difficult working in such a male-dominated field, she politely corrected my initial assumption. "There are all kinds of women doing this kind of work," she said, smiling. "In fact, we're particularly good at it."

I looked at the young, confident faces of Emily and her friends and felt a twinge of envy for their certainty, their utter defiance in the face of anyone who would dare try to clip their wings. What would I be like now, I wondered, if I had been more like them twenty years ago, if I hadn't been grounded by the weight of so much good behavior?

Such moments of regret are fleeting.

Clipped wings can grow, I've learned. We can fly at any age and any stage of life. And if we catch the wind just right, we can even soar, high above all those well-behaved women still stuck on the ground.

THE QUEEN OF SOUL STILL
RULES OUR HEARTS

When *I was seventeen,* my favorite song on the planet was Aretha Franklin's "(You Make Me Feel) Like a Natural Woman."

The Queen of Soul belted out her version of Carole King's song in 1967, when I was in the fourth grade. She was still singing it on the radio eight years later. By that time I was a senior in high school who was sure Aretha captured the sheer ecstasy of a woman in love with a real man.

I was a teenager, so this was pure conjecture on my part, and I had the metabolism of a hummingbird, so I didn't quite get why she was feelin' so tired lookin' out on the mornin' rain.

But when she cooed that her soul was in the Lost and Found 'til he came along and claimed it, I swooned. I got all goose-pimply imagining burly arms the size of tree trunks wrapped around my pale, skinny self and rescuing me from all that ailed me.

Then life happened, and I grew up.

I came of age at the height of the women's movement. I aged a whole lot more through career and marriage, midnight breast-feedings and car pools, divorce and starting over. And I could fill a dump the size of Pittsburgh with the mistakes I made along the way.

Well into my forties now, I know a thing or two about what a woman—or at least this woman—wants, in her life and in her man, and it has nothing to do with being gathered up like a soggy mitten found once the snow thaws.

I'm like most other women I know: We're not lost, we don't need to be rescued, and we long ago stopped defining a man or our good fortune by the size of his muscles.

We're not teenagers anymore, but we're not dead, either, and we're inclined to feel signs of life whenever a special someone smiles in our direction. How smart he is to know there is magic behind our smile lines. How happy we are to share it.

Which is why my favorite song is still Aretha Franklin's "(You Make Me Feel) Like a Natural Woman."

That's what a few years of living will do to you, I guess.

My friends and I listen to that song now, and as often as not, we sigh, hearing its wisdom as well as its yearnings.

We can ignore the needy parts and appreciate the lyrics that telegraph how alive she feels with the one she loves. The tired part? We get that one now. But we also understand that sharing a life with someone who smiles at the thought of us can make us want to face another day, no matter how much rain is comin' down.

Some of us have learned there's also a whole lot to be said for belting out how we feel at the top of our lungs.

Some of us like me, anyway. And I urge all you women out there to try this, particularly in those moments when you're starting to feel real—oh, what's the word?

Old.

Last week, I got into my tired old car and plugged in the new CD converter a friend gave me for my birthday. Inch by inch, I'm nearing another milestone, and, friends, it ain't thirty.

You know what the first song had to be.

Over and over, Aretha went at it as I drove through my orderly little neighborhood brimming with sculptured hedges and inch-high lawns and headed downtown. Right about Chester Avenue, something came over me.

Now, mind you, I was dressed in Suburban Tidy. My black polka-dot dress was freshly ironed, my nails were freshly polished, and my hair was freshly combed just so, which is why I was driving with all the windows up.

Once I started singing about feeling like a natch-a-ruuul woman, though, hermetically sealed seemed wrong, just plain wrong. (Granted, I was also wearing a hot-pink sweater, and I'm not saying you need one, but it pretty much screams at you to loosen up.)

Whirrrr went the sunroof. *Rummm* went the windows.

I was a sight: My hair was whipping around my head and sticking to my lip gloss, and people stared as I, this middle-aged woman in the soccer mom minivan, howled, "Ohhh, baby, what you've done to me" louder than a calving heifer.

I felt like a teenager again.

With a whole lot more sense.

MORE WOMEN NEED TO RUN FOR OFFICE

he moment the Vietnam War became the hot issue in this presidential race, the women of America became invisible.

For weeks, we were eliminated from the debate as two privileged men from Yale and their minions duked it out: Who fought and who did not? Who's a hero and who is not? Were the medals for true courage or a fraud?

Most women shook their heads in disbelief and disgust. Worriers that we are, we had other concerns on our minds:

We are a country at war. We've lost more than a thousand of our soldiers, who left behind thousands more who grieve. Millions of Americans have no health care. We've abandoned entire public school districts. Jobless numbers are staggering. The poor and many elderly are forced to choose between basic necessities and lifesaving medication.

But there they were, fighting over who fought and who did not in a war we lost thirty years ago.

There is only one way women will ever steer the direction of this country. We can't do it from the sidelines. We must risk center stage, which is a big leap for most women who are socialized to blend in.

Right now, women are only 14 percent of the U.S. Senate and 13.6 percent of the House of Representatives. And if you think it's usually a bunch of guys yakking on those all-important Sunday-morning political talk shows, you're right. Only 11 percent of the guests are women, reports Rutgers University's Center for American Women and Politics. We are a whisper in a world of shouts.

More women must run for public office, and more women must work to help them win.

Marie Wilson, president of the White House Project and the Ms. Foundation for Women, has written a sobering but inspiring book for anyone interested in transforming the culture of our country. *Closing the Leadership Gap: Why Women Can and Must Help Run the World* is packed with data that illustrate why women don't run for public office and why we must.

"We set the bar so high for ourselves," Wilson said last week. "We think we can't run for office unless we know absolutely everything about that job. Men don't do that. They figure that what they don't know, they'll learn."

Men "wake up in the morning and ask themselves if they should run for president," she said. "Women need a drumroll and a draft before they even begin thinking about it."

Wilson cites a study by three political scientists confirming this gender difference. Thirty-seven percent of male candidates polled said it was their own idea to run for office. They saw or met an elected official and concluded: I can do that.

Only 11 percent of female candidates, though, said they decided on their own to run. Nearly 40 percent of the women candidates said they didn't even think of running until someone else brought it up.

Many women, Wilson said, fear that running for office makes them look ambitious. Too often, it's their female friends who are quick to put them in their place.

"It happened to me," Wilson said. "I'd mention my interest in a particular position, and my women friends would say, 'Do you really think you can do that?' "

We need more women who can answer that question with an unequivocal yes. Research shows a direct correlation between the number of women in a legislative body and the passage of bills that benefit women and children.

And so, on the eve of this most important election, I have a request.

When you leave the polls tomorrow, think about the few women who were on the ballot. Then think of the strong, capable women you know who could change that equation.

Most of us can name the women leaders in our community. They are the PTA president and the entrepreneur, the community activist and the full-time volunteer. These women raise money and hope, but never the possibility that they themselves could be the answer.

We can change that with a single conversation that begins with, "Have you ever thought of running?"

Let's start that conversation today.

7.

Keeping the Faith

Last fall, our Cleveland newsroom was abuzz after learning that a journalist in Minnesota was suspended for joining his fellow church members in a silent antiwar demonstration.

Tim Mahoney is a part-time copy editor with the *St. Paul Pioneer Press,* which means he edits other reporters' stories and writes headlines for them. On the last Saturday in September 2005, he boarded one of three buses sponsored by St. Joan of Arc Church in Minneapolis, where he is an active member, and headed for Washington, D.C.

"On our part it was a silent march," Mahoney told the online alternative weekly *City Press.* "We just marched around the White House, period."

When editors found out, though, he was suspended for three days without pay and ordered not to participate in any more political events.

Mahoney insisted he wasn't being political, but acting on his faith.

"There is an issue of conscience, of religion," Mahoney told *City Press.* "I'm not trying to put myself forth as any kind of pious person at all. I'm not. But it's a matter of personal belief."

What most interested me about this story was my colleagues' reaction to it, especially from those who are active in their own churches. Almost to a person, they wondered aloud whether it was possible to be equally vigilant in their practice of journalism and that of their faith.

That this conversation even took place in a newsroom might surprise a lot of Americans who think we are a Godless bunch, what with our impertinent questions, our apparent disregard for social graces. A newsroom, though, reflects the same hodgepodge of religious beliefs found in communities all across America.

In our newsroom, for example, an ordained minister works on the copy desk. Two others in the newsroom—a reporter and an editor, both middle-aged—are part-time divinity students. An editor in our op-ed department works with prisoners through a program at her church, and dozens of other colleagues serve communion, usher during Sunday service, and give Scripture readings from the pulpit. As a community of colleagues, we pray together at funerals, belt out hymns at weddings, and thank God for the babies being baptized.

In all kinds of ways, big and small, we are keeping the faith.

At most newspapers, only the designated religion writers weigh in publicly on issues of faith. Often these stories focus on rituals and practices and the history behind them. These are important stories, usually predictably planted in a designated space on a designated day.

Faith, though, threads through every hour of every day. Our country has become deeply divided over religion, with the far right co-opting Christianity to the point where many of us raised in the faith no longer feel comfortable claiming it. It seemed to me that there was a greater conversation out there.

So I described how the congregation of a church that was set on fire after its leadership voted to welcome gays and lesbians gathered together on the front lawn and praised God the very next Sunday. I wondered aloud why so-called Christians thought it was God's work to demand that hourly wage earners bolster our faith by saying "Merry Christmas" with each swipe of the credit card. I wrote about an innocent black man who spent thirteen years in prison, leaned hard on his Muslim faith, and forgave the man who finally confessed to the crime.

Some of the reader response was fast and furious, and by furious I do mean angry. I was raised to believe God casts a wide net, but saying that in a newspaper doesn't sit well with those who claim there is but one set of rules and they bind and constrict us in ways only their particular house of worship understands.

Most readers, though, weighed in with a grace that fuels my own faith in ways that all that chest-thumping never will. One of my favorite letters came from a fifty-three-year-old reader named Donna, who lives in Mansfield, Ohio, a small town near Columbus.

Her first few letters had outlined how she didn't agree with me about much of anything. Over time, though, she began sharing stories about her own life, including how—and why—she prays. I saved her letter as a reminder of how an abiding faith in God can stretch our reach in this troubled world.

"When I pray at night," she wrote, "I ask God to let me pray for those who feel as if they have no friend, for those who hurt, for those who are desperate and are without hope.

"Does he hear my prayer? My faith tells me that he does and that he counts it unto me as good. Although I can't physically be there to give those in need a helping hand my thoughts are with them.

"For those who say they don't know where their strength comes from during the hard times, I like to think it is the answer to my prayers."

IT'S NOT CHRISTIAN TO CHAMPION HATE

he drive to my daughter's elementary school used to take about fifteen minutes, and back then we used the time for morning prayers.

We always prayed out loud. Sometimes she was a chipper little prayer girl, her head bobbing with enthusiasm as she thanked God for her many blessings and asked for a special nod to those in need. Other mornings, she'd mumble something like, "Well, God, you know the list," and we'd have a little chat about right intention.

Our morning prayer was a way to teach my daughter that she is never alone and that God hears "amen" wherever we are. I also wanted her to understand that we pray in private because faith is something you live, not lecture, and we should never force our version of God on anyone else. God answers to all sorts of names, I told her, and there are all sorts of paths that lead to his front door.

Too bad I didn't see the current climate of ugliness coming. Christians around the country tell me they feel their faith has been co-opted by right-wing conservatives who depict all liberals as soldiers of Satan.

Had I known this New Rage movement was on its way, I also would have taught my daughter how to say, gently but firmly, "He's my God, too."

We caught a glimpse of these New Ragers in action when, immediately after the September 11 terrorist attacks, Jerry Falwell told Pat Robertson on national television that liberals' advocacy for abortion rights and gay rights and keeping religion out of our public schools brought on the devastation. The carnage and suffering were evidence of God's wrath at liberals, Falwell said.

"I hate to admit this," one longtime Lutheran activist told me, "but it's gotten to the point where I'm embarrassed to say I'm a Christian. I don't want anyone associating me with them."

This is a woman who, alongside her husband, has spent decades working for social justice on behalf of some of the most mistreated and neglected among us. She is living the answer to that Christian jingle, *What would Jesus do?* And yet she shrinks from the label "Christian," for fear others will mistake her for a champion of hate.

"Maybe we need another word for who we are," she said. "Maybe we should call ourselves"—she shrugged her shoulders and winced— "Jesus-ites?"

Or maybe it's time we took back our faith from those who had no business co-opting it in the first place.

I was raised to believe that being a Christian meant fixing ourselves and helping others, not the other way around.

The Christians I admire try to respond to differences with compassion, not anger or judgment. God knows I'm working on that one myself, and so I appreciate the role models.

They are the Christians who search until they find the common threads of decency and kindness that weave through people of every faith, and no faith at all. They live and work side by side with Jews, Muslims, Buddhists, and atheists without ever thumping their chests or their Bibles, claiming they own the only map to Salvation.

So-called Christians who show up at a gay person's funeral or a gay pastor's church with signs reading GOD HATES HOMOSEXUALS do not speak for the God I know.

When Pat Robertson asked Christians to pray for the demise of three liberal Supreme Court justices, he was not my idea of a Christian.

And those demonstrators protesting when the Ten Commandments were removed from an Alabama courthouse did not shout on my behalf. My faith is far too sturdy to be threatened by laws designed to protect the rights of every American.

New Ragers often call or write to assure me I've bought myself a one-way ticket to hell. "I pray for your soul," they say, but I don't think they mean it, at least not in the way I was raised to pray. Sometimes I wonder what God thinks of these folks who are so sure they've got him all figured out and then get so angry about it.

At such moments, I rely on my faith, which assures me God loves every last one of us.

Then I ask him to show me how he does it.

HARRY CHAPIN INSPIRED
GOODWILL TOWARD MEN

*A*t least once a month, it seems, I attend a charity event meant to inspire all of us to activism but that instead leaves me feeling like an unworthy slug of a human being.

These are the best of causes where the intentions are good and the crowd empathetic. The speakers are inevitably earnest and dedicated to the cause. Just as inevitably, they walk slowly to the lectern and proceed to let us have it.

People are suffering, they lecture, and we, yes we, have abandoned them.

Now, I haven't personally abandoned them. Most of the time, I don't even know them. I do care about them, which is why I'm there in the first place. But so often the message is less about how we can help and more about how we have already failed as human beings, because we haven't committed enough acts of self-sacrifice to lay claim to membership in the same species.

This voice-of-God finger-wagging from the lectern doesn't bring out the best in me. By the end of the speech, I just want to bury my head under the covers of my queen-size bed and stay there until the first robin sprints across the front yard.

I miss Harry Chapin.

Now there was a guy who knew how to make you care that you haven't cared enough. By the time he was done, you even felt worthy of his faith in you.

I'm going to force myself to believe that someone, somewhere, doesn't already know who Chapin is and tell you that he was a folksinger, storyteller, filmmaker, and tireless activist for social justice until he died too young in a car crash on July 16, 1981. He was thirty-eight.

I went to several of his concerts during high school and college. He even kissed me once on the cheek after signing my brand-new World Hunger Year T-shirt, which he sold to raise money for the organization he founded.

What I still most cherish about Chapin is his lesson about how to change people's hearts. He shared it once during a chat with the audience between songs.

When he first started writing folk songs, Chapin said, he was the guiltmaster: People are starving! People are suffering! The world is falling apart! And you—yes, you—are doing nothing to help!

Nobody cared.

Then he started writing and performing songs in which he was the screwup, the jerk, the one who couldn't get it right.

In "Cat's in the Cradle," he was the father who never had time for his son who now never had time for him. In "Taxi," he was the cab-driver who'd run out of dreams when a girlfriend from his past handed him the fare and said, "Harry, keep the change." He was the morning disc jockey who abandoned his family for W-O-L-Dee-dee-dee-dee.

Millions cared.

He'd figured out, he said, that if you don't mind being the fool, you can help people face their mirror image. His songs gave us the space to identify our own missteps, our own regrets, without ever having to admit to them.

Then we wanted to change.

"He started writing good songs when he made himself the villain," said his brother, Tom, who still performs and also serves on the World Hunger Year board. "His best stuff is where he's the 'everyman' and the audience gets to learn along with him."

At least half of Chapin's concerts were free, either for a charity or a benefit. Whenever he talked about the world's hungry, he told stories about the people and just assumed we'd want to help. My radar for grown-up disapproval was finely tuned, and I never felt he was lecturing.

Tony Kornheiser wrote Chapin's obituary for *The Washington Post.* He told a story about joining Chapin for a late-night snack after one of his fund-raising concerts in the nation's capital. Kornheiser knew how dedicated Chapin was to wiping out world hunger, so he razzed the singer when he ordered "a big, thick sandwich."

Chapin didn't miss a beat.

"Look," he said, "I'm not asking you to starve; I'm simply asking you to try and spread the word that we grow enough food each year to feed the world easily. You've got access to a great newspaper here. For God's sake, use it."

I miss Harry Chapin.

MERRY CHRISTMAS EVERYONE—OR ELSE

When did corporate America become responsible for my Christmas cheer?

In my forty-seven years on this earth, it has never occurred to me that I should look to advertising or store clerks for affirmation of my faith. That's what church is for. Family and friends are handy for that, too, not to mention the little miracles of daily living.

Newspapers around the country, though, are full of stories about disgruntled Christians insisting that their Christmas is spoiled because cashiers don't say "Merry Christmas" anymore. They're also grumbling that store ads have dropped "Merry Christmas," trumpeting "Happy Holidays" and "Season's Greetings" instead.

A California group is boycotting Macy's and its corporate parent, Federated Department Stores, accusing them of banning "Merry Christmas" signs, even though the companies insist they have no such ban.

In Raleigh, North Carolina, a church pledging to keep "Christ in Christmas" paid $7,000 that could have clothed the poor and fed the homeless to place a full-page ad in the November 24 issue of *The News and Observer* newspaper.

"Attention Christians!" began the ad, which then urged "all Christians to spend their hard-earned dollars with merchants who include the greeting 'Merry Christmas' in their holiday advertising promotions this Christmas."

A lot of readers objected to the ad, in part because it also pointed out that only 5 percent of Americans celebrate Hanukkah and 2 percent celebrate Kwanzaa. In other words, we're bigger than they are—they being Jews and African-Americans—so let's start acting like it and throw our weight around.

I'm confused.

If we really want to go after what corporate America has done to Christmas, shouldn't we stop buying all these—dare I say it?—*things*?

If what we long for is the Christmas of yore, shouldn't we return to the days of baked goods tied up with bows and presents no larger than stockings hung by the chimney with care? Threatening to withhold our Visa or MasterCard only until they say what we want them to say doesn't strike me as getting us any closer to the manger.

I'm also trying to figure out why store clerks should have to make me feel good about Christmas.

When I shop, I have to wait at their counter for ten, maybe fifteen minutes, tops. They have to stand there all day.

I make a generous living and have health care. They rarely make a living wage and most have no benefits.

I'll get the whole week off. At best, they get only Christmas Day, and then they're back for the mobs on December 26.

Seems to me I can afford to take the lead on Christmas cheer.

I want to live my faith, not enforce it, and I can start by remembering there's a beating heart beneath every store smock and name tag. We get plenty of reminders on that one, especially during this season of giving.

Last week, for example, I stood in line and watched a middle-aged woman with a Christmas angel pinned to her lapel berate two young clerks because the store didn't have her favorite brand of gum.

"I've been in here three times in the last week, and three times you haven't had it," she hissed, pointing to the rack that held dozens of other brands of gum. "This is outrageous."

The clerks apologized several times. Her only response was to threaten never to return to that store if they didn't stock her gum. I was willing to lead a round of applause on that one, but they just continued to apologize and assured her they would order it that very day.

Those two clerks taught me a lot about the spirit of Christmas. They reminded me that we keep the Christ in Christmas every time we're kind when we want to be angry, generous when we want to be selfish, patient when we want to scream.

We don't find joy by demanding it, and I for one have no interest in joining the faith police. Insisting on carols while we shop and clerks chirping "Merry Christmas" at the checkout counter suggests a fragile faith, one that could fall prey to corporate control.

Surely, the spirit of Christmas is stronger than that.

FROM THE MAN WHO DID THE TIME:
"I HARBOR NO BITTERNESS"

M*ichael Green leaned forward* in his seat and called out to the judge in the courtroom.

"Your honor?" he said. "Can I please speak?"

Cuyahoga County Common Pleas judge Judith Kilbane Koch looked over at the jury box, where Michael sat with various reporters and photographers. Then she glanced at the defendant, Rodney Rhines, whom she was about to sentence to five years in prison.

"Sure," she said, motioning for Michael to stand.

The moment both men had been waiting for had finally arrived.

Almost fifteen years ago, their lives had intersected when Rhines committed a crime and Michael was ordered to do the time.

Yesterday, Rhines went to court to be sentenced for the 1988 rape of a terminally ill patient at the Cleveland Clinic Hotel. Michael went to that same courtroom to tell him what has been on his mind ever since Rhines confessed on October 21 after reading a *Plain Dealer* series chronicling Michael's ordeal.

Michael stood up in the second row of the jury box and walked to the railing. The two men locked eyes.

"I didn't come out of prison with a bitter heart," Michael said, "and I won't leave here with a bitter heart. I harbor no bitterness toward you, and I hope you can continue to walk the path you're on now."

Rhines's eyes teared and his lips trembled as he silently accepted the forgiveness he had been waiting for.

Since last October, Rhines has called me periodically from Cuyahoga County Jail, where he awaited sentencing. He talked about how his faith was holding him steady, how sorry he was for the rape victim, who died eleven months after the trial. And he always wanted to talk about Michael.

"I hope he can find it in his heart to forgive me for what I did to him," Rhines would say, often sobbing. "I hope he doesn't hate me." My assurances that Michael had indeed forgiven him weren't enough.

"I guess I need to hear it from him," he said. "I guess that's what I need."

Over those same months, Michael often said he wished he could talk to Rhines. "I need to let him know I harbor no ill will toward him," Michael said repeatedly. "I did the time for him. I don't want to see him go to prison. And I want to tell him that."

Yesterday, he finally had his chance, but it almost didn't happen.

At first, Michael said he couldn't come to the courthouse for Rhines's hearing, which was scheduled for 1:30 P.M. "I'll never make it in time," he said in a morning telephone call from his job with troubled youths at Lutheran Ministries on Cleveland's East Side. He hasn't re-placed his car, which was totaled last month after a driver ran him into a telephone pole and took off.

About 1:15, though, Michael changed his mind.

"I'm coming," he said after reaching me on my cell phone at the courthouse.

"Why?"

"I have to do this," he said. "I have to let him know I've got no prob-lem with him. I can't let him go off to prison with me as one of his bur-dens."

A friend offered to drive Michael from East 100th Street to the Jus-tice Center, but after a few blocks, the car died. Michael jumped out and caught the No. 6 RTA bus on Euclid Avenue and made it to the courtroom around two P.M. It was another hour and a half before Rhines entered.

Before Rhines's arrival, his lawyer, Ralph DeFranco, approached the reporters and photographers gathered in the jury box, unaware that the man who paid for Rhines's crime was also sitting there. When he was introduced, DeFranco let out an audible gasp.

"That's amazing," he said to Michael. "You two don't look a thing alike."

Michael just nodded and smiled.

A few minutes later, a deputy sheriff escorted Rhines into the court-room. His hands were cuffed behind his back, and at first he stared at the floor, his lips moving in prayer. When someone told the judge that Michael was in the courtroom, Rhines's head shot up and he looked timidly toward the jury box. Michael met his gaze and nodded once.

After Michael spoke in the courtroom, the judge turned to him and smiled. "I commend you for the kindness in your heart for this man," she said, and then she looked at both men and shook her head. "I'm sorry," she told Michael. "You don't look alike."

She then sentenced Rhines to five years in prison and ordered that he be classified a sexually oriented offender for ten years after his release.

"All rise," shouted the bailiff.

As a deputy sheriff led Rhines toward the door of the holding cell, he turned one last time, looked at Michael and spoke in a near whisper.

"Thank you," he said.

THE UGLINESS COMES FROM BOTH EXTREMES

I *looked around* the crowded room and knew there was no way everyone was going to agree with what I had to say.

In fact, a few of them told me so before I even stepped up to the lectern.

"Sometimes you make me mad," one woman said. The man behind her nodded his head.

Not one of them was under sixty. A good number of them were probably over seventy. Some of them, I was sure, would disagree with me on abortion or gay rights. Others might argue with me about Wal-Mart or the war in Iraq. Chances are we wouldn't even agree on who should be allowed to vote.

We knew what we were getting into, but we agreed to come together anyway on a rainy afternoon in May because we also knew we'd find plenty of the common ground you stumble on whenever you go looking for reasons to like another human being.

Anyone taking a stand is someone willing to care, and it was our mutual interest in the state of the world that carried the day. We didn't part in total agreement, but we didn't leave screaming either, and that was a nice break from the vitriol that is so pervasive these days.

The path to common ground isn't that long of a hike, but lately it sure seems to be sprouting a lot more weeds. So many detours, to the left and to the right, where lines are drawn and paths never cross.

I used to blame the far right for most of the decline in public discourse. Not long after I started writing a column, I discovered they could be a mean, ugly bunch.

The hate mail was fast and furious, often clearly organized and frequently personal, or as personal as you can get when you've never met the person on the receiving end of your malice. They were especially keen on attacking my appearance, my faith, and my children. When it came to spewing venom, the far right could spit for miles.

Lately, though, I must admit the far left can be just as mean and ugly. I learned that firsthand after writing about a young wife who was worried about her husband, an Army Reserve captain stationed in Afghanistan during the recent riots there. She was angry at *Newsweek* for any role it may have played in sparking the riots after publishing a story it later retracted, and she wanted journalists to please be careful with their facts.

I spent the next two days weeding through mostly anonymous calls and e-mail accusing me of selling out to the Bush administration. In a heartbreaking moment of clarity, I had to admit these messages were just as awful as the ones I often get from the right.

I was a moron for focusing on the suffering of one military wife instead of the massive casualties of war. I was an idiot for not stating the obvious, that it is this awful war, and not *Newsweek,* that has damaged the U.S. image abroad.

Where was my heart? My conscience? My soul?

It didn't matter that I opposed this war from the beginning. It didn't matter how often in the past I've championed so many of the causes dear to the left, either. What mattered was that, on that day, in that particular column, I didn't say what they wanted me to say.

Lost was the message that this young wife's anguish was a human face on the pain shared by so many who grab for the nearest railing every time bad news from the war reaches home. Lost, too, was my belief that liberals are always a kinder, gentler folk.

People yell when they feel they aren't being heard. But if righteous rage is our only tongue, our reach never stretches beyond our own small tribe. Think back to the last time someone's screaming and name-calling inspired you to listen.

That'd be a big, fat never, I suspect.

Are we meaner than we used to be? Or do we simply have more outlets for the unnamed rage we used to just take out on the kids and the family dog?

The anonymity of voice mail and e-mail now allows us to live in absentia, like bomber pilots who never see the shells land or feel the flames rise.

We need that crowded room, where little by little, we soften in the listening.

And little by little, the flames die down.

ANSWERING HOSTILITY WITH AMAZING GRACE

*A*ny person who's found solace in a house of worship knows why this is a wound that hurts an entire congregation.

St. John's Reformed United Church of Christ is a 225-year-old church in rural Middlebrook, Virginia. On Wednesday, the outgoing message on the church phone still invited you to buy tickets for May's spaghetti supper, but that has to be the last thing on the minds of its grieving congregation.

Vandals set fire to St. John's just five days after the United Church of Christ's General Synod met in Atlanta and passed a nonbinding resolution to endorse gay and lesbian marriages. News reports called it a "small fire," but there's no such thing when the flames are in your sacred home.

A church member was about to mow the lawn on Saturday when he spotted graffiti on the outside of the church declaring that UCC members are sinners. When he ran inside, he found a fire in the sanctuary.

The vandals burned a stack of hymnals, the same books that members opened week after week for funerals and weddings, Sunday services and urgent prayers. The fire damaged the choir loft, too, and one of the pews where sleepy children used to lean against patient parents and folks in trouble listened hard for what God had to say.

Why, church members asked. Why would they do this to us?

They found their answer in the antigay graffiti left behind.

After the Associated Press reported the fire, one weblog led with the headline CHRISTIANS PREFER TO BURN CHURCHES THAN TO LET GAYS MARRY.

What Christians might these be?

It reminds me of recent coverage of ABC's decision to cancel its ill-conceived reality show *Welcome to the Neighborhood* after both liberal and conservative groups complained that it promoted prejudice. Neighbors in a quiet cul-de-sac near Austin, Texas, voted on which household of the following would be allowed to move in: a black family, Wiccans, Latinos, a white family with a stripper mother, or a white gay couple with an adopted black infant.

Apparently, for some this is quite a quandary.

Much of the coverage, including that of *The New York Times* and *The Washington Post,* described those neighbors willing to cast judgment as "Christians."

Again, I ask: What Christians might these be?

"Clearly, there are at least two competing versions of interpreting our Gospel," said the Reverend John Thomas, president of the UCC, whose headquarters are in Cleveland. "There are those who are Jesus-centered, focused on outreach to those in the margins with a message of inclusion, and there are those who are real judgmental, more rule-bound with boundaries for who is welcome and who is not."

Both, he said, can find biblical text to support their brand of Christianity, and he has heard from plenty on both sides since the General Synod's vote. His voice sounded weary as he recounted some of the ugly mail. In the face of such vitriol, he said, it is best to take the long view.

"In 1833, we ordained the first woman," Thomas said. "It caused deep divisions in the church back then. Now it's not even an issue. If you think only in weeks, it can be very difficult."

Thomas first heard about the fire at St. John's Saturday afternoon. "I had this stunned, sickened feeling. I said, 'My God, is it starting?' Part of your mind tells you it is an isolated incident. But still, you worry."

Less than forty-eight hours after vandals tried to destroy their church, about one hundred members of St. John's gathered on the lawn to celebrate its 225th anniversary.

The Staunton *News Leader* described the scene: Children used discarded strips of yellow police tape to bind their legs for a three-legged race. The Reverend Dorcas Lohr urged her congregation to remember their long history, including the church fire they survived in 1978.

The latest act of vandalism, she said, wasn't personal, but "a symptom of what is happening in our nation."

When she was done, the congregation sang "Let There Be Peace on Earth."

There was no music, no choir in the loft. No pews, even.

And still, these Christians sang.

NO PLEDGE NEEDED TO SHOW OUR FAITH

O nce again, we're arguing over whether we should keep God out of our public schools.

As if we could. I don't think God takes marching orders from us.

So, I do not share the anxiety of those who claim that a U.S. federal judge's recent order to remove the words "under God" from our Pledge of Allegiance is just one more step in a steady march toward a heathen nation.

In a letter to the *St. Louis Post-Dispatch,* reader Pamela Muich Jearls echoed the apparent sentiment of many:

"For those individuals who call themselves Americans, if you do not like the words 'under God,' please pack your bags and leave. Please obtain citizenship in China, a Godless country, it will be perfect for you. These so-called Americans are a disgrace to the USA, to their families and children, their fellow co-workers. . . . Then you wonder why terrorists state that 'we are a Godless country.' "

There's that word: *godless.* As if the failure to display publicly our faith proves we have no faith at all.

The court ruling places responsibility for faith where it belongs, on the private individual. Surely people of faith don't need the rote recitation invoking God's name where it doesn't belong to believe God still shows up every day in America, with or without the invitation. In fact, my own faith has been bolstered in recent weeks by witnessing acts large and small throughout our country. God's will be done from sea to shining sea.

Consider, for example, the cavalcade of rescue efforts since Hurricane Katrina hit the Gulf Coast. Financial contributions to the American Red Cross have surpassed those donated after the September 11 terrorist attacks. And that is just the beginning of the heroism of Americans reaching out to save total strangers from the grip of despair.

All you have to do is scroll through some of the images captured by photographers covering the Gulf Coast tragedy to see God at work.

Amid so much suffering and loss, acts of compassion and selfless courage make my spirits soar.

We saw Terrence Gray, a police officer in Gulfport, Mississippi, waist-high in water as he pushed to safety a boat holding Lovie Mae Allen and her oxygen tank.

We saw a tattered rooftop in New Orleans' St. Bernard Parish, where someone painted in large, white letters these names: AVARESE, SACCO, HARRIS, SCORTINO, BRANDON, G.U.M., DAQUINE. Next to this list were two more words: ARE ALIVE.

We saw a large, unnamed man holding a tiny infant over his shoulder as he gently draped a blanket over the body of an old man in New Orleans who died at the convention center.

Schoolchildren held fund-raisers, servers donated their tips, businesses posted prayers of support on their front-yard signs. Celebrities stepped out of their zones of self-absorption and engaged in hands-on rescue efforts, and if that isn't a miracle, I don't know one.

And we in the media found our spine when one journalist after another—even at Fox News—beheld the horror and demanded to know why the federal government had abandoned so many of its own people in need.

"I am called to protest the injustice against my neighbor," the Reverend Dr. Michael Kinnamon said Sunday in a visit to our church. He is professor of mission and peace at Eden Theological Seminary in St. Louis, the same town in which that reader wrote such an angry letter.

Kinnamon's interpretation of God's work resonates with those who embrace Christianity as a call to action on behalf of those who don't have it in them to fight. Every day, I meet Americans who live this faith by offering a reservoir of hope and encouragement in a land parched from anger and neglect.

I see God in the faces of those who protest the war, and those who show up for the services of fallen troops they never met.

I see God in the healing touch of doctors and nurses and volunteers who care for the swelling numbers of the poor.

And I see God in the righteous fury of those who champion the homeless, advocate for the overworked and underpaid, and demand that every citizen's vote be counted.

I don't know if each and every one of these people believes in God, but they help me believe every single day.

SEDER OF HOPE: JEWISH RITUALS
FEED THIS GENTILE'S SOUL

Seven years ago, my daughter and I were fresh recruits to the ranks of single parenthood, weak-kneed and wobbly as we navigated the sudden sweep of changes in our lives.

We were immersed in strange surroundings I was determined we'd call home without that catch in our voices. Our new life was brimming with unfamiliar things, a forced homeyness emblematic of flight. Our address was different. So were our beds, our dishes, and the curtain we pulled across the shower. I envied friends' scratched flatware, the sunken corners of their favorite sofas, their stained oven mitts with singed thumbs.

We were so steeped in the unfamiliar that when my friend Joan left a message on our new voice mail inviting us to her parents' Seder, I didn't immediately feel anxious in the way I would have even a year before.

I was raised a small-town Presbyterian. There was only one Jew in my high school class. I didn't know Passover from Poughkeepsie. Imagining myself at the Seder table, I looked at our new kitten, Winnie, and said, "I would have no idea what to do."

Then I laughed. Not knowing what I was doing? That was familiar. I said we'd be there.

Joan's parents are Gloria and Laurie (short for Laurence). I had met them only a couple of times and gave them no reason to care about us the way they immediately did. They hugged us hello, then whisked my normally shy child off for a tour of their art gallery of a home. They showed Cait pictures of their family, answered her questions about their many paintings, and told her stories about why Jews celebrate Passover. By the time Joan and Jeff and their two kids arrived, we were family.

That night, we learned about the struggle of the Israelites in their journey to freedom. We took turns reading from the Haggadah. We dipped parsley in salt water to remind us of the tears of the Jewish slaves. Our eyes watered when we swallowed the horseradish meant to reflect the bitter affliction of their captivity.

We recited the Four Questions, too. My favorite: On all other nights we eat sitting up; why do we lean on a pillow tonight?

"To be comfortable," read Lia, the youngest child at the table. "And to remind us that once we were slaves, but now we are free."

I swallowed hard, grateful for the reminder that many people far less fortunate than I have started their lives over and made it under God's watchful eye.

It was a magical night for me. I stared at my little Gentile daughter as she sang in Hebrew without looking at the phonetic key. She sang loudly, as if joyfully remembering her ancient tongue. As if, finally, she were at home in the familiar.

We have been invited to their Seder ever since. The rituals of Passover are now as familiar to us as our own at Easter and Christmas. We are changed in other ways, too. Six years ago I interviewed Miep Gies, the woman who helped hide Anne Frank and her family until they were captured and murdered by the Nazis. Cait went with me to hear Gies speak. For weeks afterward, she pored over Anne Frank's diary.

One night Cait came running into my bedroom, fresh from the shower, her hair wet and matted to her head.

"We would hide Gloria and Laurie, wouldn't we, Mom?" she asked, her eyes dark with fear. I looked quizzically at her. "From the Nazis, Mom. We would hide them from the Nazis if we knew them back then?"

I pulled her close. "Of course we would."

"And Jeff and Joan, and Peter and Lia, too?" she said. "Even though we could be killed, right?"

"Yes," I whispered as I kissed the top of her head and tried to force the horror from my own mind.

And so our lessons of Passover continued.

This Wednesday, we will join our friends again. We will know where to begin reading in the Haggadah, how to dip the parsley, and when to leave the door open for the prophet Elijah. I'll sneak a peek, ever hopeful that this time he might show up.

I will listen to Lia's sweet singing, bask in Peter's enthusiasm, and watch Gloria putter in the kitchen as Laurie shares a story or two. I'll ask Jeff about his writing, prod Joan into telling me about her latest project. I will look at my teenage daughter aglow at the table and re-member her frightened face the night she first realized these people we love could have been killed in another time, another place, simply for who they are.

Then I will do what I always do. I will silently thank God for guiding the Israelites to safety so long ago, and for leading us to these, our beloved friends, who became our familiar, our family, when we needed it most.

NEVER DOUBT THAT SANTA'S THERE

t has come to my attention that some children are no longer sure they can believe in Santa.

An older brother or sister, a know-it-all classmate, or even their own snooping selves have produced what appears to be irrefutable evidence that someone else has been behind this whole ho-ho-ho thing. With quivering bottom lips and a tightness in their chests, they are running to Mom or Dad and asking, "Is it true?"

Oh, boy.

For most parents, this is the moment when the whimsical in us does silent battle with our role as truth bearer. We want our children to turn to us when facts are murky. We want them to trust that we'll always play it straight with them. But we also want never to break their hearts.

That's why we can go ahead and tell them the truth: Even if you don't believe in Santa, you can believe.

You can believe that something greater than yourself looks out for you and cheers you on. That love, kindness, and generosity are your greatest gifts to the world, and the more you give them away, the more they come back to you. That the same spirit that makes your hairline tingle also visits the grumpiest of people, even the man honking from the car behind you who's so angry his face looks like a monkey's behind.

Now, granted, it's sometimes hard to believe in something you can't prove. And there will always be those wise guys who want to point to your lack of evidence as proof of your foolishness. They sweep in with their unsolicited version of re-AL-i-ty, pummel you with it like a mallet and then say it was for your own good.

Personally, I don't understand such unkindness. Why would anyone want to talk us out of our epiphanies? Perhaps they feel left out because they've never high-fived an angel or heard that invisible whisper in their ear that everything will be all right. Maybe they're just too cranky to believe in anything but their own bad moods, like Ebenezer Scrooge. But we know what happened to him, don't we?

Even other believers will sometimes pick on you. They'll say what you believe doesn't match what they believe and so what you believe is wrong, which only goes to show you that even believers sometimes carry mallets. This is a complicated world.

But it is also a magical world, and sometimes Santa surprises even us grown-ups. Just last week, I was rushing through a mall with my hands full of bags and my neck on fire from the wool scarf I wished I'd left in the car when I dropped my keys and fell over trying to pick them up.

"Perfect," I mumbled. "Just perfect."

A red flush crawled up my face as I stretched to reach for the keys and saw two big black boots stop right at my fingertips.

Not now, I thought. *Not a good time.*

I looked up. The ample man in the red suit was surrounded by little believers who were following him on his way back from a dinner break.

"Hi, Santa."

He laughed, extended his hand, and pulled me up to my feet.

"You shouldn't rush so much," he said, smiling as he gathered up my bags. Then he pointed to the many gifts I'd bought. "You must have a lot of people who love you."

I nodded and returned his smile. All the little kids were staring at me, the woman Santa had just picked up off the floor. Something more than, "Well, seeya Santa," seemed to be called for.

"So, Santa," I said, "how's Donner?"

"Oh, he's just fine, real fine. Ready for the big night, you know."

I nodded again. "Merry Christmas."

"And Merry Christmas to you, Connie."

Stunned, I stared at him as he walked away, a child's hand tucked in each of his. He looked back, gave me a wink, then belted out, "Ho, ho, ho."

I felt that familiar tingle tug at my hairline. Suddenly, I forgot why I was rushing. I didn't feel hot and bothered anymore, either, even with the scarf still wrapped around my neck.

I just stood there for the longest time, oblivious to the work ID badge dangling from my neck and wondering: *How did Santa know my name?*

8.

The Perfect Couple

In the last presidential race, my home state earned the dubious distinction of passing the most hateful of the eleven antigay ballot issues in the country. By an overwhelming majority, we told gays and lesbians we don't like their brand of love and robbed them of their partners' health benefits. Not that they ever had these in Ohio, but some legislators felt the need to hammer that one home with a blunt instrument.

For me, this is personal.

The high school guidance counselor who convinced my daughter she was greater than her low expectations is gay. So is the medical director who treats the growing number of the working poor at Ohio's largest free clinic. The banker who handled our mortgage loan is gay, too.

And then there are Kate and Jackie, two of our closest friends. It was Jackie who knew before I did that I would one day marry my husband, and it was her partner, Kate, who donned her pastor's robes and tenderly guided us through our wedding vows.

Jackie and Kate are family, in no small part because they never saw anything but potential in my kids and stood by me when others didn't have the stomach for it. You tend to love friends like that, and once you do, silence just isn't an option when others take aim at them for loving each other.

We columnists like to think we have all the answers. Give us a problem, we'll solve it; a puzzle, we'll supply the missing piece. But I struggle mightily when otherwise decent people visit their vitriol on an entire group of people they're so sure they don't want to know. Some readers angrily insist, "I don't even want to *think* about what those people do in their bedrooms." I don't know about the rest of you, but I don't want to imagine the bedroom gymnastics of anyone, straight or gay, so that particular bit of logic is lost on me.

Column by column, I tell the stories of extraordinary people who also happen to be gay. Story by story, they chip away at that imaginary wall that divides us.

That's my prayer, anyway.

A PERFECT COUPLE, AN IMPERFECT WORLD

I *n so many ways,* Jack and Kate are the perfect couple.

They are proud parents deeply involved in their adult children's lives. They are productive members of society, too. Jack works in upper management for a realty company; Kate is an ordained minister with the United Church of Christ. Jack sings in the church choir and serves on its board; Kate preaches and holds funerals for those who have no church home.

Last spring, they moved out of their cozy suburban cottage and built a house in one of Cleveland's oldest neighborhoods because they wanted to be a part of the city's revitalization.

Kate and Jack are a promise that love can bloom long after temples gray and waistbands beg for a little give. This is a second marriage for them both, and their love for each other is palpable. I feel it whenever they laugh at each other's jokes. I see it when they snuggle in the movie theater after the lights dim.

And I heard it just yesterday when Jack—or Jackie, as many call her—described what happened the night she took Kate to an emergency room.

The clerk looked up at Jackie and asked, "What is your relationship to the patient?"

"I'm her partner," Jackie answered.

The woman frowned and wrote, "Friend."

With one stroke of the pen, the perfect couple was put asunder.

"I try not to think about what would happen if Kate or I were on our deathbed," Jackie said. She has reason to worry.

Jackie and Kate exchanged vows and rings in 1996, the same year the Defense of Marriage Act codified gays and lesbians as second-class citizens. Their church commitment ceremony in front of two hundred friends and some, but not all, of their family, was both a public pronouncement of their devotion and a direct rebuttal to the notion that love can be legislated.

Their house is in both their names, they have living wills and power of attorney forms, but they are not legally a couple because the law won't let them be.

Any hospital could deny either of them access to her dying mate. And even if they live together for the next forty years, when one of them dies, the other will not receive a penny in government survivor benefits.

It can get worse, and sometimes it does. I lived next door to a gay couple on Cleveland's East Side who spent nearly ten years together before one of them died of AIDS. The man, a doctor, died believing he had left his home and personal belongings to his partner.

His family, though, had other ideas, even though they had cut off all contact with him years ago when they found out he was gay. With the force of law behind them, they swept in, evicted his devastated partner, held a garage sale and split the profits from the house sale.

Recently, the American Law Institute, an influential private organization of lawyers, judges, and scholars, recommended sweeping changes in family law as it is currently practiced in this country. One of the recommendations was to extend to gay couples the rights long enjoyed by even the most dysfunctional of married heterosexuals.

Predictably, some immediately declared this an erosion of traditional family values and a threat to the institution of marriage. This was a bit confusing to all of us divorced heterosexual parents who thought we were to blame for the demise of the American family. But I quibble.

Allowing gays and lesbians to marry doesn't mean that straight Americans will suddenly dump traditional marriage for a gay one. It means that an entire group of Americans who've been denied their constitutional rights finally will be able to marry those they love and shed the fears that shroud their every day and night.

Most readers, I suspect, initially agreed that Kate and Jack were the perfect couple. Some changed their minds once they realized both Kate and Jack were women.

That bigotry, not their gender, is the only thing that keeps them from being the perfect couple.

SPONGEBOB CAUGHT IN A SQUEEZE PLAY

here's something fishy about that boy SpongeBob SquarePants.

Some conservative Christian groups are sure of it, and they are makin' waves.

For one thing, SpongeBob is mighty chirpy as he flits around the streets of a town called Bikini Bottom.

He's been spotted holding hands with his best friend, Patrick, too, and likes to watch the imaginary television show *The Adventures of Mermaidman and Barnacleboy.*

And.

Aaaaaand.

He vacuums and even cooks. In fact, he is so masterful at the grill that he is the chief fry cook at the Krusty Krab, where he whips up the Krabby Patty faster than you can say Squidward Tentacles. (He's the cashier, and let's not even get started on how grumpy *he* is.)

Of course, there's one other little detail about SpongeBob.

He's a cartoon. As in animated. As in *not real.*

That doesn't deter conservative leaders like Dr. James Dobson, founder of Focus on the Family, from pointing his damning finger at Nickelodeon's porous little guy and accusing him of being an absorbent propagandist for the homosexual agenda.

SpongeBob is out to brainwash America's children, Dobson warns. Before you know it, children watching him cavort with his pet snail, Gary, will smack their tiny brows and squeal, "Oh, tartar sauce, I, too, am a homosexual sponge."

Dobson denounced the sponge at a black-tie dinner in Washington, D.C., to celebrate the election results. He was particularly worked up about a new video produced by the We Are Family Foundation. In it, SpongeBob, along with about one hundred other children's characters—including Barney, Winnie the Pooh, and Kermit the Frog—sing and dance to the song "We Are Family."

"This is my worst nightmare," wails Oscar the Grouch in the video. "I'm in the middle of a heartfelt anthem."

Nile Rodgers, who wrote the 1970s disco song and formed the foundation by the same name after the September 11 attacks, said the video will be mailed to 61,000 public and private schools to affirm diversity.

That there's a code word, Dobson said. It's "a pro-homosexual video."

Peter Sprigg of the Family Research Council agreed. The video was clearly meant to convince kids that even children of gay parents live in a family, too, he said. And we can't have that.

"Ultimately we feel that this is being used as propaganda to indoctrinate very small children to accept a different definition of family," said Sprigg, sounding suspiciously like the paranoid Sheldon Plankton, owner of the Chum Bucket in Bikini Bottom.

Seems to me that everyone living under one roof in the name of love is a family. In this particular video, *Sesame Street*'s Count identified family as 89 sisters, 13 cousins, 7 uncles, 14 grandmothers, 15 grandfathers, 261 friends, and one cousin five times removed. He didn't identify them by sexual preference, but then puppets seldom have sex.

There are others, though, who are apparently fascinated with who is sleeping with whom. Takes up all their days and nights. Which is why everyone from *The New York Times* to the *Today* show is publicizing the latest attacks on SpongeBob's sexuality.

I feel the need to step up and launch a defense.

I visited the foundation's website at wearefamilyfoundation.org to view the video in question, and I'm telling you right now, SpongeBob is not gay. I say that in defense of gay men everywhere. Please, let's not give the boy credit where credit ain't due.

For one thing, I saw him dance, and he does it like just about every straight guy I know. His feet are planted like oaks in the ground as he makes goofy faces and flaps his arms like a seagull. He is one frame away from mouthing, "You-da-man, I-da-man, we-da-man."

We've all been to that wedding reception.

And let's talk about the boy's clothes. He always wears brown shorts with that teeny-tiny tie. Except when he's running around the house in his underwear.

They're tighty-whities.

I repeat: He is not gay.

Finally, SpongeBob has a girlfriend for whom he pines. Her name is Sandy Cheeks, and she's a hell-raiser of a squirrel with a Texas twang that could bend rod iron to her will. He loves her so much that one time he went several whole minutes without water just so he could woo Sandy in her hermetically sealed bubble under the sea.

"Water is for sissies," he chanted as his face shriveled. "Water is for sissies."

Is that a man's man or what?

SOMETIMES LOVE TAKES COURAGE

They are like most newlyweds, still flush with memories about how they got here and eager to tell the stories. Their stories.

Mutual friends introduced them. Their first date was really two on the same day, June 22, 1991: shopping in the afternoon, then a long walk-and-talk late into the warm summer evening.

By that December, Dave Wittkowsky knew this was the one. The day after Christmas, he told his parents over tuna sandwiches. He hated making anyone uncomfortable, and he knew his news would be hard for them. They're conservative, "buttoned-up," he said. His father used to be the Republican mayor of his hometown in suburban Buffalo.

"I've met the man I'm going to spend the rest of my life with," Dave said.

His mother cried; his father was stoic. Their only son was twenty-eight years old, and he had finally worked up the courage to tell them he was gay.

Over time, his partner, Dr. James Anderson, became a beloved member of their family. So much so, jokes Dave, "that they like him more than me."

James is the only son in his family, too. He was never athletic like his father, never loud and tough like him, either, and there was pressure to succeed. But he is a neurosurgeon, he had made it. He hoped that would be enough to cushion the blow when he finally told his parents in 1986.

"Don't tell them," his sisters had pleaded. "It'll kill Dad."

James sat his parents down and said, "I want you to know I'm gay."

"What do you mean by that?" asked his father. For a brief moment, James thought, *Okay, he's going to listen to me.* Then his mother started to scream.

James's parents asked him to leave by morning. They did not speak to him for two years. Then James's father sent him a Thanksgiving Day card. "You're my son. We'll never stop loving you."

When one of James's sisters married, his parents insisted that James not bring Dave to the wedding. James took it in stride. He made a real effort at the wedding reception. "I schmoozed, I danced with all the women."

Later, he told his parents, "You got the last performance out of me."

The following year, James's parents celebrated their fortieth anniversary with a family reunion in Hawaii. Dave was invited.

"That's all behind us now," James said. "We understand why it was hard to fully accept us because we had a hard time accepting ourselves."

Dave and James bought a house together in Cleveland Heights, where an American flag flies over their front stoop. Their flower garden in the front yard brings cars to a crawl. Couples, both gay and straight, rave about their cooking at their frequent dinner parties.

Like any responsible couple, they drew up a will, filled out papers for power of attorney and living wills, named each other as their beloved who will make decisions for them if they cannot. Ohio law, however, makes it possible to ignore all their wishes if family members protest, but James and Dave are two of the lucky ones, and they know it. They live only blocks away from where another gay couple used to live. When one of them died of AIDS, his family ignored his wishes and ordered his longtime partner to leave.

Last month, the state of Massachusetts said that gays could legally marry. On the thirteenth anniversary of the day they met, Dave and James exchanged vows and rings in Provincetown. Their families showered them with loving cards, letters, and e-mail they will cherish the rest of their lives.

Marriage changed them.

"I would have said, before we were married, that I never doubted Dave's commitment to me," James said. "But now I feel the commitment of marriage is a little bit reassuring."

Dave nodded. "I'm the luckiest guy in the world."

James calls Dave his husband. He likes saying, "You've met my husband, haven't you?"

Dave isn't quite there yet. "Someone will ask, 'Are you married?' I'll say, 'Well, yes, but . . .' "

James smiled at him. "It's okay."

Dave returned his smile. "It's who I've always been," he said, his eyes wide. "I still don't want to make anyone uncomfortable."

OHIO PULLS AWAY THE WELCOME MAT

The Sunday after the election was like any other morning at Pilgrim Congregational United Church of Christ in Cleveland's Tremont neighborhood.

The choir director cheerfully led us in a Latin chant. Another member urged us to dig deep so that poor children in the neighborhood will have a Christmas. Pastor Kate Huey preached about stewardship as a way to let our light shine.

The mood turned, though, when head pastor Laurie Hafner talked about the passage of Ohio's Issue 1.

This amendment, which had the support of many priests and pastors, is the harshest such legislation of its kind in the country. It bans gay marriages and all civil unions and strips health benefits to unmarried couples—gay or straight—at public colleges, including Cleveland State and Ohio State.

In word and deed, Ohio told thousands of gay and lesbian couples that they, and their kind of love, aren't welcome here.

Pastor Laurie asked everyone in the congregation who was affected by Issue 1 to stand.

Silently, more than fifty rose to their feet.

Pastor Kate stood. So did the choir director, and the man leading the children's Christmas drive. The doctor who has dedicated his life to caring for the poor stood, too, as did many church volunteers who always greet me by name.

And there was Jackie, dear Jackie, one of my oldest friends, who called me the day after the election, unable to summon one ounce of her usual fire.

"I'm scared, Con," she told me. "I'm honestly scared."

One after another, the gay members of our congregation stood. They didn't look angry or defiant. They looked abandoned.

Many of us still sitting in the pews began to weep.

Pastor Laurie, her own voice breaking, rattled off the many ways our gay members enrich our lives. Then she made a promise that brought the entire congregation to its feet.

"We promise again, this day, to each and every member of this community of faith: You have our love and support," she said. "We promise never to take it back."

William Sloane Coffin wrote, "God dwells with those in America who feel geographically at home and spiritually in exile." That is my prayer.

We keep hearing that Issue 1 supporters voted on "moral values." Well, I took my values to the polls, too, and they are grounded in my own Christian upbringing. My mother's only bumper sticker read, MY BOSS IS A JEWISH CARPENTER. She told anyone who'd listen that she was born again, and her rule for us was simple: "Love anyone God loves," she'd say. "That'd be everyone, no exceptions."

Days before my mother died, she grabbed my hand and assured me she was ready to meet Jesus. Were she alive today, she would not have voted for Issue 1.

"No exceptions," she would have said.

I learned from my mother that those who are most secure in their faith feel no need to hammer others with their certainty. The walk of faith begins and ends with the journey within, and that's a path fraught with mystery and best guesses. My own faith makes me neither right nor righteous because it demands so much of me that I am still trying to find. Empathy, forgiveness, compassion—I never have enough.

Mom would say that's okay. As I've said before, she taught me that being a Christian meant fixing ourselves and helping others, not the other way around. It's a lifetime of work—for me, anyway, especially as I try to find a gentle way to respond to those who supported this hateful amendment that rewards only some kinds of love and punishes others. The God I know insists I try, but I do struggle.

Issue 1 advocates insist that gays pose a threat to traditional marriage. A curious claim, when the Bible Belt has the highest rate of divorce in the country and Massachusetts, where gay marriage is legal, has the absolute lowest.

The only threat I feel from gays is that so many of these kind and talented members of our community will now leave us.

Who am I to ask them to stay?

SURVIVOR DISPLAYS A DOGGED RESOLVE

Christmas Eve marks a year ago that our friend Kate was diagnosed with cancer.

Some calls you never forget. Jackie was crying into her cell phone, saying Kate's doctor had just called and the news was worse than any of us had expected because we all thought the lump in Kate's throat was more than stress-related but not a lot more.

Only a few hours before Christmas Eve service, though, we knew Kate had thyroid cancer. My husband and I sat with them at church, and most of my memories of that evening are the muted images of peripheral vision. Jackie dabbing her eyes, over and over. Kate still nodding in prayer after the rest of us had stopped. Their hands clasped tightly right up until we held candles to sing "Silent Night."

A few weeks later, nurses poked and prodded Kate as she lay on a hospital gurney minutes before surgery. She sighed, turned to Jackie and said, "I need more fun in my life."

It was a plan. While recovering, she came up with a motto:

Play more in '04.

Her list included a zippy new car, a real vacation, bicycles, a Ping-Pong table, and an adoption. That last item on the agenda explains why I was stuffed in the backseat of Kate's zippy new car on Monday, zooming into Ohio's snowy hinterlands to pick up their brand-new baby boy.

His name is Fletcher Zebedee. Jackie swears the name Fletcher came to her in a dream. The meaning behind Zebedee depends on whom you ask. Kate, a minister, says it's from the Bible, book of Matthew. Jackie, not even close to being a minister but a veteran of community theater, says it's short for zebedee-doo-dah.

Fletcher is a dog. Don't tell Jackie and Kate I said that, though, because the photo they just e-mailed me of the tiny Yorkshire terrier resembles one of those hospital newborn photos. I see a baptism gown in his future and lots of ruffles, poor guy. I predict this with confidence after witnessing more preadoption consumption than was heaped on the birth of Prince Charles. I'll spare you the list, but let me just say I'd never heard of a piddle pad before, and I wince every time I think of the Velcro turtleneck waiting to stretch him stiffer than a No. 2 pencil.

The funny thing about Fletcher, besides the way he slides across the wood floors I swear Jackie polishes with her own spit, is how he brings out a side of Kate I've never seen. She always insisted she was not a pet person, not one for cooing over four-legged fur balls. Understand, her graduate studies included working with both deaf and blind people. Then she became a minister. She fusses over people, not pets.

But there was one Yorkshire terrier named T-Rex from her past. He was named T-Rex, the neighbor said, because he was a "giant of a dog on the inside," which is what owners of yippy little things always say when you ask why a dog the size of a sock is named after dinosaurs, wrestlers, or gods from Greek mythology.

T-Rex always hopped in delight at the sight of Kate, and that memory kept making her smile after she was diagnosed with cancer. Maybe having something small to adore her might just help her play more in '04, she said. Jackie found the breeder within days. They picked Fletcher out of a litter earlier this month. Then Kate rushed back to lead a service for World AIDS Day.

And so, there we were on Monday, driving into the country, past a shop called "Hookers Only" with a sign promising live bait and gun ammo, to the breeder's home, where Fletcher awaited a life of pampering guaranteed to make him the biggest sissy on the block. The breeder, a woman possessing the rural mix of no-nonsense and kindness, didn't know Kate had survived cancer, that a year ago we couldn't imagine this day. She had to smile, though, when she saw Kate scoop Fletcher into her arms and promise to love him for the rest of his days.

"He can live for seventeen years," Jackie said on the drive home.

"Is that right?" Kate cooed.

The puppy in her arms looked into her eyes with the adoration of a child.

"Well, then, we're just going to have to love each other for a long, long time."

CLASPED HANDS CAN OPEN HEARTS

D*an was paying* for a car wash when he overheard two men behind him talking about what kind of guy wears pink shirts.

"You know where you can never find a pink shirt?" the car wash owner said to the other man. "In San Francisco . . . in Lakewood, too."

The men chuckled, and Dan felt his collar tighten.

"I wish they'd all wear pink shirts so we know who they are," the man added.

It was the "they" that got to Dan. He turned around. "You should be more aware of who's in your presence before you make a comment like that," he said.

"Why, are you one of them?" owner Sterling "Bud" Kassoff said.

Dan said that, yes, he's gay, and he always brings his two cars to Bud's Mr. Magic Car Wash on Carnegie.

The two men disagree on who started shouting and swearing first, but it's clear that Dan left thinking Bud didn't want his business any-more because he is gay.

Reeling from the volatile exchange, Dan wrote an e-mail to several friends describing what happened. One of them forwarded the message to me, and I immediately called Dan, who asked me not to use his last name.

"You can Google my name, and my address pops right up," he said. "It only takes one nut."

I asked Dan if he was willing to return to the car wash and take me with him. He didn't hesitate, but when he picked me up in his Volvo convertible Tuesday, he admitted he was nervous.

At first, Bud was angry and defensive. Yes, he remembered Dan. And yes, he said that about men in pink shirts.

"I was kidding," he said, his voice rising. "It was a joke. I was talking to a good friend of mine, and you had rabbit ears and heard something that wasn't meant for you."

Dan said it wasn't a joke to him, that it was a slur directed at gays and he resented such comments at a car wash where he spent more than $100 just last month.

Both men were red-faced, toe-to-toe, then Bud suddenly softened.

"If it offended you, I'm really sorry," he said. "I apologize for what I said."

Dan listened as Bud continued.

"I get very defensive when someone says, 'I'm never coming back here.' I've been in business for forty-five years, I've run this car wash for fourteen years. I don't discriminate against anyone. I'm seventy-three years old. I've lived in Cleveland all my life."

"Me, too," Dan said softly.

Bud held out his hand, and Dan shook it. "I truly apologize," Bud said.

"I hope you mean it," Dan said.

"I do."

Bud shrugged his shoulders. "I was probably ashamed of myself for what I said and how you saw it. I shouldn't have said it."

He shook Dan's hand two more times before we left.

For Dan, what-ifs linger.

What if Bud said he was sorry only because I was standing there with my reporter's notebook?

What if his apology was insincere?

"I don't know if I'll go back there," he said. "If I thought he really meant it, I would."

Dan's resistance is understandable, but I hope he'll give Bud another chance. Asking someone to change and then refusing to give him the chance to do so only widens the chasm.

I'm reminded of the elderly man who called me last year about his earnest wrestling with gay rights.

"I was raised in a conservative home, attended a conservative church, lived in a conservative community all my life," he said. "I want to see this issue differently. I'm trying. But please be patient. This is a big leap for some of us."

I can't forget his plea, in part because I, too, have to rely on the patience of others when I am unable to see as clearly, or kindly, as they.

We don't make it to the high road in the face of withering judgment. It is the open heart and outreached hand that pulls us up.

This week, Dan and Bud discovered they had far more in common than either had suspected.

They are equally passionate men, born and raised in the same town, willing to shake hands over an ugly exchange both of them wished had never happened.

All right, where are they?

Where are all these gay couples threatening my heterosexual marriage?

I know they're out there. Why else would our state representatives have spent this much time and energy in the middle of a budget crisis, a health-care crisis, and a schools crisis to pass the Defense of Marriage Act, which robs gays of rights they never had in the first place?

And how stupid am I? When I agreed to marry a man, I didn't realize all the happily coupled gays we know were rooting against us.

They sure seem happy for us. In fact, every time one of them finds out we're getting married, they say such nice things like, "What a perfect couple!" and "Congratulations!" and "Let's see the ring!" (I normally don't use exclamation marks, but they sound so excited I have no choice.)

Pretty clever, these homosexuals.

But I'm no fool. I'm a journalist. So, I went in search of the Lesbian, Gay, and Transgendered Attack on Marriage Task Force.

I called Patrick Shepherd, president of the gay Stonewall Democrats.

First words out of his mouth: "Congratulations on your engagement!" (See what I mean? Clever.)

"Don't mess with me, Patrick," I said. "I want names. Who are the gays threatening my marriage?"

Immediately, he started laughing.

"I love you, Connie."

Now how confusing is that?

"I mean it, Patrick. How many gays do you know?"

"Five."

"Patrick."

"Okay, make that five hundred."

"How many of them are actively seeking the demise of my hetero-sexual union?"

Patrick hesitated. "You want exact numbers?"

"Exact."

"There aren't any."

"Not one?"

"No, sorry. Not one of us cares about your marriage. Some of us are jealous, but that's because your guy is hot."

Big help he was.

So, I called Patti Harris, managing editor of the *Gay People's Chronicle*. She knows thousands of gay people. Surely she could identify the gays threatening my marriage.

"You're engaged?" she said.

Nice try.

"How?" I asked. "How could you be a leader of the homosexual agenda and not know I'm engaged?"

"Well," she said, "right now my agenda is as follows: Pick up dry cleaning. Pick up eggs, milk, and bread. Mail brother's birthday card, which is already late."

"That's it?"

"Yeah, sorry."

"You don't care about my heterosexual marriage?"

"No. I've been too busy worrying about how Ohio's Defense of Marriage Act is the most antigay legislation in the country."

Oh, *that*.

I asked her how many gays she knew of who were trying to under-mine marriage.

"Let me think," she said.

I let her think.

"Okay, I've counted."

My heart started pounding. "How many, Patti, and don't fudge the numbers."

"Less than zero."

"Zero?"

"Yeah. Zero."

Maybe, I said, the Lesbian, Gay, and Transgendered Attack on Mar-riage Task Force was an underground movement that fell under her gaydar.

"Well," she said, "you could be right. We're pretty sneaky, you know. At least that's what the far right tells me."

Her words haunt me: *We're pretty sneaky.*

I started thinking about our dear friends Kate and Jackie.

These two women have been a couple for ten years now, and they've been way too happy about our engagement. Congratulations, this. God's blessings, that.

They've even invited us to dinner.

Yeah, that's right. Dinner.

Oh, we're going. You'd better believe we're going.

I'm on a mission, see. And I'm keeping my eyes on them.

9.

Battle Fatigue

L ast summer, five couples who live near our new home held a cookout to welcome us to the neighborhood on Cleveland's far West Side.

It is always comforting when your neighbors want to like you, but my husband and I were especially heartened because we were fairly sure most of them diverged from us in our political views—and they knew it.

As a newspaper columnist and a member of Congress, our beliefs are as public and accessible as the union-made cars parked in our driveway. It didn't require much effort to know that both of us opposed the war in Iraq and the administration that waged it.

Our neighbors were far less transparent, but there were glimpses. Some cars on the street still sported "W" bumper stickers left over from the election, often pasted next to magnetic ribbons declaring support for our troops in Iraq. The former owner of our home, whom we never met, left behind an autographed photo of George Bush, thanking him for all the money he had raised for the Republican Party. We found mischievous comfort in knowing that he had just moved his family to the blue state of Pennsylvania.

And then there were the computer printouts of our new precinct's election results—the sort of documents you find tucked in the stack of warranties and appliance manuals when you're married to a politician—which left no doubt that the majority of residents around us were more conservative than their brand-new neighbors.

On a breezy Sunday evening in August, though, our neighbors offered a warm embrace. At the beginning of the evening we chatted about sports and kids, and we peppered them with questions about our home, which they knew far better than we did because they had been good friends with the previous owners.

In the time between appetizers and dinner, the men wandered out to the patio and all of us women retreated to the kitchen. We were a range of ages and professions, but our gender united us in the ways it always does once you get a few women together. After the inevitable oooing and ahhing over our hostess's cooking abilities, our conversation turned to what is on so many minds these days. We talked about the war, and any political differences between us dissolved into our universal concern for our troops. But, then, we are all mothers, and most of us have sons.

Many who oppose this war complain that we're too far removed from its horrors to feel any personal sacrifice. It doesn't really feel like our war, some say, and they have a point. We aren't rationing food and fuel, and Hummers that devour enough fuel to power a village still come with a tax break when you buy them. We aren't skimping on vacations, either, unless you count the temporary travel dip after Hurricanes Katrina and Rita when gas prices spiked. So, yes, the war sometimes seems far away indeed.

Increasingly, though, the war is creeping into our daily lives. Many parents of college-bound children shared similar feelings of gratitude after I wrote about my own daughter who was leaving, not for Iraq, but for a campus only a few hours from home. I had been in such a sorry state of abandoned motherhood until Cleveland lost thirteen Marines in a single week. Suddenly, the war was right here at home, flag-draped caskets filling one front page after another in my newspaper and the nightly newscasts.

Increasingly, Americans are opposing this war. Always, the majority of women have, and when a grieving mother named Cindy Sheehan took her protest to the president's vacation in Crawford, Texas, even Karl Rove's spin machine could not bring her down. Her son had died in Iraq, and no matter what her detractors flung at her, the majority of Americans, particularly women, supported her right to protest. She was a mother driven by raw grief, and that is a language we speak only too well.

As we mothers stood in the suburban kitchen on that warm August night, we shared our fears for the children, the ones whose necks we can still nuzzle at night, the ones we pray will never have to fight. One mother with two young sons talked about how she can already see the lure of the military in one of her boys.

"I don't want him to join, but I want to support him if he does," she said. "Let's face it, if he really wants to go, I can't stop him."

We were quiet for a moment, supportive with our silence.

A few minutes later, all twelve of us sat down to dinner. One of the men led us in prayer.

For a little bit there, we weren't liberals or conservatives. What we did for a living didn't matter. We were just neighbors on a quiet street in America, bowing our heads as we thanked God for friendship and food and then pleaded for the safety of our troops.

Amen, we said in unison.

Amen.

THE DRUMBEAT OF WAR
IS A SORROWFUL SOUND

For the women of America, the time to grieve has already begun.

We watch as the men in power turn into breast-beating gorillas, lobbing the wartime euphemisms "sacrifice" and "casualties" like hand grenades aimed straight for our hearts.

We listen to them debate whether war against Iraq is about Saddam Hussein or avenging Daddy or powering our SUVs.

We read about George W. Bush getting all teary-eyed last weekend as he stood in front of four thousand young soldiers breaking into boisterous song: "The Army's on its way. Count off the cadence loud and strong. Two! Three!"

Women watch all this, but it isn't what we see.

We see the bodies of our babies, the boys and girls whose battle fatigues can't camouflage the baby-soft down trailing the back of their necks and the pimples that still pop out on their cheeks. We see a president who never served on the front lines prepared to send off children—our children, not his—to kill and be killed. And we see that we are increasingly powerless to stop it.

Certainly, there are men who are angrily and vocally arguing against war on Iraq. And there are men who, when calculating the cost of war, include the loss of human life in their equation. For most women, though, that is where the equation begins and ends.

Women tend to view life in its minutiae, where the real living goes on. We look at those soldiers and consider the arc of their young lives. We imagine them as toddlers, tearfully weaving tiny fingers through their mothers' hair when they kneeled to kiss their skinned knees. We wonder if they freckle in the sun, have they ever seen the ocean, do they know the breathlessness of falling in love?

Just as men have enduring memories of war, so do women. Except for our sisters in the service and medical corps, ours are the homegrown kind, the recollections of those left behind.

As a kid, I knew several boys who fought in Vietnam because, in our blue-collar neighborhood, there was no such thing as college deferments. I remember watching my mother's hands shake as she hung up the phone and cried out that my cousin Norman had his air mattress shot out from under him, but he's alive, he's alive.

I remember my best friend's sister, Patty, who would start to sob and run into the house whenever a police cruiser came down the hill because she was sure it was bringing bad news about her fiancé in Vietnam. He eventually came home, but not really. "Don't look at him," she always told us, her eyes dark and sunken from lack of sleep. "And don't talk loud."

My single most enduring memory of Desert Storm is of a three-year-old Israeli girl whose name I never knew. I was alone in a hotel room watching the continuous coverage on TV when I learned that the little girl had just suffocated in her gas mask, which her mother had dutifully strapped to her face during an air raid. When the Scud missiles stopped, her relieved parents turned to their child and found her dead.

Until that moment, my fears about the war had congealed around my teenage son. But I was also the mother of a three-year-old girl, and I was inconsolable that lonely night, imagining that poor mother across the sea. I thought of her again just yesterday, when NPR reported that Israelis are trading in their old gas masks for new ones.

If we go to war with Iraq, some, maybe many, of our young soldiers will die. The folded flag, the solitary bugle crying out "Taps," the assurance that he or she "died a hero"—these manly gestures bring little comfort to women.

We define heroism so differently. To us, acts of bravery come when we know the risks and consequences but plow ahead anyway. These young soldiers have no idea what lies ahead and all that they can lose.

We do, though. That's our burden. We've been caught up in the wondrous minutiae of life long enough to know just how much they can lose, how much they can miss. And while we are trying desperately to stand up and be heard, it is that sense of loss that can bring us prayerfully to our knees.

O*n October 27, 1969,* Marine Pfc. Alvin Blanton sobbed as he stared down at death and saw his own face.

The nineteen-year-old dead man was his identical twin brother, Marine Pfc. Calvin Blanton.

"The only thing different about him was he was three minutes older," Alvin says. "When I saw him lying there, it was like looking at my own dead self."

The Blanton twins were in the same Marine company, same unit, in Da Nang, Vietnam. They enlisted on the same day, went to the same boot camp. Alvin slept on the top bunk, Calvin on the bottom.

From the morning they landed in Vietnam, there wasn't a day they didn't talk, because one of their combat duties was to look out for each other.

"We were very close," Alvin says. "We had that vibe that twins have, and we always knew how each other was doing."

All these years later, Alvin, fifty-four, still grieves his brother's death. That's how it is when a young soldier dies in war, he says. That's how it was then. That's how it is now.

Our young soldiers are dying again, this time in Iraq. Three of them—Brandon Sloan, Robert Dowdy, Christian Gurtner—were from this area. Government officials call them casualties; their families call them Brandon, Bob, and Chris.

Those who loved these young men will need the support of their friends and families long after the lone bugler plays "Taps" over their open graves.

"This is just the beginning of their separation from their children," Alvin says. "They're going to need support for years to come. If they're lucky, they'll survive intact. My brother's death tore my family apart. We were never the same."

Minutes before Calvin died, the brothers were approaching the Da

Nang River and talking about how good it felt to be short-timers. They had been in Vietnam for nine months during the brutal Tet offensive. In less than three months, they would rotate and go back to the World— back to Lorain and the night shift at the Ford auto plant.

It was a short conversation, but one that made them smile. Then they waded into the turbulent river, loaded down with equipment as they prepared to swim to their camp on the other shore.

At first, no one noticed that Calvin was gone. Several soldiers saw Alvin and mistook him for his brother. Fifteen minutes later, though, Alvin began shouting.

"Where's my brother? My brother! Where's my brother!"

Calvin's body didn't surface until the following day. Bearing a full pack, weary at the end of a long day, he was no match for the angry undertow.

Alvin sat vigil next to his brother's casket for the sixteen-hour flight to Okinawa and the eight-hour flight to Cleveland Hopkins, then took a cab home to Lorain, where his parents and five younger siblings were already choked with grief.

They never recovered. His parents divorced, and most of the siblings picked sides. Years after their parents' deaths, the ties remain severed.

It took Alvin, who blamed himself for his brother's death, fifteen years to pull his own life together. Finally, he asked God for help.

"Take this burden off me," he prayed.

And so God did, he says, a wide smile breaking across his youthful face.

"I'm sixty-five percent healed now. Maybe that's as good as it gets, but that's pretty good. Maybe that's as good as it ever gets for those of us who lose someone in the war."

Some days, before Alvin heads to work on the night shift at the Ford plant, where he has worked for thirty-five years, he stares at the wall in his Elyria home that is dedicated to his brother.

He looks at the painting depicting the ghosts of soldiers reaching through the Wall to touch mourning loved ones at the Vietnam Veterans Memorial.

He stares at the clock displaying the figure of three Vietnam soldiers.

And sometimes, Alvin swears the eyes in his brother's portrait are looking right at him, assuring him that he's going to be okay.

"It's as if he's telling me, 'You're moving on. You're doing real good.'"

At such moments, Alvin dares to believe him.

A SOLDIER SALUTES HER FALLEN FRIENDS

S*gt. Cheri L. Brown* was sitting in her living room on Cleveland's near West Side last Thursday when an ad for the war exhibit popped up on her television screen.

The traveling exhibit, "Eyes Wide Open: Beyond Fear—Towards Hope," was headed to the Coventry Village Library in Cleveland Heights. For four short hours, more than eight hundred pairs of military boots would stand in silent tribute to the American soldiers who have died in Iraq.

Two of those soldiers she knew by name. They served alongside her in Iraq, fellow soldiers in the Ohio National Guard's 135th Military Police Company.

Spc. Todd Bates died trying to save Staff Sgt. Aaron Reese from drowning in the Tigris River.

They were her comrades, and her friends.

She knew what she had to do.

The forty-four-year-old single mother of two sons grabbed her tan desert boots by the door and threw them into her 1981 Suburban Scottsdale. She drove to the Cleveland Heights–University Heights Main Library on Lee Road, where she found the informational part of the exhibit, which is sponsored by the Quaker-affiliated American Friends Service Committee.

"I'm looking for the boots," she told a volunteer, who gave her directions for the short drive to Coventry.

When she pulled up around 2:30 P.M., volunteers had just begun to set up the boots exhibit, which included walls representing the eleven thousand Iraqi civilians who've been killed.

She grabbed her own boots and headed for the small patch of grass at the corner of Coventry Road and Euclid Heights Boulevard, only a hundred feet or so from a school playground built in the name of peace.

Sergeant Brown introduced herself and told AFSC local director

Greg Coleridge that she wanted to donate her boots to the exhibit. When he explained that the black boots there represented soldiers who had died, she nodded her head.

"I understand that," she said. "But I served alongside a couple of the men whose names are on those boots. I'd like to leave mine in tribute."

Coleridge immediately agreed.

She looked at the tubs of boots. "Do you need any help setting up?" she asked.

The volunteers eagerly welcomed her. She reached into the nearest tub of boots and read the name tag on the first pair she pulled out: STAFF SGT. AARON REESE.

Sergeant Brown sucked in a breath and started to cry.

She still remembers the first time she ever saw Aaron. She had arrived for deployment to Iraq in February 2003, and as she walked toward the armory, she noticed a soldier standing with his wife. His toddler son was playing in the snow. Aaron wept as he cradled his baby and tried to say a few last words to his wife.

"He didn't even know then that was the last time he'd ever hold his baby," Sergeant Brown said, her voice breaking.

Last Thursday, she thought about that moment again as she held "his" boots in her hands, then wrapped them around her neck. She wore them for the entire time she helped set up the other boots.

She watched the volunteers randomly place the boots in the grass. She sucked in her breath again and asked a favor.

"Could we please line them up in formation?" she asked. "Could you straighten them out, make sure they're placed together right? Whenever we stand together, that's how we do it, in formation."

When the exhibit opened at four P.M., the empty soldiers' boots were neatly lined up like headstones, row after row. A single pair of tan desert boots rested near a tree in stark contrast to the hundreds of black boots from army-navy stores.

They were Sergeant Brown's tribute to the fallen, and a prayer of gratitude that she came home alive.

"I wish everybody could come home now," she said. "I hope no one else has to die. When you see all those boots . . ." Her voice trailed off.

Sergeant Brown pulled away from the exhibit around 4:30.

Less than an hour later, the local public radio station announced that three more American soldiers had died.

FOR PARENTS, WAR IS TOO CLOSE

A*t least once a month,* the military tries to snatch up my kid.

Tucked in among the bills and college solicitations, the catalogs and the postcards, are the letters to my high school senior that feel like a punch to the solar plexus.

One month the letter is from the National Guard. Another month it's from the Navy. Last week, the Army ROTC tempted her with "merit-based scholarships worth up to $68,000."

My reaction was visceral: *Not my kid.*

I tore and I tore and I tore until the fragments fell through my fingers like confetti, the cheap kind that lands in clumps instead of sprinkling like dandelion fluff after a child's hopeful breath. Like my daughter's barefoot wishes when she was six, seven, eight . . .

I buried the letters' remains deep in the kitchen trash and repeated my mantra, this time aloud: "Not my kid."

Inevitably, though, my conscience turned on me: Why not your kid? Why someone else's kid?

It's a question I cannot answer in any way that is right or just. Whenever the discussion turns to this war and who should fight it, I am at my most limited, my smallest self. I am reduced to the parent who has spent most of her adult life promising God she can handle anything. Except.

Except, please don't make me outlive one of my children. Please. Not that.

Not all high school seniors are getting these recruitment letters. My friend whose son attends private school doesn't get them. Nor is the son and daughter in the two-parent family with the "better" zip code getting them.

My mind races. Why, I wonder, has our household been deemed susceptible to the promises of free tuition and a chance to see the world?

Is it because we're only three blocks from the city of Cleveland, where the neighborhoods brim with poor, black teenagers?

Is it because I rent the duplex where my daughter and I have lived for the last eight years? Not a lot of stability in that, you know.

Or is it because, until very recently, ours was a single-parent home? Is it this, our perceived economic and social vulnerability, that makes my daughter such an attractive military target?

I repeat: *Not my kid.*

The conscience pricks: Then whose?

There is no solace in knowing I opposed this war from the beginning. So did millions of others, but our troops went anyway, their ranks populated with somebody else's sons and daughters. Nearly nine hundred of them have died so far in a war with no end in sight, and every week my e-mail is increasingly peppered with letters from mothers—always, it's mothers—asking, "Is it true we're going to have a draft?"

Nobody knows the answer for sure, and that uncertainty stokes a fear rich in rumor.

Canada won't take anyone, mothers write. And have you heard about our daughters?

"They'll have to go this time," one mother wrote, echoing dozens of others. "There's no way they'll make only the boys go this time."

Will there be a draft? Maybe.

Will our daughters have to go? My prayers become more frantic because my fear is so fundamental: I do not want my child to die.

And so, I am like every parent I have ever known.

Too many parents, though, have already had to consider the unthinkable. Day after day, month after month.

On Memorial Day, I spent time with an Ohio National Guardsman who had just returned from his second tour of duty in Iraq. He is our friends' son, young and full of dreams. He does not complain about the second tour of duty he did not want, and he is modest about his achievements.

At a veterans' service, he reluctantly stepped forward when the speaker asked for Iraq war veterans to move to the front of the crowd.

I watched him shyly toe the ground, and then I looked at his mother. Her shoulders were shaking. She was not crying, but sobbing, even though her boy made it home.

I came face to face with my most selfish fear about this war. Even if my daughter survived, I know I would never be the same.

THE HORRORS OF WAR REMAIN

BOTTLED UP INSIDE

We got a glimpse, but only a glimpse, into what our returning soldiers went through in Iraq when they heard the names of their two fallen comrades.

In two separate ceremonies in a cavernous hangar at Cleveland Hopkins International Airport a week ago, the 180 Ohio National Guard soldiers stood in formation as the officer onstage recited the names of the two men who died: Spc. Todd Bates and Staff Sgt. Aaron Reese.

Many of the hundreds of family members and friends surrounding the soldiers began to tear up, staring at them as the Cleveland Police Pipes and Drums Corps played "Amazing Grace."

The soldiers of the 135th Military Police Company, though, were true professionals. The women, shorter and more diminutive, stood out like black keys on a piano, but otherwise the camouflage uniforms and rigid postures rendered them all nearly identical.

They wore the expressionless faces of returning warriors. Except for the blinking. Dozens of them were blinking, blinking, blinking as the bagpipes wailed. When the song finished, a few made quick swipes at their eyes, and that was that.

Only it isn't, and only now their families may be finding out just what these young men and women went through in Iraq. For all their worrying, many of them had no idea just how awful it was because their soldiers protected them.

That's what soldiers do.

I learned that after sharing a flight last month with a young man the same age as my son, twenty-nine, who recently had returned from Iraq.

I didn't know he was a soldier until I offered him the bag of Doritos from my lunch tray. He snatched them up.

"I haven't had these in more than a year," he said. "I can't get enough of them now."

He laughed at my confusion. "I just got back from Iraq," he said, grinning. "They don't have these there."

His name is Brendan, and he is a corporal in the National Guard. With little prodding, and without bitterness or anger, he described the hell he'd just seen.

The heat, I'd heard about. The lack of adequate water in a place where you can never drink enough, I'd also heard about. I'd even heard that some soldiers, particularly those in the National Guard and the Reserves, lacked adequate protective gear. I had a hard time believing that, though, until Brendan started telling his story.

His job was to attract sniper fire as he drove a light-armored vehicle in the dead of night. The idea was to draw lone gunmen out so they could be killed or captured before the Army convoys drove through.

His flak jacket was designed to carry protective plates in the front and back of the chest. Each jacket in his company, though, arrived with only one protective plate.

"Each of us had to decide whether to wear it in the front or back," he said, laughing. "We figured, we're not going to run away from them, so we decided to wear them over our hearts."

When I asked him if he had been scared, he laughed again. "You're scared all the time. You'd better be."

Over the next two hours, we talked. He was a handsome, animated man. He told his stories as a soldier on an adventure. I heard them as a mother. When I asked how his own mom dealt with his hardships, he shook his head.

"I didn't tell her. I didn't tell anyone until I got home. None of us did. You don't want to put your family through that, you know?"

Brendan came home from Iraq in October. He brought his stories with him, in a dusty journal he wrote in nearly every day. One by one, his family members read it. Their reactions, he said, were always the same.

"I didn't know," they said, usually with tears in their eyes.

"You never told me."

"I had no idea."

I thought of Brendan as I watched the soldiers of the 135th flood into the hangar and into the arms of their tearful families. I thought of his stories when I saw many of them tear up for their fallen comrades.

They, too, have their stories.

My prayer is that they also have someone willing to listen.

Fourth-class cadet Tim Gaydosh had just folded his lanky six-foot-four frame into an aisle seat at the back of the plane when he locked eyes with the civilian headed his way.

Tim, a first-year student at the Air Force Academy, was on his way home to Cleveland for spring break. As always, he was in uniform, and he'd been on the receiving end of enough strangers lately to stiffen just a bit as the man plowed through the busy aisle.

Would this guy be one of those nice folks who shook his hand and thanked him for his service to our country? Or was this going to be like that day in Wal-Mart, when another customer took one look at Tim's uniform and shook his head in disgust?

The middle-aged man headed his way wore blue jeans, a sweatshirt, and a few extra pounds on his tall frame. He came to a stop at Tim's outstretched knee and extended his hand.

"I really appreciate what you're doing for our country," he said.

Then he handed Tim his ticket.

"I want you to sit in first class," he said. "I want you to take my seat."

The soft-spoken Tim politely protested. "You paid for it, sir," he said. "I can't sit in your seat."

The man would not be deterred.

"I said I want you to have it, and I mean it. You go up there now, and take my seat."

After a little more wrangling, Tim finally agreed. He heard other passengers thanking the man and praising his generosity as he walked up the aisle.

"It gave me such a good feeling," Tim said later. "And it's quite an experience up there in first class. They come up to you every five minutes asking if you need anything."

He sighed ever so slightly. "I had to say no to the wine, being only eighteen."

I first learned about Tim's flight upgrade from his father, Joe, an electrician at the Ford plant in Avon Lake, Ohio.

"I just want to thank all the people who've been so nice to my son since he put on a uniform," he said in a phone message. "You hear so much evil about people, but there are so many nice people out there, and many of them are coming up to my son."

Joe is especially grateful to that man named David who gave up his first-class seat for Tim. "I wish I could tell him, 'Sir, I appreciate that you saw what you saw and did what you did for my son.' "

Tim insists that "the real soldiers"—the ones coming home from active duty in Iraq—are the ones most deserving of Americans' kindness.

"They shouldn't have to come home to a Vietnam," he said, referring to the ridicule and hostility many soldiers of that era experienced upon their return to American soil.

Long after that war ended, Vietnam veterans finally found the courage to speak out about the torture they endured, not in Asia, but at the hands of an angry and condemning public in their own hometowns. Their honesty about that unspeakable pain forced us to face our own ugly past, and they are the reason that, this time, most of us know the difference between the men who plan the war and the soldiers who fight it.

Recent polls show that most Americans now oppose the war in Iraq. Our support, though, for the men and women risking their lives in that guerrilla warfare remains strong.

Earlier this month, I was standing in a long line at Cleveland's airport. There must have been a hundred of us slowly winding our way through the maze of straps and posts just outside the waiting area where all arriving passengers eventually exit. Most of us couldn't help but notice the jolly band waiting to welcome a soldier named Ryan.

WELCOME HOME, RYAN! read one sign.

YOU'RE OUR HERO, RYAN! read another.

Several were holding small American flags, and all of them eagerly peered with stretched necks, waiting for their soldier.

Finally, a young man wearing camouflage and boots and a grin wider than the bill of his cap bounded through the entryway.

Without a word, nearly a hundred strangers put down their bags and purses and started to clap.

Welcome home.

"WE DIE ALONG WITH THESE KIDS"

As *Jeanette Schroeder* rounded the corner of her front yard with the lawn mower, she spotted two Marines standing at her brother Paul Schroeder's front door.

Immediately, she knew.

"Oh, no!" she sobbed. "Oh, no! Oh, no!"

The two men looked at her, then stepped away from the door and started walking toward her.

She froze.

Her hands released the safety bar on her mower. The street went silent.

As they walked closer, she almost told them, "You've got the wrong house."

But she knew.

Fourteen members of Brook Park's Twenty-fifth Regiment, Third Battalion Marines were killed Wednesday by a roadside bomb in Iraq.

It was the same battalion that lost six Marines on Monday.

It was the same battalion in which her nephew Augie served.

Jeanette just knew.

She nodded when they asked if she knew the family next door in her Cleveland neighborhood.

"He's my brother," she said. "They probably didn't hear the doorbell."

She was sure her brother and his wife, Rosemary Palmer, were upstairs, hovering over their computer as they frantically searched the Internet for any news about the latest group of Marines who had been killed in Iraq.

Earlier that morning, Rosemary had given Jeanette a printout quoting skeletal news reports about the attack on Marines in Haditha. After reading it, Jeanette had a bad feeling. She prayed all the way to her doctor's appointment. She prayed on her drive to the grocery store, too, and all the way home.

Please, God, not Augie.

Now, about 10:30 A.M., two Marines were standing in her yard, asking to speak to Augie's parents.

Aunt Nettie, that's what Augie always called her, offered to run into her house to call his parents.

"No," one of the Marines said gently. "We have to talk to them in person."

Jeanette ran through Paul's back door and started to scream.

"Paul! Paul! Get down here. Just get down here now!"

Paul and Rosemary saw the grim faces on the men at their door and they knew, too. They stood motionless as one of the Marines began to speak.

"We regret to inform you that Edward August Schroeder II . . ."

And they knew.

Two weeks ago, Augie had called home from Iraq after spending twenty-six days in the field. They had not heard from him for five weeks, and their son's voice seemed to reflect a change in his convictions about this war.

"When he first arrived in Iraq in March, he was full of optimism about what his good intentions could accomplish," Paul said.

But Augie's enthusiasm eroded over time, and his father said he will never forget what his son told him.

"The closer we are to departure, the less 'worth it' this has become," Augie said.

In a way, Paul was heartened by his son's words.

"When you first get there, you think everything's hunky-dory," he said. "But after four operations, the insurgents were still there. He didn't think they were having any effect. I heard him and thought, 'Well, the bloom is off the rose.' I was opposed to this war before it even started, and my son is a sharp kid."

He caught himself.

"Was," he said, as he started to sob. "My son *was* a sharp kid.

"Oh, Jesus."

Augie was twenty-three years old. He was six weeks from coming home.

While we don't yet have exact numbers, we now know that Ohio has lost about one hundred soldiers and Marines to the Iraq war. Its death toll in this war will soon rival the numbers of Texas and California.

And there is no end in sight.

That haunts Paul Schroeder.

In the first hours after he learned that his son was dead, Paul wrote a short statement.

"I hope people forgive me for what I have to say," he began. "I just don't care anymore."

He listed who he blamed for Augie's death.

"I hold the Bush administration responsible, from the president through the secretaries of state and defense and all those who have had a hand in starting this war.

"I also hold every Democrat in Congress who voted to authorize this misadventure as accomplices."

His son, he wrote, "died doing his duty. So have some 1,800 other Americans.

"Augie did his duty at every turn, from being an emergency medical technician while still in high school, a lifeguard, a Boy Scout, an active church member, and, of course, as a Marine. For all this, we consider him a hero.

"To honor him, I no longer can sit still, just keeping quiet and being politically correct."

In her own way, Augie's mother also issued a statement. She made the call about two hours before she learned that Augie was dead.

Rosemary had sobbed the day Augie enlisted. She had begged him not to go to Iraq. When she made the call that morning, hers was the desperate plea of a mother trying to find out if her son was still alive.

She left this phone message for Brian Albrecht, a reporter for *The Plain Dealer* of Cleveland who has steadfastly chronicled the war's impact here:

"This is Rosemary Palmer," she said. "I'm the mother of one of the many Marines who are deployed right now. My son is currently in Haditha and we just heard the news story this morning that fourteen Marines in Haditha were killed.

"We are all obviously going nuts. . . . I know you can't give out the names of people who haven't been notified, but if you have those names of the ones who have died, if you could let us know as soon as possible, I would really appreciate it because we die along with these kids . . ."

Her voice broke.

She recited her number.

Then she hung up the phone.

A CARING EMBRACE FOR THE HURTING

WAR HITS OHIO

t doesn't matter that we don't know what to say.

It doesn't matter that we're afraid or uncomfortable.

It doesn't matter that we're busy.

What matters is that we show up anyway.

In these long, sad days following last week's deaths of twenty Marine reservists, thousands of area residents are showing up.

They show up for the wakes and the funerals, the memorial services and the public prayers.

They show up at the Brook Park headquarters for the Third Battalion, Twenty-fifth Regiment Marines, too. Fourteen of the dead were from this battalion. By the hundreds, the mourners deliver homemade tributes and handwritten letters to the fallen sons they hope can somehow, somewhere, feel the gratitude of this grieving community, where so many homes now display small American flags in their front windows.

Bundles of flowers line the headquarters fence. Some people dropped off American flags with scrawled messages of thanks or promises to remember. A veteran donated his Purple Heart. Somebody took the time to tie red, white, and blue ribbons to the chain-link fence— twenty in all, in remembrance of those who died.

Then there are the pictures, single snapshots of Marines in uniform, group photos of kids with no idea what is coming. Public officials pay tribute to them as men, but privately, with both affection and disbelief, we call them boys. They were young enough to be our children, our grandchildren. This is every parent's unthinkable, our unbearable. And yet, for a growing number of parents, it has come to pass.

And so, day by day, the gifts mount. The memorial takes shape, the fence fades. With each small act, a community's embrace grows.

The majority of mourners who show up are older than the fallen

Marines will ever be, driven by the hard lessons of life. It takes a lot of living, and dying, to see the role we can play in other people's times of sorrow. Most of us discover our capacity for such grace only after enduring our own paralyzing loss.

Who forgets such a moment when it happens to us? We stand near the lifeless remains of our beloved, so grief-stricken we can barely breathe when, suddenly, we look up and behold the face of someone we can't quite believe took the time to find us in our darkest hour.

Our grief is still raw, our shock not yet absorbed, but we are ennobled by the simple gesture of another's footsteps in our direction. Our loss is registered, our despair acknowledged. They don't have to say a word. Just standing there, right in front of us, or sitting in the pew behind us, they tell us what we need to hear: Our beloved mattered, his memory matters still.

That's how most of us join the ranks of those who show up.

On Monday evening, thousands of area residents changed the course of their daily lives to honor a group of Marines most of them had never met.

They rushed home to get dinner on the table early or just skipped it, maybe snacked on the drive through heavy traffic. They missed their favorite TV shows, too, the beers on the porch at sunset, and that precious downtime with kids before baths and bedtime stories.

For one night, they changed their schedules and where their minds usually wander on a hot summer night to show up at the International Exposition Center for a service honoring Ohio's latest war heroes.

At one point, the crowd grew silent and still as giant screens flashed photographs of each and every one of the Marines who died. Somber music played as a faceless voice recited each man's name and hometown. Most of them were boys, just boys, really, looking combatant fierce or grinning like the crazy kids you hope they got to be.

Twenty-year-old Marine Jeff Gulley, a Brook Park mechanic, stared at the screen. He expects to be in Iraq by January.

If he gets killed, he told *Plain Dealer* reporter Brian Albrecht, he's sure the same kind of memorial service would help his family.

"Nothing can replace a loved one," he said. "But I know it makes me feel good to live in a community that supports the troops this much."

That's why he showed up.

Already, the prayers for Marine Gulley have begun.

A MOM BURIES HER FEARS
ALONG WITH HER SON

At an age when most women become invisible in this country, fifty-seven-year-old Rosemary Palmer is emerging for all the world to see.

Over the past two weeks, her face has become a map of where she's been and where she is going. Photographers have chronicled her journey from grief-stricken mother of a fallen Marine to a woman of courage resolved to fight the war on her own terms.

She's a little nervous, but she's going public. The way she sees it, the worst that could happen already has.

Palmer's twenty-three-year-old son, Lance Cpl. Edward "Augie" Schroeder II, was one of the fourteen men in the Third Battalion, Twenty-fifth Marine Regiment who were killed on August 3 by a roadside bomb in Iraq.

What she most feared had come to pass.

"There were so many days when I would continue working until they finally kicked me out and told me to go home," she said, recalling her son's time in Iraq. "I was just so afraid to find that car in my driveway."

That car she feared, the one bringing two Marines and the news that changes a parent's world forever, pulled up to her Cleveland home on the morning of August 4.

Palmer and her husband, Paul Schroeder, responded differently in the first hours after the devastating news. Schroeder issued an angry statement that morning condemning the war and those who support it.

Palmer granted a few tearful interviews, but her activism percolated. She waited until her son's casket was lowered into the ground.

The day after his funeral, Augie's mother held a news conference.

With Schroeder at her side, Palmer attacked the strategy of the war. "We have to fight this war properly or get out," she said.

Both parents spoke, but stories around the country focused on Palmer. She had come a long way from the young woman too afraid of public scorn to protest the Vietnam War.

"I was a scaredy-cat back then," she said. "I was young with a new mortgage living in a conservative town."

She was not media savvy, either.

"When I lived in New Jersey, I did a short stint on a school board," she said. "Every time they pointed a TV camera at me, I thought I was going to throw up. I was very uncomfortable, very nervous."

This is different.

"This is not my story," she said. "This is about Augie, and about all the men and women still fighting in Iraq. Now I feel like, 'You got a microphone? I've got something to say.' "

She attracts comparisons to another outspoken mother, Cindy Sheehan, whose son was killed in Iraq last year. Sheehan camped outside the vacationing president's ranch in Crawford, Texas, vowing to stay until Bush met with her. Sheehan left Thursday after her mother suffered a stroke.

They are different mothers, different women, Palmer said.

"I don't have the same message. She's willing to be a lightning rod. What's happening to her now, with all the criticism, is starting to make me nervous."

So far, the response to Palmer has been positive. She knows that could change.

"People start thinking 'enough already,' and they start looking for the clay feet, which we all have," she said.

It's a risk Palmer continues to take.

When she and her husband learned that more than a thousand vigils were planned last week to support Sheehan, they decided to attend one of them in Cleveland Heights.

"I was actually a little nervous," she said. "Some of us are having flashbacks to the whole Vietnam thing."

This is different, she decided again.

"I was hoping the vigils would embolden others to speak out."

She quoted the line her son loved from a song by Social Distortion: "Reach for the sky, 'cause tomorrow may never come."

Her voice softened as she recalled sharing that message in an online chat room with other mothers of young Marines.

"Even though my son has no tomorrow," she told them, "I hope your children have many tomorrows."

That is the hope that drives Rosemary Palmer now.

That is why she is no longer afraid.

When you love someone who is grieving, you'll do almost anything to bring them a moment's reprieve.

For Steve Wright, that meant he had to somehow, some way, find the proper sword to bury with his stepson, Marine Cpl. Jeffrey Boskovitch, who was killed in an ambush in Iraq on August 1.

It's the Marine's NCO sword, shorthand for the ceremonial weapon of the noncommissioned officer. Steve and his wife, Kathy, didn't even know how important it was to Jeffrey until his girlfriend told them he'd always wanted one. As soon as she heard that, Kathy wanted the sword for her son.

But reality trumped yearning, it seemed. The Marine NCO sword, which costs more than $500, has to be custom-made. Shaped like a saber, the length is based on the Marine's height, and each sword is engraved with the Marine's name.

Wright found out that the Ames Sword Company, a small operation in New London, Ohio, made the exact sword they needed. When he listened to the company's voice-mail message left in response to his query, though, his heart sank. The normal waiting period is eight to ten weeks. Jeffrey would be buried in seven days.

Jeffrey's stepfather, an Air Force veteran, called the company president, Russel Sword. All Sword needed to hear was that a Marine had been killed.

"I'll get it to you on Monday," Sword promised.

"As soon as I talked to him, I knew he'd keep his word," Wright said.

What he didn't know was why.

In 1967, nineteen-year-old Russel Sword escorted the body of his best friend and fellow Marine home from Vietnam.

"His name was Davis Jones," Sword said. "He was from Wellington, and he was only twenty years old. I hadn't even shipped out yet. But when his mother asked me to do it, there was no way I could say no."

Sword went to Vietnam the following year. He earned a Purple Heart and a Bronze Star.

Now, thirty-eight years later, the parent of another fallen Marine needed his help.

Sword called three employees who would have to work weekend overtime if he were to keep his promise to the grieving family in North Royalton. He knew their answers before he asked.

Marine Vietnam veteran Lewis Collins, the finisher, said he'd be there.

Lloyd Yates, the artist, said he'd be there, too.

Production manager Keith Bailey didn't hesitate.

"There was never any question we were going to do our best," Sword said. "I know how much I hurt when I lost Davis. We were going to do this, and we were going to do it right."

They worked through the weekend on the thirty-two-inch sword for Jeffrey. At Wright's request, they made two others with blades in stock: a thirty-two-inch and a twenty-eight-inch, which Wright also paid for and donated to the Third Battalion, Twenty-fifth Marine Regiment, in Jeffrey's name. Just in case.

Wright said he would pick up the sabers. Sword had another idea.

His future son-in-law is a Marine recruiter in Lima.

"I thought, 'I'll bet Chris would do this, and it would mean so much to me if a Marine delivered this.' You know, once a Marine, always a Marine. I'm fifty-six, but no matter what your age, you always trust another Marine."

So he called Marine Staff Sgt. Christopher Mulet and asked if he could help.

"Let me double-check," Mulet said.

Permission granted.

Around one P.M. on Monday, August 8, Mulet and Marine Gunnery Sgt. Terranfus Williams, both in dress blues, rang the doorbell at the Wright home.

The family was overwhelmed.

"So many people have been so kind to us in the last two weeks," Wright said. "This one really blew us away."

His wife, sitting next to him at the kitchen table, nodded. "This is maybe hard for some to understand, but there have been small blessings since Jeffrey was killed. He's home. He was viewable to the public.

Some of the boys come home in pieces. Maybe he was tortured, we'll never know. But he was whole."

And Steve Wright was able to come through for his wife in her darkest hour.

The sword's simple engraving reads: CORPORAL JEFFREY BOSKO-VITCH.

10.

Growing Away

A *few days before* my daughter left for college, my friend Joanna sent me a gift to remind me that I still had plenty of my own adventures up ahead.

For weeks, she had been watching me mope around like a plaintiff who'd just lost her last appeal. Truth be told, I felt no more ready for my baby's departure than I was for her first day of preschool, her first dance, or even the first time she could reach for her favorite cup without the step stool. If parenthood has taught me anything, though, it's that children insist on growing up no matter how many times we try to freeze them on videotape.

I don't handle change well. It takes me six months to get used to a new coffeemaker, so you can imagine all my hard swallowing as I watched my daughter shop for towels, bubble-wrap her treasured photographs, and pack all 422 pairs of her favorite shoes.

Then, Joanna's present arrived.

I tore open the shiny foil wrapping paper and couldn't help but smile. She'd sent exactly what I needed: a brand-new pair of white Keds.

Joanna knew these were no ordinary sneakers to me. A month earlier, I had noticed her wearing her own Keds, which bore the telltale signs of an eventful summer. Oh, the memories summoned by her scruffy Keds.

When I was young, my mother bought a new pair for me every spring, and I continued the tradition after I had children of my own. They were always lace-ups, always with the little blue square on the heel, and white, always white—the perfect canvas for the painted stories from your life.

That's the thing about Keds. After a few months' wear, you know a lot about the person who's been slipping them on every day. Mine would always fray where the big toes push, push, push in my rush to get to here when I was already late for there. By midsummer, you could see exactly where the round of one toe ended and the next began, fanning the shoe as wide as it could stretch.

Badges of dirt and grass stains chronicled long hours coaching my daughter's softball team and teaching my son how to throw, along with the inevitable postgame splats of color from spurting juice boxes and long, slow slurps of popsicles dripping orange, yellow, and green. Two summers in a row, my homemade tomato sauce found my left toe.

Sometimes, my Keds would take on hues borrowed from the latest load of laundry after a last-minute toss into the washer. One summer, my shoes even had an autograph, backward letters in large, dark-blue caps that only a three-year-old's mom could read. Or forgive.

My Keds did so much living that by the first snowfall, they were ready to be retired. What little padding they'd had was long gone and they had less tread than a furrowed brow, but I would hold on to them through the winter for trips to the basement and climbs up a ladder to replace a bulb or paint the crown molding.

As soon as I spotted my first robin, I'd toss out the old Keds and start over with a brand-new pair. They were a promise, I guess, or at least a hope, that a whole lot of life would happen in the months ahead.

I don't recall exactly when I let this ritual die. I just remember one day thinking, *Well, that's that, my son is grown and my daughter no longer wants to wear shoes that match her mommy's and I'm a little old anyway to be clomping around in sneakers with less shock absorption than a stick-'em note.*

Maybe it was time to grow up.

I gave it my best shot, really, I did. Even bought sensible pumps and a pair of sneakers designed strictly for walking.

But when I opened Joanna's gift, I have to admit it: I felt like a kid again, as if a whole new season of life was about to happen.

"You shared with me memories of a young mother and daughter and the Keds that walked with them on their path those many years ago," Joanna wrote in a note that she tucked between the shoes. "And once again, a new path has found its way under your feet."

She listed my many blessings, including a new marriage, a new house, a thriving career, and a daughter spreading her wings.

Then she gave me my marching orders: "These Keds are your scrap-book."

I sat down at my desk that day, kicked off my dress shoes, and slowly slid my feet into the stiff new sneakers. I laced them up—not too tight, but not so loose they couldn't keep up with me. Then I wiggled my toes, trying to imagine where the first threads would give way, wondering how much living I'd have to do to earn that fray.

My daughter is off and running.

Her mother is kicking up dirt in her brand-new Keds.

A DAUGHTER'S DOLL TEACHES MOM
A LESSON ON RACE

Sometimes our kids teach us lessons we thought we were teaching them.

That's how Addy made her way into our family's life five years ago.

Addy is an American Girl doll. She is based on the main character in a series of books about a slave girl whose family escaped to freedom in the 1800s.

Addy is black. My daughter is white. But from the moment Cait read her first sentence about Addy, she was convinced she and that slave girl were practically twins. And since her father and I had recently separated, it didn't take much lobbying on Cait's part to get exactly what she wanted from this mother steeped up to her furrowed brow in guilt: an Addy doll. An almost-$100 Addy doll, to be precise.

That Christmas morning, my then eight-year-old daughter greeted her new friend with squeals. Not only did she get Addy, she and Addy got matching nightgowns, which Cait quickly snatched up before running off to her bedroom.

A few minutes later, there they were: Addy and Cait, cheek to cheek and dressed in matching white, ruffly nightgowns. "Don't we look alike, Mommy?" Cait said, her face beaming as she wrapped her arms around her doll.

I looked at my blue-eyed daughter, as pale as a calla lily, squeezing her doll with the creamy brown skin and big dark eyes, and wondered what she could be thinking. Tread gently here, I told myself.

"How do you and Addy look alike?" I asked.

Cait just smiled as she brushed back Addy's hair. "Oh, you know," she said, nuzzling the doll's cheek. But I didn't know, and I felt left out, blinded to the bigger picture only my daughter seemed to see.

For the next two months, Cait took Addy everywhere she went. You can learn a lot about strangers by their reaction to a pretty black doll in a white girl's arms. One woman, who was white, glared at me as we stood in line at a McDonald's. "You made her buy that, didn't you?" she hissed, shaking her head as she looked at Cait clutching Addy to her chest. "There is no way she would have asked for a doll like that."

A young black woman working at a local drugstore stared at Cait and Addy and then politely leaned in to whisper to me. "Did she want that doll?" When I nodded my head, she winced. "Why?"

"We're a lot alike," piped up Cait. I looked at the bewildered woman, shrugged my shoulders and smiled.

I thought of Addy recently after talking to a mother with two adopted sons from Korea. For years, Linda has sent her boys to a camp for Korean children adopted by Americans. "I thought it was a good idea," she said. "All year long they are with kids who don't look like them, who didn't come from Korea, and everything I had heard and read said this is a good thing to do."

One of her sons, however, balked last year, announcing he did not want to go to that camp again. Her ten-year-old did this in what is all children's venue of choice for serious conversations: in the car, while his mother was driving.

Linda was surprised, but undeterred. "Don't you like to be some-place where everyone is like you?" Her son's response so startled her she nearly ended up on a lawn: "Isn't the important thing supposed to be liking who you are and not being like everyone else?"

Linda smacked her forehead in recounting this conversation. "You know, you raise them to believe certain things, to get beyond the issues of race and gender and all that, but then you're blown away when you realize they're there, all your lessons took, and you're the one who isn't getting it."

At that point I was required to welcome Linda into the Clueless Mothers Club, of which I am president. Then I told her about Addy, and how I finally found out why Cait wanted the doll in the first place.

"Addy and I are so alike," Cait said yet again as I tucked them into bed one night. "How so?" I asked. Cait reached up and touched my face. "Addy had to leave with her mom, just like you and me."

I froze. For eight years I had been teaching my daughter that it's what's on the inside that counts. Obviously, only one of us had been listening.

And you know what? Cait was right. She and Addy, they're so alike. They're practically twins.

THE VIEW FROM THE DUGOUT

School may still be in session, but there's no question the softball season is upon us.

Kids are scarfing down early dinners or snacking on string cheese stuffed in their pockets because there is no way they want to miss practice for anything as mundane as a balanced meal. They tug on their favorite sneakers or cleats, check out their batting stance in hallway mirrors, and bury their faces in their gloves to breathe in long, slow whiffs of leather. This is the hour of promise, when the season is young and untainted by grass stains, win-loss records, and parents' bad behavior. It is my favorite time of year.

For six years, I coached my daughter's team. We started with T-ball when she was in kindergarten. Parents still laughingly remind me of how my rules changed in the span of an hour. At the beginning of that first practice, they smiled as their children loudly yelled my first rule of softball: Everyone Has Fun! By the end of the practice, that rule had been amended to include And Don't Hurt the Coach! after dozens of errant balls aimed for home plate smacked instead into my head, thighs, and backside, usually in clusters of three. Thus began my coaching career.

Most of my time as a coach was wonderful, full of great kids eager to discover their gifts and show them off. There is nothing like the face of a child who's just realized she has a touch of magic. And no one can eclipse that joy faster than a parent, which I learned in those not-so-wonderful moments of coaching.

Misbehaving parents are easy targets for our wrath. Most of us wince when we hear a parent scream at a child. We squirm when they bark orders that contradict the coach or they argue with an umpire. We want them to sit down and shut up. What I learned as a coach, though, was that indifference hurts children, too.

A child scoops up a grounder, hurls it to first base, and the runner is out. It is a glorious moment, a few seconds when one little kid feels like a superstar. Nine times out of ten, the first thing young players do is look to see if their parents were watching. Far too often, their faces fall. Mom is reading a book. Dad is talking on his cell phone. Oftentimes, a whole group of parents are laughing and gabbing, oblivious to their kids on the field.

It was heartbreaking to watch my kids' faces go from a grin to a pout in the time it took them to look over their shoulders. I'd pat them on the back and tell them how great they were, but I was no substitute for their parents. Usually, they'd lower their heads and kick the dirt before muttering a barely audible, "Thanks."

Coaches aren't immune to the seductive powers of a lazy summer night. On most game nights I performed my own bit of magic as I wriggled out of pantyhose and into shorts while driving home to scoop up my daughter and forty pounds of equipment before heading to the field. Occasionally I pulled out the schedule at my desk, counted how many more games remained, and sighed. Not often, but often enough that I regret it now.

Summer softball is a thing of the past in our house. I knew this day would come, but still I am rattled to discover that kids—even my kids—grow up and move on. My daughter is fifteen now. She no longer plays ball, and the only time she seems to care if I'm watching her is when she's trying to slip out the door before unloading the dishwasher.

I miss those summer nights when her hair was pulled through the loop in her baseball cap and her jersey fell to her knees. I miss pitching ball after ball to her as she stood in front of the giant oak tree with her bat poised and her face screwed up like a trucker behind schedule. Back then, we'd play catch until the streetlights clicked on, then collapse on the front stoop, gulping water and comparing biceps.

We still sit on the front stoop. I'm typing, though, and she's poised on the porch swing, her knees up to her chin as she paints her toenails metallic lavender. I look up from my laptop, watch her dab at her toes, and remember how hard she used to throw the ball, how she'd pump her arm and say "Yesssss!" when it smacked into my glove. I glance at her freshly ironed blouse and recall how we used to peel off our dusty jerseys and toss them together into the washer.

She catches me looking, asks what I am thinking. I tell her I miss playing catch. To my delight, she tells me sure, she'd love to.

As soon as her nails dry.

STARTING THE DAY WITH A BANG

he clock radio erupts into the NPR theme song, signaling that my own personal hell is about to begin.

It is seven A.M. Time to wake the teenager.

I've been up for at least an hour already, pumping myself full of coffee and treadmill-induced endorphins so that I am up to the challenge.

This is the morning, I tell myself.

This is the morning when I will not scream, threaten, or plead. I will be calm. I will be patient. I will be so serene that a passerby could mistake me for the Dalai Lama himself, were he ever to start his day in fuzzy platform slippers and a red terry cloth robe from Victoria's Secret.

I open the door to the debris-laden stairs leading to my daughter's third-floor bedroom. I pretend I don't see the dirty spoon nestled in the far right corner of step No. 3.

"Cait?"

Silence.

"Caitlin?"

I hear Gracie the pug snort from under my daughter's flannel sheets.

I try again. "Cait. Lin."

"Mmmmmm."

Ah, signs of life. "Time to get up."

"I'm up."

Thus begin her lies.

I walk downstairs to the kitchen and wait. Ten minutes, I tell myself, trying not to think about how much I'm talking to myself these days. Give her ten minutes.

Seven minutes later, I am back at her stairwell.

"Cait."

Silence.

"Caaaaaaait."

"I'm up."

"I don't hear any movement."

Thump. Thump. Thump.

"Nice try, young lady, but it isn't going to work." She has simply thrown her left leg over the side of the bed and stomped. I know this. She knows I know this. She is unrepentant.

"Just calm down, Mom."

Calm down? Calm *down*? I look at my watch. It is 7:27. We must leave in twenty-three minutes. "All right," I say. "That's it!"

I scream. *I can't believe you're doing this to me.*

I threaten. *If you don't stop doing this to me.*

I plead. *Please in the name of God stop doing this to me.*

Abruptly, the floorboards over my head start vibrating as rapper Eminem bleats out something heinous about his mother.

I don't even care that the sole intention behind this musical interlude is to drown me out because, clever me, I know she had to get out of bed to flick it on.

I feel as victorious as Muhammad Ali after his Rumble in the Jungle until I catch a glimpse of myself in the hallway mirror. I am reminded of the words of another wise Buddhist monk, Thich Nhat Hanh: When we are angry, our faces look like a monkey's butt.

Yeah, but. I'll bet the good monk's mornings never begin with a mad dash in the minivan next to a scowling teenager who can't quite believe she has to join the living. Again.

I know this isn't her fault. I know that adolescents need nine hours and fifteen minutes of sleep but can't fall asleep until just before dawn because they have the metabolism of a hummingbird.

I know Minneapolis changed the starting time of its high schools to 8:40 and their students' performance improved.

I even know that my daughter doesn't mean it when she tells me three mornings a week that I'm meaner than a plantar wart.

I know all this, but, geez, it used to be so easy. She was the little preschooler who insisted on waking me up at 5:30 most mornings by counting the freckles on my chest: "Twenty-one, twenty-twooooo . . ."

I look at my watch: It's now 7:47.

"Caaaait!" I scream.

I immediately shriek when the stealth teenager shouts into the back of my head, "I'm right here."

I turn and there she is. Eyes open. Not yet focused, but she'll find the stairs.

I turn her toward the door and can't resist. I sneak a kiss to her forehead, confident that she'll never know what hit her.

LOOKING BACK AND AHEAD AS A CHILD GROWS UP

The morning started yesterday with my sixteen-year-old daughter taking one look at me at the kitchen counter and cracking up.

"Oh, wow, Mom," she said, pointing to my brightly patterned silk shirt. "I was just going to ask you if I could borrow that shirt for Wacky Wednesday."

Did I mention I was dressed for work?

"Whoa, sorry," she said over the drum of my fingers on the counter. "Didn't mean to offend you or anything. It's just that today's theme is a Hawaiian thing."

That's when I noticed that my normally too-cool-for-words daughter was wearing a gaudy, yellow-and-orange lei with fake flowers the size of pompoms. This on a girl whose fashion sense exceeded my own by the time she was seven.

It was my turn to laugh. "Look what they've done to you," I said. "You'll do anything for those kids."

She grinned and grabbed her lunch bag. "*My* kids, Mom," she said. "They're my kids."

This is Cait's third summer as a counselor at the day camp she used to attend as a child who always looked back when I drove away. Now I drop her off and watch the ponytail swing from the back of her head as little kids light up like fireflies at the sight of her.

There are milestones in every kid's life that nudge us parents into realizing they are growing up and moving on. My daughter's summer job—and the way she embraces its many responsibilities—has been a two-handed shove.

So much has changed. Before camp started, the same daughter who can't remember to jot down a phone message was writing little notes to all her future charges, welcoming them and insisting she couldn't wait to meet them.

On school mornings, I was the screamer and she was the slug, rolling out of bed just this side of tardy day after day, week after week. Now, every morning we vie for shower rights, each of us whining that we have a job to get to so hurry up.

Dinnertime, usually a fishing expedition for even the slightest snippet from school life, is now a bounty of tales about her kids. She sounds like the proud parent, so many of her stories beginning with how yet another child said the cutest thing today.

Sometimes she wants to brainstorm problems at work: How should she handle a clique she thinks is underfoot? How can she help a shy little girl find her courage? What should she do about the child who always wants to hold her hand?

"It's so important that she learn she can let go and I'll still be there," she said.

At such moments, her job seems harder than mine. She tends to injured knees and wounded feelings, smiles even when she doesn't feel like it, and is ever vigilant for those who might be ignored or teased because they're plump or timid or different in some other way that sets her heart pounding. Once a shy child herself, she is now their safe place, the wise grown-up in the room.

I came face to face with that same grown-up the evening she described the little girl who pointed to a prominent birthmark and said, "This means I'm special."

"She has a good mother," Cait said. "She knew exactly how to handle that one."

I felt the shove as I stumbled over this latest milestone, the one where a parent realizes she admires her own child.

Last week, Cait came home and announced that the fourth-graders sat her down for a conference.

"They said I was giving too much attention to the little kids," she said, grinning. "They said they weren't getting enough 'Caitlin time.'"

I know the feeling.

Not so long ago, she was mine, all mine. I would pull into the camp's circular drive and there she'd be, nut brown and happy, her hands full of the day's crafts that were all presents for me.

Now, as often as not, she's already on the phone making plans for the evening by the time I get home. The crafts heaped on the dining room table are the love offerings from her own little kids, for her, not me.

And most mornings when she is dropped off to camp, now I am the one who hesitates. I am the one who looks back before driving away.

This is our third mother-daughter trip to the Ohio Bureau of Motor Vehicles in our quest for a temporary driver's license.

Two of these ten-mile drives have occurred in the last two hours.

All of them have occurred because we were missing yet another piece of paper documenting the existence of the child who has filled all my days and nights and most of my anxiety dreams for the last fifteen years, eleven months, and three days.

This latest trip we are making by way of the local Social Security office.

The mood in our car is not, shall we say, effervescent.

"This is soooo not my fault," says my daughter, her arms crossed as she stares out the window.

She's got to be kidding, I think.

"You've got to be kidding," I say.

She is unrepentant.

"You'd think a mother would know where her daughter's Social Security card is."

"Well, you'd think a daughter would have called ahead and known that she needed the card in the first place."

"Well, you'd think a mother who's had her license for decades—"

I stop the car.

We look at each other. Hard.

Then we start to laugh. If we'd done half this much thinking even an hour ago we wouldn't be in this fix.

Our first trip to the BMV was a bust because we didn't have her birth certificate.

Not to worry.

Being the dutiful and blissfully happy new mother that I was in May 1987, I had immediately filed my baby's birth certificate away as proof of my maternal do-goodness, which had already been well documented by my vow to boil any and all toys that came within three feet of her precious little lips.

Open the file box, there it was.

The next trip to the BMV we found out we needed her Social Security card, too, and wouldn't it have been nice if they'd told us that during our little chat about the birth certificate?

"You have her Social Security card, right, Mom?" the clerk asked with a smile.

Time to worry.

By the time I filed for Cait's Social Security card in May 1989, I was the harried mother of a speed-demon toddler who regularly shared chew-toys with our dog, Max. The card arrived in the mail and I promptly squirreled it away.

Somewhere.

Open the file box, there it wasn't.

Let's skip the part about how long it took us to find the local Social Security office. And how important it is that at least one of the parents remembers her own Social Security number to order a replacement card for her child. (I was hungry, okay?)

Hours later, we were once again driving to the BMV, during which time I realized there are far too many rules of the road with which I am completely unfamiliar. This is a most unfortunate discovery to make while your daughter is firing questions at you from her handy-dandy *Digest of Ohio Motor Vehicle Laws.*

"Mom, did you know you're supposed to honk when you pass someone?"

"Huh. No."

"Mom, did you know you aren't supposed to park between a safety zone and the adjacent curb or within thirty feet of points on the curb immediately opposite the ends of a safety zone, unless the traffic authority indicates a different length by signs or markings?"

"Huh. No."

"Boy, Mom, here's something I know you don't know: Veee-hicles are not supposed to be parked more than twelve inches from the curb."

Would this hell never end?

We arrived at the BMV with enough documentation for Cait to enter any country in the Western Hemisphere and at least one parallel universe.

"Oh, good," said the clerk, looking at the official piece of paper documenting that, yes, this pretty young lady does indeed have a Social Security number but her mother lost the card.

The clerk smiled at Cait.

Cait smiled back.

She took the test.

She posed for the picture.

She complained about the picture.

She walked toward the car.

Straight for the driver's side.

I see my hell has just begun.

IT'S HARD TO KNOW WHEN NOT TO PARENT

It's a good thing there was a woman of maturity and grace in our home during this grueling process of college applications.

I just wish I could say that woman was me.

The overwrought mother in me, however, did her best to turn what ought to be an exciting time in a high school senior's life into a seemingly endless period of purgatory in which every day began with, "Have you?"

Have you decided where to apply?

Have you requested your transcripts?

Have you filled out the applications?

My daughter combated these rants with her usual arsenal of sighs, foot-stomps, and protests that somebody needed to get a grip. In the end, though, she complied.

Then I asked her about her writing sample.

"Have you written—"

"No."

"You haven't written it?"

"Yes," she said. "I've written it, and no, you cannot see it."

"But—"

"Mom. I mean it. This is my writing, my applications. I want to do this myself."

Okay, not to state the obvious here, but I write for a living. Reams, in fact. It seemed to me that if there was anything I could have a hand in, it was my daughter's attempt to write her way into college.

"I don't want to rewrite it," I said. "I just want to take a look—"

"Mom? No."

And that was that. My career as the meddling, overmanaging mother had come to an abrupt end.

Mother angst is as enduring as it is disabling, and it has proved to be the mother lode for recent publications eagerly illustrating how many of today's moms are both suffering and insufferable. Last week alone, the covers of both *The New York Times Book Review* and *Newsweek* showcased Judith Warner, whose new book, *Perfect Madness: Motherhood in the Age of Anxiety,* argues that "American moms are turning themselves into physically and financially depleted drones," to quote the *Times* review.

We're also turning on our kids. Take the pressure for academic achievement. Why is it okay for us not to be perfect, but we expect our kids to excel in everything? Why aren't they ever allowed to be average when we so clearly are?

Warner's lens focuses on mostly well-to-do mothers, and their litany of complaints wear on the majority of mothers who never have the chance to endure such supposed hardships as extravagant birthday parties at the finest clubs or lining up at five A.M. to enroll their children in the perfect preschool.

Most mothers spend their days deciding in mid-act which balls they can drop as they juggle bills and diapers and homework and dinner plans they hope won't revolve around pizza more than three times a week. There's not a lot of sympathy for the high-profile television anchor who whines in *Newsweek* that she can't change her own clothes before she has to dress baby Sasha.

I was not an affluent mother, but I certainly had my share of privileges, including a car that always ran and a job that paid the bills. And I winced as I read about some of these mothers, realizing I tried too hard to protect my daughter from every disappointment after her father and I handed her the disappointment of a lifetime. We adults call it a divorce. Kids tend to think of it as the end of the world.

After all those years of fighting off the dragons, what do I get? A daughter on the verge of eighteen telling me to back off.

And so I did.

The first college that accepted her called before sending the acceptance letter. The woman leaving the message said she wanted to talk to my daughter about her writing. I remember hearing the word "amazing," then "fabulous," and then it suddenly dawned on me the message wasn't for me but my daughter.

I yelled for her to come to the phone.

"It's for you," I said.

I watched my daughter's face as she listened to the message. She smiled. And then she laughed. And then she looked at me and smiled some more.

She'd just opened a gift I could never have given her, no matter how hard I tried.

A PARENT'S DISORIENTING TRIP

U*ntil last week,* it never occurred to me that boys will be attending my daughter's college.

Everywhere, there they were: tall boys, short boys, skinny boys, burly boys who could lift a Hummer over their heads—all of them looking right past my don't-even-think-about-it scowl to fasten their gaze upon my daughter. My baby. My about-to-go-to-college little girl.

Fine time to find this out.

Last week, my daughter and I drove to her college orientation. In retrospect, I think I can safely say it was a bad idea to spend the last hour of that trek listening to National Public Radio's Diane Rehm interview an author about all the clever ways underage students find to drink themselves into a stupor on campus.

But enough about me.

Let me tell you about all the other parents. And me.

Remember the movie *Night of the Living Dead*? They must have cast every one of those zombies from parents at college orientation.

There we were, dazed and lost as we wandered hither and yon, our footsteps a steady *thump-thump-thump* as we bumped into one another following all the orders from children who only a few months ago still had a curfew.

Go sit over there, they said.

I'll meet you back here later, they said.

I can spell my own name, Mom, they said.

Actually, only my daughter said that one, and I really appreciate how all the nice people at the registration table kindly averted their eyes. Nice trick, that one. I used it myself later when I noticed a father's face drain of color as his daughter said, "I don't need you right now. I'll come back for you later."

"But I thought I'd—"

"Dad. If you can't let me walk on my own now, what are you going to do when you leave me here for good?"

Ouch.

He shuffled his feet, glanced at the floor, and then looked right at me. Not only did I avert my eyes from his ashen face, I smiled real big and waved to an imaginary person across the room. This did not amuse my daughter, but, quite frankly, I wasn't auditioning for that job by the time she walked over to where I'd been exiled to announce she was going to go register for classes.

"Great!" I said, gathering up the newspaper, two books, lined notepad, and six pens I'd brought along just in case.

"No," she said. "I'm going. You're staying."

"I knew that," I said.

She frowned.

"No, really. I'm just changing tables. See? Here I go."

So then I had to actually stand up and switch tables. More change.

"See?" I said, settling at a table identical to the one I'd just left. "Perfect."

Her eyes narrowed, but I swear she almost smiled. Then off she went to plan a future without me.

For a while, I'd say at least a good six minutes, I was fine, even though I'd lost the perfect table and was now wedged between two mothers who just realized they were from the same county.

This is a fairly common event at college orientation. Say you're from Shaker Heights, and you overhear someone mention something about Rocky River—which is all the way across town.

Until you're at your kid's college orientation.

"Rocky River?" you say. "Did you just say Rocky River? Why, we're practically neighbors."

Before you know it you're exchanging e-mails and dorm-room assignments and acting as if you're the only two Americans on the streets of Moscow.

In the face of all this cooing and hugging, my mind wandered. I suddenly remembered a friend's son who had to pick a language in college.

He grew up in Miami, so naturally she thought he'd pick the language he'd been hearing, reading, and speaking since he was a toddler.

Spanish, she thought. *He'll take Spanish.*

Silly mom.

He took Italian.

"The line was shorter," he said.

I gathered up my newspaper, two books, lined notepad, and six pens and waved good-bye to the two Americans.

"*Ciao,*" I said.

I THANK MY LUCKY STARS FOR
A CHILD AT COLLEGE

For the last eight years, the ceiling in my home office has been plastered with plastic stars that glow in the dark.

They were leftovers from my daughter's childhood nights, when her bed used to lie right beneath the made-up sky. Sometimes, after kissing her good night, I would hover outside her door and listen to her count the stars. Once in a while she would make a wish. It was a child's hope for what could never be, the kind that breaks a single mother's heart.

She had a thing for stars, and for the moon, too. Once, when she was five, we sat outside the old Arabica coffeehouse on Shaker Square during one of those summer nights when I let her stay up past bedtime.

She munched on a chocolate croissant and drew with the crayons she always carried in a pink travel case. I sipped the house regular as we talked about our friend the moon shining oh-so-brightly overhead.

"Do you think he sees us?" she asked.

"Mm-hm," I said, nodding.

"Does he see me?"

"Especially you," I said. "I think he followed you here."

Her face glowed.

After a while, we gathered up her crayons and drawings and headed for the car. She looked up at the sky and frowned.

"I hate to leave him, Mommy."

"Don't you know?" I said, buckling her in. "The moon's going to follow you home."

And don't you know? He did.

"Good night, moon," she whispered to the open window as I tucked her in. "Good night, stars."

Today I will drive my daughter to college and will leave without her.

She is not a little girl anymore, and I can no longer comfort her with a made-up sky or stories about a moon that hangs on her every move.

The best I can give her is a mother's performance that masks every qualm, hides every fear.

We had a dress rehearsal at orientation. I have practiced my lines.

I'm only a phone call away.

This is the biggest adventure of your life.

I'm only a phone call away.

College was some of the best days of my life.

Did I mention I'm only a phone call away?

A month ago I was bundled in that mother's cliché, teetering on the edge of an empty nest, wondering why I'd ever taught my chick how to fly.

Oh, poor, poor me. My baby was going away.

Then, in one week, twenty young Marines were killed in Iraq. Fourteen of them were Ohioans, thirteen of those from the Third Battalion, Twenty-fifth Regiment, which has its headquarters in Brook Park.

And just like that, the earth shifted.

Like thousands of others, I attended the wakes and funerals where animated faces smiled from video screens and poster boards. I went to memorial services and candlelight vigils where hope showed up in the tenderness of strangers. I interviewed grieving parents whose stories made me cry on the drive home.

What got to me most was the certainty that this was it, their last chance to make memories with their children. In a final embrace, they reached out to touch flag-draped coffins holding the lifeless bodies of their children, who had so much to live for.

Today, my daughter is leaving for college.

Just that, and all that.

How blessed can one parent be?

I gave her a children's book by Cooper Edens titled *If You're Afraid of the Dark, Add One More Star to the Night*. My favorite page: "If one day you must leave home, draw stars on the bottom of your shoes to light your way back."

I don't know how long it will take her to look on the bottom of her flip-flops, but I know that she'll smile at the stars her mother put there.

Tonight, she will sleep in her dorm room for the first time. She might be homesick, maybe even a little scared. Knowing my daughter, she'll probably look out her window and stare into the night sky.

Fortunately, the moon and I had a little chat.

He'll be there for her.

Especially for her.

ACKNOWLEDGMENTS

Some people, particularly those who populate newsrooms, love to make fun of the lists of acknowledgments tucked into writers' books. Not me. I relish the reminder than not one of us goes it alone. Besides, I've lived long enough to know my own voice would be but a whisper without the many people who've egged me on.

From the beginning: My mother, Janey Schultz, taught me how to find the punch line without taking a swing at someone else. My father, Charles Schultz, made sure I never gave up. My sister Leslie is the first strong single mother I ever knew. My sister Toni's devotion keeps me humble. My brother, Chuck, proves there really is a second act in life, no matter what Fitzgerald said.

Every high school kid should have a guidance counselor like Joe Petro and a teacher like Tom Carr. Kent State University professors Fred and Kathleen (Kitty) Endres ignored my fears and heard my heart, instead.

Lisa Hearey's short life changed my own; her husband, Clem, and sons C.J., Michael, and Christopher continue to drive the lesson home. I will never give up because of Erin Jones. By word and deed, Michael Green never lets me forget.

A colleague once described a newsroom as the Land of Misfit Toys. Maybe that's why I fit right in at *The Plain Dealer,* like a Chatty Cathy whose cord never retracts. So many there have invested in me.

Clint O'Connor pushed me to put it in writing. Joe Frolik made my hiring his cause. David Hall and Gary Clark took a chance on me, and then Lou Mio stubbornly reminded me why. Jane Kahoun was God's gift to a nervous newbie. Harlan Spector talked me off the cliffs. Christine Jindra lobbied for me. Steve Koff saw the spark, and Jean Dubail fanned the flame. Ellen Stein Burbach insisted I had something to say. Betsy O'Connell staked the trail, and Elizabeth McIntyre moved the mountain. Doug Clifton changed his mind and greeted the outcome with abundant grace. Tom O'Hara has endured more than his share of my speeches. Alex Machaskee paved the way for the book you're holding.

I happily concede that Sue Klein is The Boss of Me, and that the features copy desk has rescued me more times than I deserve. The ever-so-kind Jo Ann Pallant keeps me on track. Mark Rapp takes care of the details. Greg Burnett reminds me why it matters. The front-desk clerks are heroic on a daily basis. The cafeteria staff, the guards, and the maintenance crew make it worth showing up.

Tom Gaumer never gave up on me. Ted Diadiun proves friendship ain't about politics. Sincerity by any other name is Susan Jaffe. John Luttermoser reminds me to poke the bear, and Grant Segall cheers me on whenever I do. Joe Crea is my sturdy compass. Andrea Simakis gives me hope for the future. Mark Naymik sets the standard. Chuck Yarborough's loyalty keeps me honest. Michael McIntyre keeps me on my toes. Merlene Santiago forces me to call it what it is.

Rosemary Kovacs has been my quiet champion since Day One. Richard Conway gave me the crucial pep talk early in my *Plain Dealer* career. Margie Frazer always picks me up and brushes me off. John Gruner's personal courage makes it impossible for me to give up. Chris Sheridan is the voice at my back that's always whispering, "Go for it." Jeff Greene keeps me sane, Bill Gugliotta makes me stretch, and David Kordalski makes me do it all over again. The photographers—artists, every last one of them—force me to aim higher.

Sandy Livingston carries the torch. Sandy Theis always knows when I need the boost. Tom Feran is my buddy in crime, and Evelyn Theiss is my friend on the journey. Sam Fulwood III makes me think it through. Mark Dawidziak shares the wealth. Sheryl Harris is fiercely by my side. Regina Brett always props me up. Jim Sweeney refuses to let me take myself too seriously. Bill Lubinger saves me from myself almost every day.

Stuart Warner, my editor at *The Plain Dealer,* steered me in another direction and changed the trajectory of my career. I wish every writer could benefit from the gentle precision of his genius.

My ability to practice journalism and earn a decent living is due, in large measure, to the tireless efforts of the Newspaper Guild, especially Local 1.

Gaylee McCracken's energy and wit still leave me breathless. Hope and Stanley Adelstein make me miss my mom a little less. Gloria and

Laurie Goldstein are beacons of hope. Fleka Anderson knows too much about me but loves me anyway. Kate Huey's vision lifts my own sights. Karen Sandstrom makes me braver. Buffy Fillippel sees where I'm headed before I do, and Mark Fillippel draws the map. Karen Long keeps me tethered to what's real. Jackie Cassara is so right about so much that it scares me.

Pete Kotz insists that I laugh at myself. Frank Lewis offers to do it for me. Thank you both for the surprise of friendship.

The Ohio 13 family keeps me laughing and learning at the same time.

Kate Medina, my editor at Random House, reaches back and pulls with every step she takes. She improved my writing, and me. Associate editor Robin Rolewicz deftly sanded the rough edges and never let me down. My lawyer, Robin Davis Miller, should have been my sister, I swear. Photographer Izabela Viktoria sees everything differently, lucky me.

Cleveland: I LOVE YOU.

My new family stretches my world in all directions, especially my mother-in-law, Emily Campbell Brown; my two stepdaughters, Emily Montgomery Brown and Elizabeth Clarke Brown; and Michael Stanley and Kristina Torres. Add Bob and Charlie, Catherine and Anne, Marcia Grace and Tara—blessings, all.

My children, Caitlin Schultz Gard and Andrew Christopher Gard, give me all the reason I need to keep trying.

My husband, Sherrod Brown, makes it all worthwhile.

CONNIE SCHULTZ, whose column runs twice a week in the Cleveland *Plain Dealer,* won the Pulitzer Prize for Commentary in 2005. Her other accolades include the Scripps-Howard National Journalism Award, the National Headliner Award, the Batten Medal, and the Robert F. Kennedy Award for social-justice reporting. Her narrative series "The Burden of Innocence," which chronicled the life of a man wrongly incarcerated for rape, was a Pulitzer Prize finalist. After the series ran, the real rapist turned himself in, and he is now serving a five-year prison sentence. Connie is married to Ohio's popular congressman Sherrod Brown.

ABOUT THE TYPE

This book was set in Bembo, a typeface based on an old-style Roman face that was used for Cardinal Bembo's tract *De Aetna* in 1495. Bembo was cut by Francisco Griffo in the early sixteenth century. The Lanston Monotype Machine Company of Philadelphia brought the well-proportioned letter forms of Bembo to the United States in the 1930s.